D0843453

CHILDHOOD'S PATTERN

The little pleader.

Gillian Avery

CHILDHOOD'S PATTERN

A study of
the heroes and heroines of
children's fiction
1770–1950

HODDER AND STOUGHTON
LONDON LEICESTER SYDNEY AUCKLAND

ISBN 0 340 16945 1

TEXT COPYRIGHT © 1975 GILLIAN AVERY

FIRST PUBLISHED IN 1975 BY HODDER AND STOUGHTON
CHILDREN'S BOOKS, SALISBURY ROAD, LEICESTER

FILMSET BY KEYSPOOLS LIMITED, GOLBORNE, LANCASHIRE.
PRINTED IN GREAT BRITAIN BY
TINLING (1973) LIMITED, PRESCOT, MERSEYSIDE.

Contents

For A.O.J.C.
whose learning, judgement and sympathies
have contributed so much

Preface

THIS book has arisen out of one that I wrote nine years ago. *Nineteenth Century Children* was published in 1965 when a new interest in the history of children's reading was beginning, but comparatively little had yet appeared in print. Since then the whole aspect has changed. Children's books now have their own niche in the study of English and of education. Journals are devoted to them; for a graduate to produce a thesis on Ballantyne or Mrs Molesworth is regarded as in no way eccentric, and the ancient university of Oxford has even gone so far as to include the subject on its lecture list. To repeat my trite remarks on the better-known nineteenth-century authors would be, in the light of the present interest taken in them, superfluous to say the least, though there was a stage when I would have liked the chance to correct some of the errors of fact and of judgement that I had made.

But in spite of the avalanche of words that has been poured out during the last ten years, the great work that Harvey Darton wrote as long ago as 1932 – *Children's Books in England* – does still remain the best study. Only he has had the knowledge, the judgement and the detachment to stand back and take a long, cool look at the whole landscape without getting lost in the trees. He provided literary assessment and bibliographic details – all part of the subject – but his real interest in children's books was because they represent 'a minor chapter in the history of English social life,' not because they play a great rôle in English literature.

'Literature', in the sense that they deserve serious and weighty literary discussion, they are not – except for a small handful. But what they do mirror is a constantly shifting moral pattern. What in any given age do adults want of children? What are their values? What are the virtues they are striving to inculcate, the vices they are trying to tread down? Do they rate learning above godliness, truthtelling above obedience; do they encourage or suppress imagination? Examine children's books in this light and even the dreariest becomes rewarding.

9

This is what, in the present study, I am attempting – having made a faint beginning nine years ago. The giants stand above this scrutiny. Lewis Carroll, Lear, *The Just-So Stories*, *The Wind in the Willows*, *The Hobbit*, *Tom's Midnight Garden*, cannot be treated in this way. They are in any case works of fantasy and imagination, a subject which lies outside my province and which I do not try to include.

I have given the dates 1770 to 1950 as marking the limits of the study, but it is in fact the middle years that have received most attention. Before the nineteenth century the publishers were not properly under way. After 1910 or so the moralists and educationalists temporarily lost interest in juvenile reading and some thirty years or so of comparatively undirected commercial production followed. No new patterns emerged, only extensions of those formed at the beginning of the century. Of this period I have given only a slight indication. Since 1950 there has been a renaissance, far too recent to assess, but one which will present great interest to future chroniclers. Not only is the output formidable, in quantity and quality, but the educational experts are once again fully involved, as certain as ever they were in the days of Richard Lovell Edgeworth and Mrs Trimmer and all their successors that their generation is uniquely equipped to form the child mind.

I owe a great debt in the preparation of this book to Sylvia Gardner, the Oxford City Children's Librarian, who has taken endless trouble on my behalf, hunting out information, answering many questions, and who has always been ready with help at the shortest notice. I must also thank Michael Turner for so readily allowing me access to the children's books in the John Johnson Collection at the Bodleian Library, from which many of my earlier examples have been taken, and to his staff who have made working there such a pleasure. Anybody concerned with the history of children's books inevitably leans heavily on the catalogue to the Osborne Collection of Early Children's Books. The details assembled there are available nowhere else, and all of us are deeply grateful to the meticulous scholarship and infinite care with which Judith St John has prepared it.

The Lutterworth Press, successors of the Religious Tract Society, have given valuable assistance about their publications and have lent books, as have Collins and the Scripture Union. The Society for Promoting Christian Knowledge, Messrs W. and R. Chambers and Blackie have all helped me with information about the history of their firms' publications of reward books. Deborah Ganz, Bernard Gross, and Rosemary Lunn have drawn my attention to particular books, and Mrs Thelma Marshall has entrusted me with the unique copy of *We Two*, the little journal about Penny Dreadfuls, edited by her father for the benefit of himself and a fellow enthusiast. Observer/Transworld have kindly allowed me to quote the poem by Robert Jones in the last chapter. Bernard Gosling of the Clarendon Press (who died before I was able to thank him formally) was as kind as ever in arranging about the photography of books from my own collection. To these, and to my own family for their patience and interest, I offer warm thanks.

Oxford, 1974.

The parting of the ways

'DAMN them! I mean the cursed Barbauld Crew, those Blights and Blasts of all that is Human in man and child,' wrote Lamb to Coleridge in 1802. He had been to Newbery's bookshop to try to buy some children's books, and had found that the new educational reading had banished all the old classics that he knew, and that 'Mrs Barbauld and Mrs Trimmer's nonsense lay about in piles'. It was hard to find even a copy of Goody Two-Shoes.

'Is there no possibility of averting this sore evil? Think what you would have been now, if instead of being fed with Tales and old wives' fables in childhood, you had been crammed with geography and natural history?'

There never has been an age which did not mourn the good old days, and hardly anybody who could make an objective assessment of

Little Goody Two-Shoes.

the state of things in his childhood. This is particularly true of our first books. There are certain details that we seize on, cherish and perhaps add to over the years, and completely forget the longeurs of the rest. The story of Margery Meanwell, alias Goody Two-Shoes, the trotting tutoress, is a very moral tale indeed. It exemplifies, according to an edition of *c.* 1830 (it was first published by Newbery in 1765) 'the good consequences of early attention to learning and virtue,' which in Margery's case is rewarded by her being made a village schoolmistress and later by marrying a country squire.

There is not much of the stuff of childhood in it, certainly less than in *Lessons for Children* which Mrs Barbauld wrote in 1778 for her nephew, or even in that meaty, if fundamentally serious hotch-potch of information which she and her brother compiled in the 1790s under the title *Evenings at Home.* The first, in spite of its forbidding title, is a loving account of the small things in a small child's life, written in words that he would understand. As for the second – most children would be able to skip over the items on Cruciform Plants and Metals, and make for the autobiography of Grimalkin the Cat, and the story of Phaeton Junior which begins:

> *Ye heroes of the upper form,*
> *Who long for whip and reins*
> *Come listen to a dismal tale*
> *Set forth in dismal strains.*

What Lamb was lamenting was the new professional seriousness that had overtaken the juvenile book-trade. But instead of kicking the modest and diffident Mrs Barbauld, he would have done better to have damned Mrs Trimmer and her *Guardian of Education* which had started up that year and was busy ferreting out hitherto undetected jacobinism and subversion and corruption in all his old favourites. Or the whole climate of education opinion – Richard Lovell Edgeworth, Thomas Day and other disciples of the Rousseau school of thought; or Hannah More who spoke for the evangelicals – which had persuaded the public that works of the imagination could only stunt the growth of the child's mind, and that his leisure reading should be used to absorb knowledge and to improve his nature.

Lamb, born in 1775, had been out of petticoats and in the blue gown and yellow stockings of a Christ's Hospital scholar by the time *Sandford and Merton* appeared. In his infancy the juvenile book trade did not take itself very seriously. Its output consisted of a cheerful medley of old tales from the chapbooks, and lively new ones which stated how good children were rewarded and naughty ones were punished with frightful fates calculated to satisfy the most blood-thirsty infant mind. And there were alphabets and spelling books and rhymes, all gaily if crudely coloured.

Those middle years of the eighteenth century had seen the beginnings of the trade. Mrs Trimmer attributed its rise to the influence of Locke. Before his time there had been little to wheedle children into learning, then suddenly the publishers realised what money was to be made out of them. 'The youthful mind, which was formerly sick from inanition, is now in danger of a plethora,' Hannah More was to make one of the characters in *Coelebs in Search of a Wife* complain.

Mrs Trimmer too, was as churlish about the little books that had delighted her childhood: Mother Goose and Aesop and Gay's fables. Born in 1741, she was a whole generation older than Lamb, but she had enjoyed that Georgian flowering. She was in fact three years old when John Newbery, having moved from Reading to London with a stock of patent medicines and a fairish number of books for adults, set up business at the sign of the Bible and Crown, and published *A Little Pretty Pocket Book*

'intended for the Instruction and Amusement of Little Master Tommy and Pretty Miss Polly, with an agreeable Letter to read from Jack the Giant Killer, as also a Ball and a Pincushion, the use of which will infallibly make Tommy a good Boy, and Polly a good Girl.'

Harvey Darton has described this little collection of rhymes and pictures of children at their games as a key publication. It may not have been the first attempt to amuse the young reader, but it was the beginning of extended activity to do so, and the opening of forty years of amusement for children, before a new school of thought put such books under an interdict.

When we look at these little books, probably only in reproduction on the pages of Tuer and Leonard de Vries for they are now of great rarity, we get the impression of a comfortable earthy society where humour was simple and ways were insensitive. The stories had morals, but they were of a very obvious and materialistic sort. The good boy in the *Little Pretty Pocket Book* is shown riding in a coach and six, the good girl gets given a fine gold watch. It is the moral world of the fairy story. There is no difficulty about being good, you just have to be diligent; and no doubt about being rewarded for it. Any child can understand this.

It is this common touch that marks the children's book in those happy-go-lucky years in the middle of the eighteenth century. The children of the poor man, if their father could spare them the ha'pence (and always provided of course that they knew their letters) might enjoy the story of Tommy Trip and his dog Jouler from Newbery's *A Pretty Book of Pictures* just as much as Charles Lamb in the Inner Temple.

'As he rides through the town [Tommy Trip] frequently stops at the doors to know how the little children do within, and if they are good and learn their books he then leaves an Apple, an Orange or a Plumb-cake at the door, and away he gallops again – *tantivy, tantivy, tantivy.*'

No obscurity of language or sentiment there, nothing that would not be equally enjoyed in cottage or in drawing-room, or that makes it more suitable for one class than for another.

Up to about 1780 there was a single culture so far as children were concerned. The ideal child was the industrious child. Dick Whittington was a favourite hero. So was Giles Gingerbread who learned his letters by eating them, because they were made of gingerbread. His father tells him: 'Why, Sir Toby was poor once, yes, as poor as thee, Giles: do not be disheartened, boy, only when you climb, climb in a proper manner.'

Then there was *King Pippin*, the story of Peter Pippin, son of Gaffer Pippin, a poor labouring man, who goes out to work when he is six, and is seen by Lady Bountiful crying because he has no money to buy a book. She sends him to Mr Teachum's school, where the boys do not resent him as a jumped-up clod but buy him a fine cap, ornamented with white feathers, and engraved with letters of gold, 'Peter Pippin, King of the Good Boys.' His companions go out birds-nesting and for their sins are variously drowned or devoured by monstrous bears (in other chapbook versions these are lions). King Pippin, surviving, goes from strength to strength; he is sent out to the West Indies to manage a plantation, weds the owner's daughter, inherits the plantation, and at length is made governor of the island.

A successor of Goody Two-Shoes was Primrose Prettyface (pub-

TALE III.

THE INDUSTRIOUS PEASANT.

———

JOHN GRAY was the son of a shoemaker, whose idle habits and constant inebriety reduced his family
to an almost starving condition, and,
at length, obliged them to seek shelter in the workhouse; whilst he,
senseless of their sufferings, aban-

John, who by industry has achieved prosperity, meets his father,
destitute through idle habits and arrested for stealing a loaf.
(*The Faithful Contrast*, 1804)

lished under the title of *The renowned history of Primrose Prettyface* by
J. Marshall & Co. about 1783) 'who, by her sweetness of temper, and
love of learning, was raised from being the daughter of a poor
cottager, to great riches, and the dignity of lady of the manor.' When
she goes into service with Squire Homestead and his family it is little

Jemmy Homestead who is the wrongdoer and the liar, not virtuous Primrose whom he so falsely accuses.

Stories then did not hesitate to extol the poor boy, and to set the rich one in an unfavourable light beside him, or to allow the well-born to learn from the humble. In Catnach's version of *Nurse Lovechild's Legacy* (an eighteenth-century chapbook originally):

'Tom Trueby was a good and sensible boy, who neither played the truant nor kept company with naughty children. He did not like tossing up nor chuck farthing, because he thought it might lead him to love gaming when he was grown up; but he liked very well to play at ball or top, and most particularly at marbles, at which he was very clever, never cheated, and played so well that he used to teach the neighbouring children. And here you see him instructing Master Manly, a Baronet's son in the place, as he did in matters of more consequence, and behaved so well towards him, that he was his friend all his lifetime.'

But once the book trade, urged forward by the teacher and the moralist and the conscientious parent, began to take the child mind seriously, a new chasm opened between the prosperous home and the cottage. It was the mind and the person of the child of the educated classes that the book trade bestirred itself to improve according to the best modern theories; that was where the money lay. The ribald crudity of the chapbooks (or at any rate of some of them) became an abomination in the eyes of a more fastidious age; so, to a lesser extent, did anything for children that lacked a pronounced educational purpose. And when the serious-minded decided that the poor child too should be improved, the two classes had so drawn away from each other that a completely new cottage literature had to be provided. It would be decades before class distinction in children's reading vanished and it was reckoned that the same book could serve both worlds.

Even in 1887, when Charlotte Yonge published her advice on the choice of reward books and the equipping of parish libraries: *What Books to Give and What to Lend*, she included a section which she called 'drawing-room stories'. By then the children in the board schools and parish schools and those who were being educated at home by governesses and mammas might meet on common ground with, say, *The Water Babies* on the one hand, and *Little Meg's Children* on the other.

But there were still whole areas where the literary style or a background completely remote from their experience or knowledge put books beyond the range of cottage children. Miss Yonge was well aware of this difficulty; she had read scores of books aloud to her classes at Otterbourne school, and knew just what held their attention and what would send their eyes and their minds wandering.

To a certain extent the old ways lingered. There still were enough parents uninfected by the modern cult of the rational and the learned child, or too lethargic to keep up with the new prestige names, who went on buying the sort of books they had had in their childhood. John Harris, the successor of Newbery, catered for this public in the early years of the nineteenth century. It was he who published *Little Rhymes for Little Folks* (1823) with its delicately tinted pictures of children both of the gentle and the humble sort playing in gilded saloons or on cottage doorsteps: *The Talking Bird, or Dame Trudge and her Parrot* (1806) in the Mother Hubbard tradition, and the dangerously subversive *The Courtship and Marriage of Jerry and Kitty* (1814), an 'elegant engraving' and a rhyme per page, which finishes

> *And Jerry was sick of his sweet little Wife*
> *Jerry alone, Jerry alone*
> *Jerry was sick of his dear little Wife*
> *And wish'd he alone could be.*
> *So he told her the Sea was not very deep*
> *And popp'd her in when she went up to peep.*
> *Oh! fye Mr Leary, where is your deary?*
> *Just gone a bathing said he.*

To this example of boisterous humour (though this is not the adjective Mrs Trimmer would have used) we might add two other relics of an age when jokes of the rough sort were perfectly acceptable; both of them untouched by the new sensibility that had come into fashion. *The Little Boys Laughingstock, or New Figures of Fun* (Hodgson & Co., 1822) pairs grotesque handcoloured copperplates with rhymes to match. There is a tight-laced dandy, a one-legged black man, a bandy-legged 'dandazette', all for rude little boys to laugh at.

The same rude little boys undoubtedly would have enjoyed *Monsieur Tonson* (Juvenile Library, 41 Skinner Street, 1808) which records the exploits of Tom King, an actor and notorious prankster, who solemnly presents himself each night at the house of an inoffensive French couple in Soho, asking for a mythical Mr Thompson. There is a triumphant conclusion.

> *At length King's wild perplexing plan*
> *The Frenchman so did goad,*
> *That the poor persecuted man*
> *Soon shifted his abode.*

Boisterous humour – the Frenchman suffering at the hands of the amusing joker. (*Monsieur Tonson*, 1808)

But this sort of 'unimproved' coarseness is rare. Marching side by side with the new children's literature which provided for the informed, sensible being that the up-to-date parent wished his child to be, are plenty of moral tales with an earthy directness, that seem to stem from the old-style Newbery tradition, even though they are perhaps told with a simpering elegance of style that belongs to the end of the century.

There is the Awful Warning story, where bad conduct meets with immediate and violent physical results, of the sort that seems to us

The imprudent boy who climbs a tree in quest of birds' nests falls to his death. (*A Present for a Little Boy*, 1797)

now who have been brought up on Belloc's *Cautionary Tales*, to be a parody of itself. Naughty disobedient boys lose an eye or a limb or their bowels, or blow up their fathers with fireworks so that they are orphaned and obliged to become chimney sweeps instead of going to a genteel boarding school. Even Mrs Trimmer, that arbiter of all that was good and proper, wrote a fable of this sort among others in *Easy Lessons*. Julia Sandford will persist in eating the ends of her thread. It unrolls itself in her stomach 'and got a-bout her bow-els, and ti-ed them to-ge-ther in pla-ces.' She dies of course.

All the moralising in this simple-minded literature has a materialistic approach. It goes with the industry theme that was so common in the early books. Work hard enough and you will ride in your own coach. The classic tale of the idle and the industrious apprentice appears in many forms. In *Juvenile Philosophy* (Vernor and Hood, 1801), Mrs Wilson even manages to cure her son Thomas of his idle habits by showing him Hogarth's engravings on the subject. And in *A Step to Fortune* (a twopenny booklet published without any date by G. Thompson and J. Evans), George Graceful who is so diligent in learning the history of England and the rules of grammar rises to the

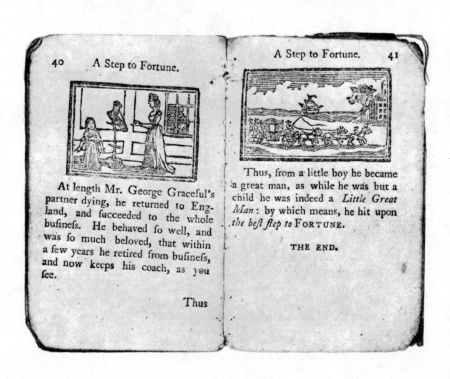

40   A Step to Fortune.

At length Mr. George Graceful's partner dying, he returned to England, and succeeded to the whole business. He behaved so well, and was so much beloved, that within a few years he retired from business, and now keeps his coach, as you see.

Thus

A Step to Fortune.   41

Thus, from a little boy he became a great man, as while he was but a child he was indeed a *Little Great Man* : by which means, he hit upon the best step to FORTUNE.

THE END.

giddy heights of a partnership with a rich West India merchant and residence in Jamaica.

An extreme example of the conflation of virtue and self-interest occurs in the tale of *A Mother's Affection* in *The Youth's Cabinet* (D. Omer Smith, n.d.). Snellgrave 'a man truly commendable for his humanity, was the captain of an English vessel engaged in the African slave trade.' He manages to bribe an African chief with the gift of blue beads to yield him a little boy he specially covets. This proves to be the child of a negress already on the slave ship, and she is so overwhelmed with gratitude that she persuades the other captives to be submissive and obedient and give him an easy passage home. 'This historical fact . . . will serve to confirm a truth which cannot be too often repeated, and that is, that virtuous actions are always conducive to personal interest.'

Conversely, materialistic arguments are used to counter wrongdoing. The social disadvantages are stressed. Take the approach to falsehood in *Early Impressions* (J. Hatchard & Son, 1828), a book distinguished by its attractive lithographs by Denis Dighton. James habitually lies to his protector and is dismissed from his service. 'Falsehoods are very soon detected . . . We must therefore take great care to avoid [the habit] if we wish to be believed and respected by others.'

In the same spirit is the condemnation of thieving in *The Half-Holiday Taskbook* (Hodgson & Co., n.d.), whose anonymous author (he signed the preface 'J.N.') recommended that his trite little reflections should be committed to memory on half-holidays. He pointed out what a drawback stealing was. 'If thieves could but see how foolish they look when detected, they would be ashamed to commit so wicked and degrading a crime.'

J.N. contents himself by showing loss of face; most of his contemporaries would triumphantly have sent their thief to the gallows. '"I think, my dear,"' says the father to the mother in Dorothy Kilner's *Life and Perambulation of a Mouse*, after rebuking his children for small deceits, '"I have heard you mention a person whom you were acquainted with when a girl, who at last was hanged for stealing, I think, was not she?"' '"No,"' says the mother casually, '"she was not hanged, she was transported for one-and-twenty years . . . but she died before that time was out as many of them do."'

Different consequences, perhaps, but the spirit is the same. Certainly there is no mention of sin, the first word that the evangelicals would have used. 'These entertaining authors seldom ground their stories on any intimation that human nature is corrupt; that the young reader is helpless and wants assistance; that he is guilty and wants pardon,' wrote Hannah More in *Coelebs*.

Be punctual and diligent, obedient and dutiful, do not lie or thieve or blow up your sister, beware of mad dogs and gaming, and you will live to be a successful sugar planter and to give your rivals a handsome funeral. This in essence seems to be the uncomplicated and cheerful message of the old-style late Georgian book. It was a message that various schools of thought found lacking.

Honest John and his wife grind their way to fortune (*The Faithful Contrast*, 1804)

[2]

The rational child

THE scene is an arbour hung with clematis at Stanley Grove in the 1800s. The inside is lined with moss into which flowers have been stuck, and more flowers have been brought out from the glass-houses in honour of the occasion. It is Kate Stanley's eighth birthday and she and her sisters are holding a tea-drinking to which the grown-ups have been invited. The estimable young Coelebs (for this is Hannah More's *Coelebs in Search of a Wife*) is led to it by Mr Stanley, his host, and little Kate, pretty as a fairy, with a birthday wreath in her hair, runs to him breathless with excitement.

"'I am eight years old today. I gave up all my gilt books, with pictures, this day twelve-month, and to-day I give up all my little story books, and I am now going to read such books as men and women read.'"

Her father explains a little further. He makes the renouncing of baby books a landmark in his children's lives, and they never think of going back. "'We have too many elementary books . . . [They] are novels in miniature and the excess of them will lead to the want of novels at full-length. The early use of savoury dishes is not usually followed by an appetite for plain food.'"

He has stronger remarks than this to offer. Children's books 'protract the imbecility of childhood'. They arrest the understanding, they give forwardness without strength, they hinder the mind from making vigorous shoots. They should be used with great caution, as an occasional refreshment from labour.

It was not just high-minded blue-stockings such as Hannah More who wanted to turn the child into a miniature adult. (It is claimed that she took her idea for Kate Stanley from the buoyant intellectual precocity of the young Macaulay, who can be said to have by-passed childhood altogether.) There were fashionable mammas of her time who had the same idea, but Miss More took a very different view of precocious sophistication. In *Strictures on the Modern System of Female Education* (1799) she was vehement about the current craze for baby

25

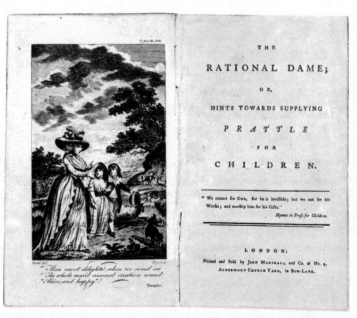

'Let us give [children] none but rational information,' the author, Lady Eleanor Fenn, said in her introduction to this compilation of facts about natural science. (*c.* 1785)

balls, held at fashionable late hours for bedizened infant guests. Only Swift could do justice to this folly, she said, this spectacle of 'lilliputian coquettes projecting dresses, studying colours, assorting ribbands and choosing feathers, their little hearts beating with hopes about partners and fears about rivals'. It was shameful to see them next morning, 'their fresh cheeks pale after the midnight supper, their aching heads and unbraced nerves disqualifying the little languid beings for the next day's talk; and to hear the grave apology, "that it is owing to the wine, the crowd, the heated room of the last night's ball"'.

But fashionable mammas had not the time to write moral tales,[1]

[1] One, though, was roused by the *Strictures* to dress up a guy as Hannah More with a rod in her hand, and to incite the children to dance round it singing:
Rouse the echoes of the hall
With your sportive Baby Ball.
Foot it nimbly on the floor
Nor heed the carping Hannah More.
(Quoted by M. G. Jones: *Hannah More*)

26

and though there are books on juvenile etiquette there are not many stories with a Chesterfieldian sort of hero. We may except 'J.N.', a disciple of Chesterfield if ever there was one, and his afore-mentioned *Half-Holiday Task-Book*. He shows us Master Webb who was one evening 'permitted to attend a dancing party. As he entered the ball-room every one was surprised at the grace and elegance with which he bowed; and, when the Ball was over, his behaviour had pleased his parents so much that they made him a present of a copy of *Hodgson's Children's Guide to Good Breeding*' – Hodgson, of course, being J.N.'s publisher.

J.N., however, with commendable openness of mind, includes a piece called *The Proud Girl*.

> *There was a young miss, who to make herself gay,*
> *At her looking-glass spent the best part of the day;*
> *There, curling, and frizzling, and patching, and painting,*
> *She labour'd until she was very near fainting.*

Pride castigated. (From Ann Elizabeth Oulton, *Juvenile Memoirs*, 1823)

How to place a white feather, or where stick a flower,
She car'd not to fritter away half an hour;
With wash-balls and scents, and pomatum and oil,
At her head, neck, and face, she'd incessantly toil.

But alas! this young girl, to her person so kind,
Bestow'd not a thought on the heart or the mind;
She was envious, insolent, haughty, and wild;
Knew no more of her book or her God than a child.

Her parents, as thoughtless and foolish as she,
Their grief, and her ruin, could never foresee;
'Till at length the small-pox spoil'd her beautiful face,
And she liv'd quite neglected, and died in disgrace!

Many were the moral tales of the time that preached against the fashionable life and against vanity. Nor were their writers necessarily all evangelicals. They were for the most part serious-minded ladies who deprecated the frivolity and worldliness of the high society of their time and constructed prosy stories to demonstrate how such a life led to the extinction of all the virtues. In many cases the girls' boarding schools were held to blame, and authors did not hesitate to tell their young readers what dangers lurked in the education they would receive there. 'French, music, and wriggling about the room,' was how Farmer Sandford in *Sandford and Merton* contemptuously described the curriculum at such establishments. An education that would fit her only 'for cutting a dash in her own carriage, receiving her five hundred friends at her assembly with the most polite in-difference, or figuring away with the most brilliant éclat in the highest circles in town,' was how Alicia Catherine Mant described that given to Caroline Lismore in the story by that name.

There was another hazard in the girls' school which Lady Fenn brought to light in *The Juvenile Tatler* (J. Marshall & Co., 1789) – the young lady might turn into 'a noted romp,' and she describes how a Miss Briskly, newly released from hers, is given to the wildest pranks such as dressing up the cat in baby linen and bringing it to the curate to be christened.

All responsible authors, then, ranged themselves against the fashionable life, and usually included in their attacks on it, an attack on boarding schools. But there was another danger in a later sort of boarding school to which Maria Benson in *Imitation* drew attention in 1817.

'She had been educated at a boarding-school, where she had picked up a great deal of grammar and dictionary. She had gone through the business of parsing in syntax . . . She had traced the maps from the nearest market-town, to the last point at which the greatest navigator had ever touched; she had read history and chronology, from the time that either had a date; she had learned to play on the pianoforte for seven years; and she had joined noses to eyes, and mouths to both, almost for as long a period, and she was, what is called by many persons, an accomplished woman.'

This was the sort of education to which Catherine Sinclair referred sadly in the preface to *Holiday House* in 1839, but it was not just boarding schools that were responsible; the home educated children suffered probably more. 'From the hour when children can speak, till they come to years of discretion or of indiscretion,' said Miss Sinclair, 'they are carefully prompted what to say, and what to think, and how to look and how to feel.'

This was what Lamb had damned thirty-seven years before, and in 1839 the cult of the 'informed' child showed no signs of weakening.

'The most formidable person to meet in society at present is the mother of a promising boy, about nine or ten years old; because there is no possible escape from a volume of anecdotes, and a complete system of education on the newest principles. The young gentleman has probably asked leave to bring his books to the breakfast-room – can scarcely be torn away from his studies at the dinner-hour – discards all toys – abhors a holiday – propounds questions of marvellous depth in politics or mineralogy – and seems, in short, more fitted to enjoy the learned meeting at Oxford than the exhilarating exercise of the cricket-ground.'

Miss Sinclair catalogued his library: Conversations on Natural Philosophy, on Chemistry, on Botany, on Arts and Sciences, Chronological Records of History, and travels as dry as a road-book. 'Therefore, while such works are delightful to the parents and teachers who select them, the younger community are fed with strong meat instead of milk, and the reading which might be a

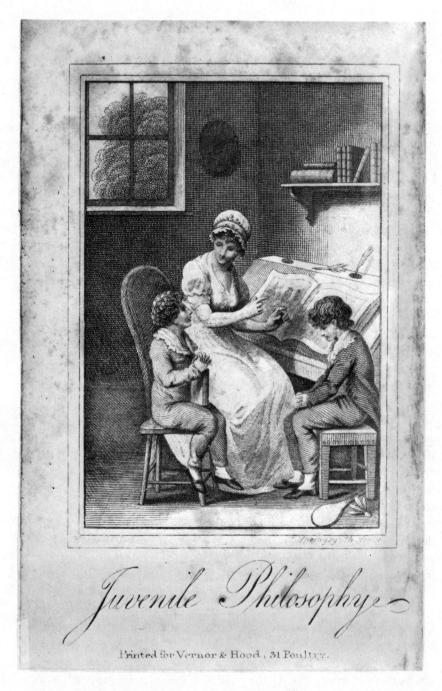

Juvenile Philosophy

Printed for Vernor & Hood, 31 Poultry.

The cult of the informed child. (*Juvenile Philosophy*, 1801)

relaxation from study becomes a study in itself.' And we remember Kate Stanley who at eight years old was going to read such books as men and women read, and her father's remarks about children's books arresting the understanding.

Not all educationalists desired children to be forcibly crammed with knowledge. Though Richard Lovell Edgeworth's ideal was a rational, well-informed child, he wished it to gain its knowledge and morality from experiment and experience. He formulated a system based on modified de Genlis and Rousseau principles, and described it in his *Practical Education* (1798). Here in the dialogue that he inserts between himself and his own children (the book is practical in the best sense since he had twenty-one, whom he taught at home) we see some of the drawbacks as well as the advantages of the system. Little Sneyd, for instance, to whom his father is trying to teach the principles of mathematics through the use of reason, says brightly that yes, he can take two away from one; he just has to wipe it away on his slate.

The Edgeworth children learned their lessons, not in a schoolroom, but in the library where the rest of the family sat. Prints and maps lay around, and the children were encouraged to handle them and ask questions. Their toys were carefully chosen to teach them skills, and they learned rural economy from going round the estate with their father. Richard Edgeworth was adamant that children should not be forced to learn or read what they could not understand, and the methods he used were described at greater length in *Early Lessons* which his daughter, the great Maria, wrote to supplement the earlier treatise. Here we see Frank and Rosamond, Harry and Lucy, discovering scientific principles through blowing soap bubbles and filling balloons, and moral truths and good sense through reason. Rosamond learns, for instance, that her day of misfortunes is directly attributable, not to the inscrutable workings of providence, but to getting up late in the first instance. She learns prudence through the famous story where she chooses a beautiful purple jar instead of some new shoes, discovers that it is only a common glass jar filled with purple liquid, and has to hobble around slip-shod for weeks to come. Her mother is apparently able, by sheer force of reason, to make her stop crying and stand still long enough to have a thorn taken from her finger.

It was a system only fully realiseable among the energetic and leisured (for Richard Edgeworth insisted that the children should never be allowed to associate with servants or any ignorant person), but it did have a great vogue among the *avant-garde*. It also had its opponents, particularly among those who detested its secular approach. Mrs Trimmer was one. She commented with disapproval that Lucy appeared to have been led into the habit of obedience to her parents, and into kindness and civility merely by finding that pleasurable sensations followed. 'But of the Law of God, which enjoins obedience to Parents, and good will to mankind, of Duties, she appears totally ignorant. She has not learned to offer up her prayers and praises to her Creator with every morning's dawn. But she has been taught to *make her bed*!' She also criticised Rosamond's mamma in the story of the purple jar. 'A child really treated in the manner Rosamond is described would have had great reason to complain of the unkindness of her mother.'

Mrs Sherwood was also outraged that a child should be reasoned into good behaviour, and wrote a story, *Obedience*, in which the child who has been taught to obey instantly, swallows her nauseous medicine and recovers from scarlet fever, whereas Robert, brought up on rational principles, refuses and dies.

But Richard Edgeworth, although he emphasised that no book should be forced on children who did not wish to read, was quite firm that they should only be offered books with a serious purpose. He recommended *Sandford and Merton*, the works of Mrs Barbauld and Mrs Trimmer, and especially Mrs Marcet's *Conversations on Chemistry* – but certainly no fairy tales, no folly, no fiction.

Nor would the evangelicals permit anything of this sort (their views were very much more vehement), allying themselves on this point if on no other with the Edgeworth school. In fact the idea that might be said to bind together the late Georgian and early Victorian writers for the young was the distrust of fiction. It was this that had banished the chapbooks from Newbery's shelves. It cast its shadow on two generations, so that Charlotte Yonge was to write in 1887 that she had found village children who were totally ignorant of Cinderella and the sort of story that in the old days had been told to them by the grandmothers. As it had so important an influence on children's books, in which there is constant reference to the pernicious influence of novels, it is worth some consideration.

It was not a new idea. The anonymous writer of *The History of Genesis* (1708) had written of the dangers of the chapbook tales.

'How often do we see Parents prefer "Tom Thumb," "Guy of Warwick" or some such foolish Book, before the Book of Life! Let not your Children read these vain Books, profane Ballads, and filthy Songs. Throw away all fond and amorous Romances and fabulous Histories of Giants, the bombast Achievements of Knight Errantry, and the Like; for these fill the Heads of Children with vain, silly, and idle imaginations.'

Now in the late eighteenth century it united minds who disagreed on most other points. The utilitarians held that reason must inevitably suffer if the imagination was cultivated, and the evangelicals that it was contrary to God's law since 'the imagination of man's heart is evil from his youth.' Joseph Priestley, who had great influence on the education of his time, thought that reading was not an end in itself but should be directed at some purpose such as that of encouraging morality or enlarging worldly knowledge.

Those who concerned themselves with children's reading – and by the last two decades of the eighteenth century there was quite a sizeable bunch – looked back with horror to a time when children had free access to the novels of circulating libraries while parents looked on complacently and did not interfere. The general charge was, in the words of the *Christian Observer* in 1815, that by novel reading the deceived imagination 'becomes itself the deceiver, and instead of embellishing life, as it is falsely represented to do, it heightens only imaginary and unattainable enjoyments, and transforms life itself into a dream, the realities of which are all made painful and disgusting, from our false expectations and erroneous notions of happiness'. The writer pointed out what a disastrous effect novel-reading had had upon the affairs of France, and drew attention to 'the dissipation, the low tone of public morals, and, I will add, the numerous and disgraceful divorces of the day' in England.

Hannah More, who held that the novel was 'one of the most universal as well as the most pernicious sources of corruption' made another telling point. 'Such is the frightful facility of this species of composition, that every raw girl, while she reads, is tempted to fancy that she can also write.' She speaks with feeling; no doubt she had been afflicted with adolescent scribblers among her sisters' pupils at Bristol.

One of the most violent evangelical denouncers of works of the imagination was the lady who wrote under the name of Charlotte

Elizabeth.[1] She could testify to their hideous danger because she had been corrupted in her youth, though when we read her tempestuous memoirs, *Personal Recollections* (1841) we may well feel that no earthly agency could have made an iota of difference to her passionate nature and her powers of imagination. Before her parents realised that their infant daughter even knew her letters she was found weeping over her slate on which she was writing a letter about some family disaster that had never occurred, but the contemplation of which was sending her into paroxysms of tears.

Charlotte Elizabeth described how 'the pernicious study of nursery tales' ensnared her imagination with dreamings of fairies and goblins. Even in those early years, she thought, the enemy was secretly constructing within her the power 'to mislead, by wild, unholy fiction, such as should come within the range of its influence. To God be all the glory that I am not now pandering with this pen to the most grovelling and the most impious of man's perverted feelings.'

But far worse was the way that Shakespeare ensnared her a few years later. The adults applauded her precocity while she drank 'a cup of intoxication under which my brain reeled for many a year . . . I revelled in the terrible excitement that it gave rise to; page after page was stereotyped upon a most retentive memory, without an effort, and during many a sleepless night I feasted on the pernicious sweets thus hoarded on my brain'. And it had the effect of her trying to be good only for the sake of being allowed to read Shakespeare.

Poetry she thought quite as dangerous: 'Parents know not what they do, when from vanity, thoughtlessness, or over-indulgence, they foster in a young girl what is called a poetical taste. Those things highly esteemed among men, are held in abomination with God; they thrust him from his creature's thoughts and enshrine a host of polluting idols in his place.'

This view of the dangers that lurked in Shakespeare and in poetry was fairly general, and responsible parents with the advent of the new seriousness of the late Georgian times were very careful in their supervision of their daughters' reading. Both the sisters in *Juliana, or The Affectionate Sisters* (by the Author of The Happy Family at Eason

[1] Charlotte Elizabeth Browne, born 1790, the child of a Norwich clergyman. She married first a Captain Phelan and settled in Ireland where she took great interest in the spiritual and material welfare of the Irish peasantry. She later separated from him, though he tried to claim the revenues from her writing. After his death she married a Mr Tonna.

House, 1800) were fond of poetry, 'but their mother seldom indulged them in reading it, as she considered if that partiality was encouraged they would lose much pleasure from other authors, and if before the judgement is formed they were allowed to read what they liked, it would be what ever offered, concluding it must be pretty if in verse'.

The corrupting power of the novel over the young female mind seems indeed to have preoccupied the authorities much as drugs and promiscuous sexual habits do in the 1970s. Many moral tales turned on this. A Miss M. Woodland devoted a whole story to the theme – *A Tale of Warning, or The Victims of Indolence* (1810). The only pleasure that Agatha enjoys is that of reading.

'The books she read, far from improving or fortifying her mind, tended to enervate her understanding, and lead her imagination astray. She could only endure romances, and such light novels as did not require the trouble of thinking. For those she had imbibed a pernicious passion; she read them night and day, and delighted to fancy herself a captive princess, whose chains some valiant knight was destined to break; or the persecuted ward of a cross old guardian; an angelic beauty who sighed for liberty and love in a cottage.'

Agatha marries, but neglects her child so woefully that it dies. At last she comes to her senses. 'Her mind and frame, rendered peculiarly weak by the fatal indulgence of indolence, sunk under the fearful conflict; she fell, senseless on the floor! ! . . . She was seized with a brain fever, and, after suffering excruciating agony for a few days, expired in the arms of her broken-hearted, but still affectionate, husband! ! !'

Even Maria Edgeworth dallied with the theme. In the story of *Mademoiselle Panache* (*Moral Tales*), an indolent French governess allows her charge to read novels. There is a carriage accident, and the young lady's suitor, going to her rescue, finds that the Lady Augusta had in her possession the *second* volume of a thoroughly reprehensible French novel. Whereupon he transfers his affections to a more worthy girl. And in another of the *Moral Tales* – Angelina, a silly adolescent even runs away to seek out her favourite novelist in the wilds of Wales, only to find that she is a raddled old soak.

The fear of the power of imagination over the mind was to persist for many years. But that the elders' attitude was resented by at least some of the young is shown by this entry from the

Journal of Emily Shore,[1] written when she was sixteen and staying with her uncle and aunt.

'Nov. 26, 1836. My uncle does not know that we are reading *Ivanhoe*, for we have said nothing about it to him; and after he had gone away this evening A., P., and I fell into conversation about it, and debated the propriety of giving it up. We were all very well inclined to do it, especially A., but we did not quite decide to do so. I confess I shall find it mortifying, and I cannot agree entirely with . . . 's opinions, because he would entirely abolish all works of imagination. Now, why has our maker given us imaginations, if they are never to be indulged?'

It was this abhorrence of fancy and the belief in 'improvement' that had driven Charles Lamb's childhood favourites from New-bery's shelves and replaced them with books with purpose. And the prototype of the book with purpose and the darling of the progressive parent with leanings towards Rousseau-ism was Thomas Day's *History of Sandford and Merton* published in three volumes from 1783 to 1789.

It must be said at once that he was no great writer. The reason for the book's popularity and survival must lie in the fact that it was the first serious full-length moral story for children, and that it reflected the new fashionable ideas on education. Day was an ardent disciple of Rousseau. Unswerving and uncritical in his devotion, he modelled his life on Rousseau's theories, condemning society, seeking the natural existence, and preaching the virtues of a natural education. The language of *Sandford and Merton* is perhaps marginally less florid than that other late Georgian classic, Mrs Trimmer's *Fabulous Histories* – later to be known as *The History of the Robins* (1786). But he has even less ability to construct a plot and his lack of humour is as unnerving. All the same, there is an endearing quality about the book which *The Robins* lacks. It is probably the personality of Day himself, so earnest, eager, warm-hearted and impractical. The story of how he reared two orphan girls in the fond expectation that one of them would surely be fitted to become Mrs Day is well-known; most of the ideas that lie behind *Sandford and Merton* belong to the same cloud cuckooland.

[1] Emily Shore, born in Bury St Edmunds 1819, died in Madeira of consumption in 1839. Her Journal was published by Kegan Paul in 1891.

Basically it is the story of two contrasted boys, Harry Sandford the worthy farmer's son, and Tommy Merton the indulged child of the rich West Indian planter, and the ideal education that they receive at the hands of the worthy Mr Barlow, the local clergyman. The good qualities of sensible Harry are enhanced by Mr Barlow's methods, and the silliness and bad habits are knocked out of Tommy, but the slender narrative is continually interrupted by stories from Xenophon and Plutarch, narrations of travels, gobbets of information, much moralising about the virtues of the simple life and the necessity of kindness to animals, and some very curious statements about natural history.

Harry, the ideal boy, is as close to Rousseau's Emile as Day's rather clumsy pen can make him. He has an honest, good-natured countenance which makes everybody love him, is never out of humour, always obliging, shares his dinner with the needy, and is always, always kind to animals.

'He would step out of the way for fear of hurting a worm, and employed himself in doing kind offices to all the animals in the neighbourhood. He used to stroke the horses as they were at work, and fill his pockets with acorns for the pigs; if he walked in the fields, he was sure to gather green boughs for the sheep, who were so fond of him, that they followed him wherever he went. In the winter time, when the ground was covered with frost and snow, and the poor little birds could get at no food, he would often go supperless to bed, that he might feed the robin-red-breasts: even toads, and frogs, and spiders, and such kinds of disagreeable animals, which most people destroy wherever they find them, were perfectly safe with Harry.'

He is incapable of being awed by pomp and wealth and fine manners, and though only six or seven if one reckons by Day's statements in the opening pages, he does not hesitate to rebuke his elders' follies in these matters. Perhaps Day liked to think of himself in the person of Harry: laughed at by the frivolous and empty-minded, but his true value recognised by the worthwhile.

Lurking modestly in later chapters of the book is Miss Sukey Simmons, Day's ideal girl, who has, one infers, been brought up in just the same way as Day brought up his orphan pair. She has been accustomed, from her earliest years 'to plunge into the cold bath at

virtue at last conquered. He promised
Mr. F. to follow his admonitions ; and he
fulfilled his promise. He shunned all as-

The reformed boy learns to eschew fashionable life. (*Edwin and Henry*, 1818)

every season of the year, to rise by candle-light in winter, to ride a
dozen miles upon a trotting horse, or to walk as many, even with the
hazard of being splashed, or soiling her clothes.' Like Harry, her
education has absolutely unfitted her for the fashionable life. Though
she is learned in the natural sciences, she can't speak a word of
French. '"My niece is to marry an Englishman,"' says her uncle
roundly. '"To what purpose then should I labour to take off the
difficulty of conversing with foreigners, and to promote her inter-
course with barbers, valets, dancing masters, and adventurers of
every description? . . . When respectable foreigners choose to visit us,
I see no reason why they should not take the trouble of learning the
language of the country."' Neither had he had her taught music
since life was too short to waste so much time on the science of making
a noise.

Set against Miss Sukey are not only the fashionable young ladies
with their attendant milliners, mantua-makers and dancing-masters,

their prinking and preening, and their adroitness at painting artificial flowers and warbling Italian airs; their inability to recognise
true honest worth, but also the new-style farmers' daughters:

'"There is fine work, indeed," says Farmer Sandford, mounted
on his favourite hobby-horse. '"They must have their hats and
feathers, and riding habits; their heads as big as bushels, and even
their hind quarters stuck out with cork or pasteboard: but scarcely
one of them can milk a cow, or churn, or bake, or do any one thing
that is necessary in a family: so that, unless the government will send
them all to this new settlement which I have heard so much of, and
bring us a cargo of plain, honest, house-wives, who have never been
at boarding-schools, I cannot conceive how we farmers are to get
wives."'

For two pins his own daughters would follow the fashionable trend.

'"My wenches, instead of Deb and Kate, would be miss Deborah and
miss Catherine; in a little time, they must be sent to boarding-school,
to learn French and music, and wriggling about the room. And,

The false values implanted at boarding schools. Engraving by Gillray of the
farmer and his wife showing off their daughter to their neighbours on her
return from school. 1819.

when they come back, who must boil the pot, or make the pudding, or sweep the house, or serve the pigs? Did you ever hear of miss Juliana, or miss Harriet, or miss Caroline, doing such things?"'

Thomas Day, as has been said, was not a very talented writer, and he was by no means an inventive one. What gives his book its individual touch is its endearing naïvety, which goes a long way towards reconciling us to the tedium when he is hammering away at his pet themes. It was a book with influence, and Harry Sandford, partly Rousseau's child, partly Day's, partly born of the spirit of the times, did become the pattern hero of the moral tale for many years; though by 1872 he had become so ludicrous that F. C. Burnand, an editor of *Punch*, went to the length of writing a heavy-handed burlesque, *The New History of Sandford and Merton*.

There are many variations on Harry Sandford, of course, and different aspects of him are stressed. Sometimes it is Harry Sandford of the questing mind, thirsty for knowledge:

> *He sought, when it was in his power,*
> *For information twice an hour*

as Belloc put it. This type of hero more often than not is a mere wooden peg on which to hang a deadweight of moralising, scientific truths, and gratuitous information according to the Barlow methods – and sometimes a bizarre mixture of scientific truth and religious teaching as in Mrs Ventum's *Holiday Reward* (J. Harris, 1814).

'. . . the cold of which you complain, Henry, and the frost and snow with which you find fault, are gifts from God to fertilise the earth, and assist the progress of vegetation . . . Snow is by experiment found to be twenty-four times lighter than water . . .' and so on through several pages, winding up triumphantly 'consider how much better you are off, than the poor Laplander.'

The Harry Sandfords were plain children. 'Miss Polly had the misfortune to have but one eye and to be very much marked with the smallpox. Little James too was a very plain child, and had a frightfully large mouth and a flat nose; but then, they were so extremely good and civil to every body; and spoke so politely if they were asked a question that every body who was acquainted with them loved them dearly,' wrote Dorothy Kilner in *The Histories of More Children than One, or Goodness Better than Beauty*. Nobody with any sense of responsibility would now address a book, as Newbery did, to *'pretty* Miss Polly,' for vanity was a failing that the late Georgians thought as insidious and dangerous as gaming. Charlotte Yonge, born in 1823, was to suffer from this.

'I never really knew whether I was not ugly. I know I thought myself so, and I was haunted occasionally by doubts whether I were not deficient, till I was nearly grown up. My mother said afterwards that I once asked her if I was pretty, and she replied that all young creatures were, i.e., the little pigs.'

Scores of fables equated the handsome with the profligate and the plain with the immaculate, but, since this was not of itself probably enough to convince the child reader, the first would be brought to a bad end through gambling or duelling or a decline, and the second plod his way through to solid affluence.

> *He rose at once in his Career,*
> *And long before his Fortieth Year*
> *Had wedded Fifi, Only Child*
> *of Bunyan. First Lord Alberfylde,*
> *He thus became immensely Rich,*
> *And built the Splendid Mansion which*
> *Is called 'The Cedars, Muswell Hill'*
> *Where he resides in Affluence still . . .*

Belloc does not exaggerate.

The vain little girl, of course, has many fingers wagged at her. The most famous of them all is probably Miss Augusta Noble in *The Fairchild Family*, so admired by Emily and Lucy Fairchild in her flower-embroidered muslin, her rose-coloured sash and shoes, her pearl necklace, but destined, like so many of her sort, to be burned to ashes through taking up a candle to admire herself in the glass.

The simple life was a cardinal feature of the Rousseau doctrine. Thomas Day is forever stepping back and asking us to admire the vigour and strength of Harry, so plainly reared, so contemptuous of rich food and easeful ways, and to mark what a poor showing Tommy Merton makes in contrast, back from the West Indies where, dressed in silk and laced clothes, he had strutted round with a negro holding an umbrella over him, and another to pick him up when he was tired.

The indulged boy. (Lithograph by Denis Dighton from *Early Impressions*, 1828)

Now, in consequence, he is fretful, delicate and ailing. 'He could use none of his limbs with ease, nor bear any degree of fatigue.'

The 'indulged child' was to become part of the mythology of the moral writers. He was a bogey of the real-life nursery too. Charlotte Yonge, brought up on Edgeworth principles, remembered how Spartan her infancy was, her nursery a dark little passage room, her diet mostly dry bread and milk, and never, never such luxuries as butter or eggs or jam. Elizabeth Grant of Rothiemurchus, born a generation before, fared worse. Even in the long Highland winters she and her sisters used to be plunged, screaming, into a frozen horse trough every morning, and she was horse-whipped by her father if she did not eat the bread and milk that made her sick. She remembered, too, the agony of practising the harp in an unheated, unlighted drawing room for an hour before breakfast in the cold, dark winter months. (One did not need a candle to play scales.)

And so in their stories the children are warned of the fearful consequences of being 'indulged': their teeth turn black, their faces yellow, and their characters are destroyed. Of Mr Robinson's children in an episode in *Idle Hours Employed* (John Harris, n.d.) three die in one year and the fourth is so weakened that by the age of twenty-four he is as feeble as an old man. Mamma in Mrs Ventum's *The Holiday Reward* tells Louisa the reason why Miss Mira Jones is shunned and disregarded by the whole neighbourhood. Her parents had been rich farmers, it seems. (This in itself is significant; the Georgians attributed every sort of folly and poor taste and ill-bred act to rich farmers, just as Victorians did to those connected with 'trade'.)

Miss Mira had been indulged in every fancy. 'She was a perfect hot-house plant, but so nursed, and such ridiculous care taken of her that she was not even suffered to go backwards and forwards to school; and in the hottest day in summer I have seen her wrapt in two or three handkerchiefs, besides a thick cloth coat . . . To be short, Louisa, long before Mira had attained her fourteenth year, she was not only esteemed the greatest liar, but most artful girl in the parish.' Her temper was a plague to all, she was abandoned by everybody and took to immoderate drinking. 'Poor woman, I pity, while I condemn her, and I cannot help regarding her parents as her greatest enemies, who by a false indulgence and bad example, have ruined the happiness and destroyed the credit of their child.'

Over and above everything else, the Harry Sandfords were kind to the less fortunate. It was not so much kindness within the family that the moralists had in mind as the suffering poor and the animals. It was part of the sensibility that was possibly the most esteemed virtue of the time. Many are the stories in which children spend money thoughtlessly on private pleasure, and then find to their remorse that they have nothing left to give a famished beggar. Little girls are told that if they want a new pelisse their mammas will have to abandon the idea of feeding a hungry family. Some of them sacrifice more than just a pelisse. Emily Mason in Mary Belson's *The Orphan Girl, or The Sweets of Benevolence* (1819), haunted by the memory of a half-starved match girl, determines to give up all toys for ever, and use the money to support six female orphans in a special school till they are old enough to be employed.

But kindness to the poor is a virtue of great antiquity; the idea that it should be extended to animals was a relatively new one, and we read, fascinated and appalled, of cruelties we could never have guessed at. Spitting cock-chafers was a favourite occupation. You stuck a pin through the insect, fastened it to a thread and watched him twirl round. Even Harry Sandford was guilty of this until it was pointed out how the poor animal suffered. Boys did not only rob birds' nests, they went 'bat-fowling' to net roosting songbirds. Any

Emma gives her shoes to a poor girl. (*Mamma's Stories for her Little Girl*, 1814)

mouse that they caught alive provided great sport and limitless possibilities. They stripped flies of their wings and birds of their feathers, and sucked the honey from live bees.

Nor were these just the idle, thoughtless ways of country children. It had become very fashionable to keep pets, and the wealthy child with his aviary of birds, his lapdogs, monkeys, squirrels and dormice was all too apt to neglect them and let them die, or keep them, according to Mary Wister in *The Adventures of a Doll* (Darton, Harvey and Darton, 1816) for the sole purpose of tormenting them.

'One pretty little dog particularly excited my compassion. His tormentors had been told, that bears were taught to dance by putting them on hot irons. Poor little Fido was carried into the laundry and made to dance on the stove where the maids were heating their irons.'

Miss Kitty aged twelve pointed out to her eight year old brother George what might be the consequences of his cruel pranks. (*The Sister's Gift, or The Bad Boy Reformed*. York, J. Kendrew, 1826). 'If you still continue to torment every unhappy being that comes in your way, you will in time (for the transition is very easy) be led to exercise your cruelties upon your own species, and Negro-like, rejoice in the blood of a parent or friend! – horrid thought.' Master George, being a rational child, sees the force of the argument, even though it is a mere sister's, and 'promised ever after to be as remarkable for generosity, compassion, and every other virtue, as he had hitherto been for cruelty, forwardness, and ill nature.'

And here we come to Mrs Trimmer and her efforts for animals. It shows her perhaps at her most genial. A good woman she certainly was, but given overmuch to lecturing, and to the certainty that what she stood for was right and what she opposed was wrong, and that there was no middle way. Life would be so simple and pleasant, she seems to be saying, if only everybody did what they were told and feared God and honoured the king and loved their neighbour (only you must first be sure that the neighbour held the right opinion).

Her efforts for the Sunday Schools are described in the next chapter. We are concerned here with the book that she wrote to promote kindness to animals, the famous *History of the Robins* on which children of all right-minded parents were reared for two generations, and with her strictures on the books of her time in *The Guardian of Education*.

This journal has already been mentioned. She founded it in 1802, and ran it apparently single-handed, the design of the work being:

'First, to caution Young Mothers, and others of the Female Sex who are engaged in the important Business of Education, against the Attempts which are making to banish Christianity from the Nursery and the School, in order to introduce Philosophy (as it is falsely called) in its stead; to direct their Attention to the peculiar Circumstances of the present Times, as they are likely to affect the Principles and Manners of the Rising Generation; and to assist their Endeavours for the Cultivation of Religion in the Minds of Children, upon the Basis of Christianity. Secondly, to assist Parents and Governesses in their choice of Books for the Instruction and Amusement of Children and Youth, as far as the Principles of Religion and good Morals are concerned.'

Naturally, working upon these principles, she was against Thomas Day (badly infected with dangerous French philosophic notions) and Richard Lovell Edgeworth whose approach to education was secular. But she was also against a great many other books as well, and is a warning to the educational pundits who unearthed corruption and perversion in Enid Blyton and other such innocuous texts.

Mrs Trimmer had a certain amount of excuse for her watchdog activities. She was writing during the time of the French wars, when revolution was in the air, and she was terrified that sedition and atheism would corrupt the English young as they had corrupted the French. Therefore she felt it her responsibility to scrutinise all their books.

She could find threats to the social order in the most unexpected places. *John Gilpin* should be barred because it 'places an honest, industrious tradesman, worthy to be held out as an example of prudence and economy to men of his rank, in a ridiculous situation, and provokes a laugh at the expense of conjugal affection.' A riddle in a joke book called *Mince Pies for Christmas* was so obviously detestable that she needed to make no comment herself. It was 'What is Majesty deprived of its Externals?' The answer is 'A Jest' (Majesty without the M and Y), and this of course is jacobinism of the direst sort. Nor did she like jokes about courtiers or great men, because these too threatened the social order, as did *The Renowned History of Primrose Prettyface*, because it suggested to girls of the lower order that they might aspire to marriage with persons so far superior to their own, and put into the heads of young gentlemen at an early age, an idea that they might when they grew up marry servant-maids.

She was whole-heartedly with those who distrusted fiction and works of imagination, and though she was tender at first towards the fairy stories that she had loved as a child, Red Riding Hood, and Bluebeard, and such, her attitude was to grow harder; 'we do not wish to have such sensations awakened in the hearts of our grandchildren by the same means . . . Neither do the generality of tales of this kind supply any moral instruction level to the infantine capacity.'

Robinson Crusoe naturally she deplored since it was so much venerated by the Rousseau-ists and those who were enthralled by the idea of the Simple Life. Besides, it led to an early taste for a rambling life, and she had known some little boys whom it had inspired to run away to sea, thereby driving the mother of one of them into a fatal illness from anxiety. So much danger lurked in so many places.

46

Even *The Book of Games* published by Tabart in 1805 might lead to an interest in games of hazard and to an increase in the numbers of gamsters in the nation.

What books did she approve of ? There was Aikin and Barbauld's *Evenings at Home*. Lamb might have forcefully damned this brother and sister, but he was in a minority. Most saw them as the supreme benefactors of the age. It was the one book on which all the pundits were agreed. Mrs Trimmer also venerated Watts' *Divine and Moral Songs,* by now nearly a century old, and mildly recommended Jane and Ann Taylor's *Original Poems,* for though she had criticism to offer as to the moral content, she thought the young authors would improve in subsequent works. She invariably praised the Kilner sisters, Dorothy and Mary Jane, whose stories, though moral, have a Smolletian and rumbustious earthiness very different from the high-flown sensibility of *The History of the Robins.* Otherwise the authors she commends are forgotten except by the antiquarian – people like

The folly of vanity. Mary paints her cheeks but only makes herself ridiculous.
(*Mamma's Stories for her Little Girl*)

Mrs Pilkington, Mrs Pinchard, Priscilla Wakefield, Mrs Hofland, Miss Sandham, schoolmistresses, most of them, who made a little extra money by their moral tales, and vented some of their irritation with girl-nature at the same time.

The Robins is probably the only other moral story besides *Sandford and Merton* that is remembered now from those years. It was published in 1786, the same year as part II of *Sandford and Merton*. (Its original portentous title, *Fabulous Histories. Designed for the Instruction of Children, respecting their Treatment of Animals*, was later discarded in favour of the more tempting *History of the Robins*.) It survived longer than Day: (my own copy is one of a series of gift books issued by Frederick Warne in the 1870s, and there is no hint that it is merely an interesting revival) and enjoyed more universal favour. Thomas Day's notions, though admittedly diluted with a great deal of harmless information, were regarded with deep suspicion by many people, whereas Mrs Trimmer could not possibly be faulted on the score of moral principles. The book is upright, worthy, and completely safe. It also turns its back on the crude, earlier Georgian notions that still to a certain extent lurk in *Sandford and Merton*, where all merit meets with immediate material reward, and Tommy Merton falls into a horsepond or a quagmire in nearly every chapter.

The Robins is a monument of sensibility. It was not the foolish, exaggerated sensibility that Hannah More and Mrs Chapone warned about, that sent the female sex into fainting fits and a vapour of tears at the death of a parrot, but true refined feeling expressed with all the cliché-ridden elegance of which the female pen was then capable. It quivers with lofty sentiments, about duty to parents, benevolence to the poor, the superior moral worth of the plain and dutiful child over the handsome and talented. Didactic and high-flown though it is, it was popular among children. After all, it was the nearest approach to imaginative literature that responsible elders allowed them, and the theme of kindness to animals is a more palatable moral than most.

There are two interwoven sets of characters: the human family and their 'pensioners,' their 'winged supplicants,' the robin family. The first is used to teach kindness to animals, the second personify the virtues and failings to which Mrs Trimmer desired to draw attention in the children of her time. (She also uses other birds for this purpose; there is a stork, for instance, who Aeneas-like carries his old father to safety on his back, and the vulgar, brawling sparrows

and to apply those useful remedies, which were afterwards of so much service to him.

She frequently observed him catching poor innocent flies, through the bodies of which he would stick pins, and then fasten them to a coach made of a card; and would thus take a pleasure in seeing them drag it along after them, till they were quite dead with pain and fatigue.

Sometimes he would amuse himself with tying an old tin-kettle or canister to the tail of any dog that was so unhappy as to fall in his way; and then with a whip set them a running and howling through the town, to the great fright and mortification of the poor tormented animal.

The farmers all round the neigh-

Cruelty to animals – a favourite Georgian theme. (*The Sister's Gift*, 1826)

who are capable of leading well-conducted young birds of good family astray.) The robin family consists of Father, Mother, and four young: Robin, Dicky, Pecksy and Flapsy. (These rather endearing names seem unTrimmeresque, and that is correct – the author apparently took over the last two from a Newbery publication.) Pecksy is the shining light of the family, the ideal daughter. She has no outward charms, of course, but the sweetest of dispositions. She is dutiful, grateful, submissive to the will of her parents. She obediently accepts the necessity of acquiring accomplishments, though a little doubtful of her ability to sing. '"I would apply to music with all my heart,"' she says to her father, '"but I do not believe it is possible to learn it."' '"Perhaps not,"' says Mr Robin, '"but I do not doubt you will apply yourself to what your mother requires of you: and she is an excellent judge both of your talents and of what is suitable to your station in life."'

The other Robin young reflect in varying degrees the failings that

Mrs Trimmer wished to castigate in the youth of her time. There is Robin himself, incautious and imprudent. (There are a fair number of Georgian moral tales that warn boys against lack of caution with ice, mad dogs, loaded guns, jumping from high places or spinning tops – pretty well everything had its dangers, it seemed). He is injured in consequence and remains something of an invalid for the rest of his life. Dicky and Flapsy are rather giddy and heedless and are trapped and imprisoned in an aviary.

The older Robins are gifted with every good quality. They are devoted to each other, wise and loving parents, and ever-conscious of the debt they owe to the Benson family. When the time comes for the young to leave the nest, the father speeds them on their way with eloquent words, ending:

'Let none of your own species excel you in any amiable quality, for want of your endeavours to equal the best; and do your duty in every relation of life, as we have done ours by you. To the gay scenes of levity and dissipation prefer a calm retirement, for there is the greatest degree of happiness to be found.'

To which his mate adds her maternal exhortations.

'"Adieu, ye dear objects of my late cares and solicitude! may ye never more stand in need of a mother's assistance! Though nature now dismisses me from the arduous task which I have long daily performed, I rejoice not, but would gladly continue my toil for the sake of its attendant pleasures. Oh! delightful sentiments of maternal love, how can I part with you! Let me, my nestlings, give you a last embrace." Then spreading her wings, she folded them successively to her bosom, and instantly recovered her tranquillity.'

There are other stories written from the animals' point of view, probably in imitation of Mrs Trimmer. With the exception of *The Life and Perambulation of a Mouse*, where the narrator manages to keep up his mouse nature in spite of his moralising, they are no more like animals than the moral tale characters are like real children, and their titles are the most exciting part of them.

Occasionally in all the welter of improvement so diligently poured out for half a century or more, we can catch glimpses of a child that seems to think and act like a real one, whose doings are set down in language that is direct and simple. There are Frank and Rosamond in Maria Edgeworth's *Early Lessons*, for instance, who quarrel and make it up, and enjoy themselves, and do foolish, childish things.

And in the simple sentences of Mrs Barbauld's *Lessons for Children*, which she intended for two and three year olds, we can put together the small world of a little boy 200 years ago, and watch Charles eating his bread and milk, stroking the cat, feeding the pigeons, hiding from his papa under his mamma's apron, riding to the hunt on papa's cane, learning to count the kisses that he gives mamma.

As the book goes on and the words get longer, Charles sees the seasons pass. There are few who can give such evocative descriptions as Mrs Barbauld with such economy. Those children whose literary style was formed from the *Lessons* and *Hymns in Prose* were fortunate indeed. Barely a page to January, but the cold and the dark close in round us. 'It is four o'clock, it is dark. Light the candles; and Ralph, get some wood from the wood-house, and get some coals and make a very good fire.' The new life of February, with snowdrops and rooks cawing in the fields; running to chase the rainbow in April; the languid heat of a hayfield in June; the little boy bathing in the river in July; August and the reapers in the field; the sound of the distant sporting guns in September, and Charles gathers enough windfall apples to make some dumplings; dark dismal November – 'Well, never mind it, we will sit by the fire and read and tell stories, and look at pictures.' 'It is December, and Christmas is coming, and Betty is very busy. She is paring apples and chopping meat, and beating spice. What for, I wonder! It is to make mince pies. Little boys come from school at Christmas. Pray wrap them up warm, for it is very cold. Well, spring will come again some time.'

Good could come out of the lesson books, even Georgian ones.

[3]

The Sunday scholar
1780–1830

As the mid-Victorian years roll past in Arnold Bennett's *Clayhanger*, two great occasions bring the inhabitants of the Pottery towns out into the streets in their best clothes, jostling and sweating under cloudless summer skies. One is the Golden Jubilee of 1887, the other the Sunday School Centenary seven years earlier. Of the two, the Centenary as described by Bennett is infinitely the bigger affair. It unites all the social strata in the Five Towns as nothing else could. It even fleetingly unites the churches – 'the princes of the royal house, and the Archbishop of Canterbury and the Lord Mayor of London had urged that it should be so'. For Darius Clayhanger, the prosperous, hard-headed man of business, it has special and poignant meaning. The Primitive Methodist Sunday School of his childhood in the 1830s had saved and preserved him. Sunday morning was the morning which he lived for. The rest of the week he toiled from five in the morning till nine or ten at night in the stinking cellars of the pot-works, making handles for beer-mugs, then on Sundays for a few hours he was lifted above those dark waters that threatened to overwhelm him. His son Edwin, born in 1856 into a life of solid middle class respectable comfort, knows nothing of this. He watches the celebrations with aloof superiority. The Centenary is just a reminder of what he had to endure as a boy – 'atrocious tedium, pietistic insincerity,' a malicious device of parents for harassing children.

Darius and Edwin would have had thousands of counterparts. Since 1780 the scope and purpose of the Sunday School had dramatically changed; so had the character of the Sunday scholars. The Five Towns were quite right to treat the affair of the Centenary with such reverence; the Queen had done far less for them. Most of those

Opposite: 1880 – the Victorian respectability of Sunday schools. A Sunday scholar presents a Bible to the daughters of the Prince of Wales at the centenary celebrations. (*Illustrated London News*)

respectable citizens marshalling the processions on that summer day in 1880, or complacently watching, had been raised from the mire by the agency of the Sunday schools. Their children's attitude now might be one of boredom or indifference, but the fact was that the manners, morals, and the condition of hundreds of thousands had been affected by Robert Raikes' movement. It alone had created the demand for the books discussed in later chapters, so it is only right that a beginning should be made by showing how Darius and his generation differed from his son's.

The ideal Sunday scholar of the 1780s was clean and orderly. That was as much as those who concerned themselves with his welfare dared hope. We hardly meet him in the pages of the children's books of the period; he still had to be taught to read, and the Bible was the book to which all his attention would be directed. The reward book, to become such a vast publishing enterprise in fifty years or so, did not exist. Robert Raikes as rewards gave his pupils combs, but even these were sometimes premature gifts for shocks of hair so matted and filthy that only fingers could be pulled through them. Edwin Clayhanger, the mid-Victorian child, was hustled to his Bible class because it was the respectable thing to do; for Darius it had been the only bright star of his grimy world. Bennett took the whole of his account of the early years of Darius from the reminiscences of Charles Shaw,[1] published in the Staffordshire Sentinel in 1892. This child had been sent to a dame school for three or four years, but his education there finished when he was seven; after that he had to go to work.

'What shall I say of the benefit I got from the Sunday school? To speak of the benefit it has been to this nation would be a joy, and all I could say would fail to tell the measure of its beneficence and inspiration, especially to the children of the poor of those days . . . Sunday brought sweetness into my life, and lifted me out of the demoralising influences of the working days. I was emancipated from the past week, and when the scenes I had to witness, as on Monday and Tuesday, were fullest of evil, I felt strongest, for the spell of the Sunday was then fresh in my soul.'

'Mr Raikes was the original founder of the Sunday schools,' wrote

[1] Signed 'An Old Potter'.

Fanny Burney only eight years after their inception, 'an institution so admirable, so fraught, I hope, with future good and mercy to generations yet unborn, that I saw almost with reverence the man who had first suggested it.' Whether or not it was Raikes who was the initiator of the movement is irrelevant; he was one of a number of people who all began to work for the same end at much the same time and who all were confronted with the same facts – the seemingly hopeless degradation of the labouring classes. Raikes, a prosperous printer and newspaper proprietor in Gloucester, was displeased by the filthy ragamuffins who idled round the streets on Sundays. He collected together as many as he could – 'botanising in human nature' he described his forays into the slums – found premises and a woman who would teach them. 'There goes Bobby Wild Goose and his ragged regiment,' Gloucester householders used to say as they watched the urchins being marched to church after morning school. Old inhabitants of Gloucester in the 1860s remembered how those first children 'were of the very lowest kind that could be found'. Some of them had to be bribed to take part. Others were strapped all the way to the school by determined parents, one or two had 14 lb. weights on their legs to stop them absconding.

The classes needed a firm hand. Josiah Harris, who collected material for a biography of Raikes, spoke to an old man who had been a pupil in 1800.

'The first Sunday I went, a boy called "Winkin Jim" brought a young badger with him and turned it loose. You should have seen old Mother Critchley jump! I laugh now . . . No writing was taught in the school in my time. We used to learn [from a] "Reading-made-easy" book, the Collects, Bible and Testament. That is those who could read, Some learnt their letters and A.B.'s.'

Raikes, said this old man, used to punish the boys himself, caning them as they were held down kicking and swearing, between the front legs of an upturned chair. 'One boy was a notorious liar . . . Mr Raikes could do nothing with him, and one day he caught him by the hand and pressed the tips of his fingers on the bars of the stove or fireplace.'

'Was he burnt?' Harris asked.

'Blistered a bit. Mr Raikes would take care that he was not much injured; but he did hate liars! Look at my book. This is what he printed for us to learn: "A thief is better than a man who is accustomed to lie." What I think hurt him most was to hear the boys cursing and swearing at each other in church. We were in church one morning and a boy named Philpotts (we called him Mugs) stuck a big shawl-pin into a boy who was nodding. He jumped up into the air with pain and yelled and swore and flew at "Mugs".'

Raikes' concern with the street arabs of Gloucester was probably as much economic and social as spiritual. His Sunday schools had none of the peculiarly evangelical flavour that was to be identified with the movement in the next century. He was not a teetotaller, for this movement had not yet begun, nor a Sabbatarian; his paper, the *Gloucester Journal*, went to press on Sunday. 'I should doubt if he was a man . . . of evangelical principles,' wrote John Powell, MP for Gloucester in 1863. 'I attribute his establishing Sunday schools rather to a benevolent than a religious motive.'

However, the teaching given in his Gloucester schools was firmly based on the Bible. He produced a manual of instruction for his pupils.

The Sunday Scholar's Companion; consisting of Scripture sentences, disposed in such order, as will quickly ground Young Learners in the Fundamental Doctrines of our Most Holy Religion, and at the same time lead them pleasantly on, from Simple and Easy to Compound and Difficult Words.

To the prudent Georgian man of business it would have seemed quite purposeless to have a secular spelling book when you could combine what the locals called 'redinmadesy' with sacred precepts. So the Gloucester children started, once they had learned their letters, with sentences such as 'God is Love,' and 'God is One,' and worked their way upwards to 'Man that is accustomed to opprobrious Words will never be reformed all the Days of his Life,' and 'All Iniquity is as a two-edged Sword, the Wounds whereof cannot be healed.'

Sarah Trimmer, in the Middlesex town of Brentford, had observed Raikes' efforts for the Gloucester poor with great interest, and in 1782, her own large family (she had six sons and six daughters) presumably by then being less demanding, she followed suit. Brentford in the 1780s, as Mrs Trimmer told her lady readers in *The Oeconomy of Charity* (1786), was a town largely populated by labourers employed in market-gardens, brickfields and farms, whose work was

CHEAP REPOSITORY.

Sunday Reading.

THE
BEGGARLY BOY.
A PARABLE.

Sold by. J. MARSHALL,
(PRINTER to the CHEAP REPOSITORY) for Moral and
Religious Tracts,) No. 17, Queen-street, Cheapside,
and No. 4, Aldermary Church-Yard, Bow-Lane,
and R. WHITE, Piccadilly, London.
By S. HAZARD,
(PRINTER to the CHEAP REPOSITORY) at Bath; and
by all Bookfellers, Newfmen and Hawkers, in Town
and Country.
Great Allowance will be made to Shopkeepers and Hawkers.
PRICE 1d. each, or 4s. 6d. per 100.—2s. 6d. for 50.
1s. 6d. for 25.
[Entered at Stationers Hall.]

Gathering in the pupils. Title page of a Cheap Repository Tract.

seasonal, and where the dirty ragged children roamed the streets from morning till night, pestering the travellers down the one main street, 'a road which is the greatest thoroughfare in England'. However, when the inhabitants were canvassed, most of the parents and children (taken from five upwards) were eager for schools, though some of them had to be provided with clothes and with brushes and combs before they were fit to attend.

The children were taught to read, questioned on the psalms and lessons that they read aloud, sang psalms (a much-enjoyed treat, this) and repeated some of Watts' songs. In her handbook for the teachers, *The Teacher's Assistant*, much emphasis is put on the catechetical method, by which miscellaneous information was rather bewilderingly to be mingled with religious instruction. *Question*. 'Suppose a man wants a coat, or a woman a stuff gown, or any flannel things, what part of God's works must they have?' *Answer*. Wool. And 'Suppose shoes are needed, can they be had without God?' *Answer*. No. There were besides many questions designed to see that the children knew how to behave in church and what to expect when the last trumpet sounded.

The Oeconomy of Charity also set out the precepts which were hung in the Brentford schools and read out to the children Sunday by Sunday. They give a fairly clear idea of the sort of material Mrs Trimmer was having to deal with.

'Before you enter the church take off your hats (or pattens) and go in without noise or clattering.'

'Do not talk in church: do not eat apples or other things either there or in school.'

'Do not spoil your hassocks, or anything else belonging to the house of God.'

'Do not sing at improper times.'

These were some of the morning admonitions. The evening ones reminded the children how to behave after school was over.

'Keep from swearing, stealing and lying.'

'Let no one tempt you to drink drams.'

'Do not fight or quarrel, call nicknames, or tell tales.'

'Come to school early next Sunday.'

'Come with your faces and hands clean, your hair combed, and your apparel neat.'

'Go home quietly.'

She also reminded her scholars to bow or curtsey to the clergyman as he came into church, and to remember to do the same when they met ladies and gentlemen. She was a lady of high principles and undoubted piety, but she did not scruple to use worldly arguments when she addressed her readers in *The Oeconomy of Charity*. After all, she needed something to counter their objections about the folly of teaching the lower orders to read. 'Do we wish our daughters to have modest, discreet, trusty maid-servants?' she demanded, and reminded them how important it was that these should be of good principles, not in league with robbers, and that they did not keep their employers in a constant state of suspicion and uneasiness with their immoralities, nor with their gross wastefulness.

Hannah More similarly had to defend her educational schemes against critics who held that the education of the poor was not only folly, but positively dangerous. Her dogmatic statements about what they should or should not learn make her sound far harsher than the personality that emerges from the Cheap Repository Tracts which were written for the people whom she had taught to read, but who found themselves without books – or at any rate without books that would improve and not corrupt. She had come in her middle age to settle quietly in Somerset, but found that instead of an idyllic pastoral life all round her, she was living in the midst of poverty-stricken and brutalised farm-workers and miners, tyrannised by the farmers, and utterly neglected by government, Church, and philanthropy. William Wilberforce begged her in 1789 to try to do something for them, and doggedly Hannah and her sister Martha set to work.

It was a daunting task, but they persevered, tramping the dirty roads between the Mendip villages, coaxing half-guineas out of subscribers, arguing with surly farmers, trying to shame an indolent and apathetic clergy into co-operation, searching for suitable teachers, and then enrolling the children.

In her Cheap Repository Tracts Hannah More did not conceal the difficulty that she had with the farmers, though she maintained a fiction of exemplary clergy. The tract *The Sunday School* describes the whole process of setting up a school. There is the difficulty of finding the right mistress. Too many of the prosperous approached for aid by Mrs Jones (this was how she referred to herself) think this is the ideal way of ridding themselves of a tiresome dependent. Eventually in a spirit of altruism which Hannah More herself alas was rarely to find among the clergy, the local incumbent agrees to

THE

SUNDAY SCHOOL.

SOLD BY HOWARD & EVANS,
(Printers to the Cheap Repository for Moral and Religious
Tracts,) No. 41 and 42, Long-Lane, West-Smithfield;
and J. HATCHARD, No. 190, Piccadilly, London,
By J. BINNS, Bath; and by all Booksellers, Newsmen,
and Hawkers, in Town and Country.
⁎ *Great allowance will be made to Shopkeepers and Hawkers.*
Price One Penny, or 6s. 6d. *per* Hundred.
Entered at Stationers-Hall.

The schoolmistress and her pupils, now decently clad in
specially provided clothing. Title page of a Cheap Repository
Tract.

give up his housekeeper for the task even though it means that his
pea-soup from now onwards will not be so well-flavoured nor his
linen so neatly got up.

There is a spirited encounter between Mrs Jones and Farmer
Hoskins who is against the whole scheme. He does not want his
labourers to learn to read, nor his maids to substitute psalms for the
merry ribald songs that they sing when they are milking, and he
detests having to subscribe to charitable objects.

'"Well, Madam, what is it now? Flannel or French? or weavers, or a new church or large bread, or cheap rice? or what other new whim-wham for getting the money out of one's pocket?"'

Patiently Mrs Jones reasons with him, but all her eloquence is as nothing beside the fact that Farmer Dobson ('"he . . . only a renter who wears his coat as threadbare as a labourer"') has subscribed a half-guinea. In a spirit of contempt, Farmer Hoskins slams down a guinea.

The History of Hester Wilmot carries on the story of the Sunday School with an account of one of its scholars. Hester is fourteen and unable to read when Mrs Jones comes to bespeak her. Her mother receives Mrs Jones with an ill-grace and says the girl cannot be spared but she can take some of the little ones.

'"No," said Mrs Jones, "I will not; I have not set up a nursery, but a school; I am not at all this expence to take crying babes out of the mother's way, but to instruct reasonable beings in the way to eternal life; and it ought to be a rule in all schools, not to take the trouble-some young children, unless the mother will try to spare the *elder* ones, who are capable of learning."'

At last Hester is allowed to go. She proves apt and diligent, but is careful never to neglect the washing tub or the spinning wheel for her new interest. Instead she gets up early and uses every spare moment to study her hymn book and catechism. 'As poor Hester had no comfort at home, it was the less wonder she delighted in her school, her Bible, and church; for so great is God's goodness, that he is pleased to make religion a peculiar comfort to those who have no other comfort.'

This may sound like pious cliché, but the Sunday school pioneers could all testify to its truth. Mrs Trimmer had noticed how the bigger girls, in particular, at her schools were eager to attend and reluctant to leave. This was because Sunday for them was the most uncomfort-able day of the week, when they might well have to endure fretful, humoursome children, a morose father, and a scolding drunken mother. The miseries at home, acute poverty, disease, death, made them eager to escape to a place where they were told of a world 'where all tears shall be wiped from all eyes;' a world 'to which the poorest wretch on earth may find access'.

We have seen how Charles Shaw, the 'Old Potter', felt about those

Sundays. Not only was he spiritually cleansed, he was physically clean as well.

'Whatever the weather on other days, Sunday always seemed to me a sun's day. It gave me the only gladsome morning of the week. I got a washing that morning such as I had not time to get on other mornings. I had poor enough clothing to put on but my oldest sister always helped me in my toilet on Sunday morning, and my hair got brushed and combed and oiled (with scented oil), so that I always carried a fragrance with me. I have a memory of that scent yet, and when I have met with it since, I know it in a moment. With this fragrance I always had the feeling of flowers about me.'

The children *wanted* to be clean and orderly. Raikes had been

14

Religion is the chief concern
Of mortals here below,
May I its great importance learn,
Its sovereign virtue know.

Religion should our thoughts
engage,
Amidst our youthful bloom,
'Twill fit us for declining age,
Or for an early tomb.

An orderly procession to church.
(*Country Scenes, c.* 1820)

astonished and touched to find how his ragged boys organised themselves to march two by two to weekday morning prayers at Gloucester cathedral. And an extraordinary improvement in the behaviour and morals of the young was noticeable – nor was it just the teachers who observed it. Raikes in a letter to the *Arminian Magazine* in 1785 could quote a Mr Church, a manufacturer of hemp and flax, about the change in his young employees, which could not have been more extraordinary, he said, had they been transformed from the shape of tigers to that of men. 'In temper, disposition, and manners, they could hardly be said to differ from the brute creation; but since the establishment of Sunday Schools, they have seemed anxious to show they are not the ignorant, illiterate creatures they were before.'

The Gentleman's Magazine in January, 1787 spoke of a local holiday in Gloucestershire, usually notorious for its disorderliness, now become a church rather than an alehouse festival, and the young people 'lately more neglected than the cattle in the field; ignorant, profane, filthy, clamorous, impatient of every restraint, were here seen cleanly, quiet, observant of order, submissive, courteous in behaviour, and, in conversation, free from that vileness which usually marks out the wretched vulgar'.

So that Hannah More, when she wound up her story *The Sunday School*, was not just providing a conventional happy ending.

'And it was observed that as the school filled, not only the fives-court and public-houses were thinned, but even Sunday gossiping and tea-visiting declined. Even Farmer Hoskins, who was at first angry with his maids for leaving off those *merry* songs (as he called them) was so pleased with the manner in which the psalms were sung at the school, that he promised Mrs Jones to make her a present of half a sheep towards her first May-day feast.'

The first Sunday school teachers had to be hand-picked for the daunting task. Ladies, however conscientious and well-disposed, had no place in classrooms where badgers might be released, or cages kept for the unruly, who were then hoisted to the ceiling in them.[1] But by 1786 Mrs Trimmer could urge her readers not just to subscribe to Sunday schools but actively to take part in their ad-

---

[1] This could defeat its purpose. W. H. Prince in *The Romance of Methodism in Old Wednesbury* describes how one boy inside it brought a class to a standstill by his cackles of 'cock-a-doodle-doo' above their heads.

ministration. 'Nothing is a greater excitement to [the children] than the hope of being noticed by their superiors.' She was also trying to calm their fears about infectious diseases. And by 1830 the Sunday school classes had become so tractable that the seven year old Charlotte Yonge could be put in charge of one at Otterbourne. It was not altogether a success, but this was due to her behaviour rather than to her pupils': she had favourites, and was tempted to cheat to bring them to the top of the class.

The Sunday school movement was no longer pioneering, it was an institution. The paid workers of the early days had given way to leisured volunteers; the children were not only drawn from the destitute poor – Charlotte Yonge had been a pupil at Otterbourne before she was promoted. From a teachers' meeting in Walworth sprang the idea of a union of Sunday schools. Before that one school was considered sufficient for a district, but now individual churches

An early Victorian Sunday School procession at the home of Samuel Gurney, MP. The girls had come to present Mrs Gurney with a writing case as an expression of their gratitude. (*Band of Hope Review*, 1857)

realised the benefit of having a school of their own. And with a new literate population came the question of what they should read.

The early books, like Raikes' *Sunday Scholar's Companion* and Jonas Hanway's *A Comprehensive Sentimental Book for Scholars Learning in Sunday Schools* were, as has been described, a combination of reading-made-easy and sacred truths, they were not intended to be read at home. But if the children were not to be contaminated with the cheap ribaldry that the pedlars hawked, and their elders inflamed by such matter as Paine's *Rights of Man*, they must be provided with something that would snatch their attention from these dangerous diversions. It was a matter of great urgency.

Hannah More was the first to grapple with the task. She felt partly responsible for the situation. Had she not been warned what might be the outcome of her foolish philanthropy? And now with the *Rights of Man* circulating among the masses as no book had ever done before, devoured by the very people to whom the Sunday schools had unlocked the mystery of the printed word, her enemies were triumphing. She was even being accused of 'sedition, disaffection, and a general aim to corrupt the principles of the community'.

With the energy and unflagging zeal that she had brought to the establishment of the Somerset schools, Hannah More settled down to fill this need. It was not just a question of countering with two or three books, but of creating a whole literature that would take the place not only of the current seditious pamphlets, but of the crude ribaldry hawked by the chapmen. It is here perhaps that the indomitable courage of the woman best shows. She was making a stand against a centuries-old tradition; chapbooks, broadsides, and ballads, bawdy and violent and delightfully pleasing to popular taste, had been part of the pedlars' stock in trade from time immemorial; it was the only contact that most people had with books. Not only did Hannah More have to oust this old and well-loved literature, she somehow had to circulate a new one at a time when there was no organised book-trade.

On March 3, 1795, the first batch of Cheap Repository Tracts was ready. She had written many herself, her total contribution was to number over fifty; friends and co-workers had provided others. They were produced with imagination, decked invitingly with woodcuts, so that they looked like the literature they were intended to supersede, and given enticing titles – *The Execution of Wild Robert, Tawney Rachel, or, The Fortune-teller, The Thunderstorm, or The History of Tom*

Watson, the Unnatural Son, Black Giles the Poacher, Betty Brown, the St Giles Orange Girl, The Story of Sinful Sally. Their attractiveness did not stop at the cover, they were written with dash and boldness, some were in ballad form, some were serials. Contributions from well-wishers made it possible to keep the prices low (a halfpenny, a penny, or three-halfpence), and a favourable discount rate meant that the hawkers and chapmen, on whom Hannah More was relying for their distribution, were willing to take them up.

Their success was staggering; 300,000 tracts were sold in the first six weeks, and by March 1796 the sales figures were in the region of two million. This in a total population in England, Scotland and Wales of under eleven million, and a literate population of far less, was success indeed.

But success did not mean universal approval. The *Evangelical Magazine* treated the tracts with reserve. 'We would recommend, as much as possible, the adoption of real facts on the ground of these little histories; as we think that danger of some kind usually lurks beneath the flowers of fiction.' And the founders of the Religious Tract Society assembled at that first historic breakfast at St Paul's Coffee House in St Paul's Churchyard, London, because they regretted that Hannah More's tracts 'did not contain a fuller statement of the great evangelical principles of Christian truth,' and felt that they should unite to promote a new popular religious literature. They wanted tracts that contained pure truth, and some account of the way of a sinner's salvation, written in plain Saxon-English that approached the sort the common man spoke, rather than the elegant literary English taught in the eighteenth-century schools.

The clerical founders of the Religious Tract Society might cavil at Hannah More's evangelical principles, but they could not fault her on simple English. Very little religious literature has been written in such a direct, easy style, and the early Committees of the RTS soon found how difficult the task was. The first year saw thirty-four tracts, twenty-seven came the next, after which the promoters felt played out, for several blank years followed. (Despite their high ideals, they had been obliged, with much interior groaning no doubt, to use catchpenny titles such as *The Fortune-Teller's Conjuring Cap* and *Rhyming Dick and the Strolling Player*). Though they all were agreed that it was vitally important to cater for the Sunday scholar's needs, it was not until 1809 that they shook themselves into doing anything to meet these.

Then in 1810 the catalogue advertised some tracts particularly adapted 'for reward books to the children of Sunday-schools'. The peculiar suitability of these seems to have lain in the coloured cuts which adorned them, rather than their content, for the titles ranged from *An Account of a Woman saved from Self-Murder* to *The Wandering Jew*. And so matters limped on until 1814, when three specifically juvenile titles were advertised: *James Steven* by the Rev John Campbell, *Bowyer Smith* by the Rev Basil Woodd, and *Early Piety* by the Rev George Burder, which had been written nearly forty years before, in 1776. Watts' *Divine Songs* which, with Doddridge's *Principles of the Christian Religion* and five others of that ilk, joined the juvenile list in 1816, was an even hoarier classic, a centenarian in fact. Obviously the task of finding writers for the young was proving a weighty problem.

It was not until William Freeman Lloyd joined the Committee in 1816 that the Society's children's list began to have less of a jumble-

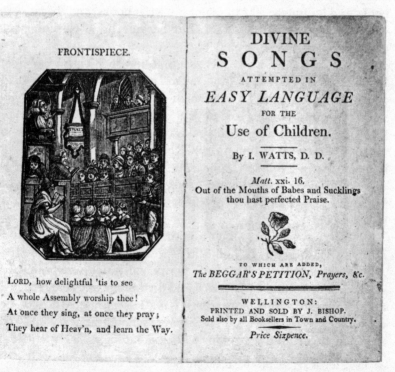

A Sunday School classic. The frontispiece shows Sunday scholars in church with their teacher.

sale appearance, and to acquire some stories specially written for young readers. Lloyd, besides editing and selecting material for them, himself wrote such matter as *The History of Joseph Green, a Sunday Scholar*, and *Susan Green* and *Betsey Green* which appeared in early numbers of *The Child's Companion or Sunday Scholar's Reward* which was founded by Lloyd and George Stokes in 1824.

It was not then until comparatively late that the Sunday scholar could be provided with stories – Hannah More's tracts apart. But books were not given so much as rewards in those early days as clothes and urgent necessities. Hannah More doled out pennies and gingerbread to the meritorious who performed well on Sundays, with a Bible as first prize at the end of the year, a Prayer Book as second, and her tracts as consolation prizes. Mrs Trimmer distributed caps, handkerchiefs, pincushions, huswifes to girls, halfpence if they repeated their catechism well in church. Then, as they began to read fluently, she lent them *The Christian Scholar*, *The Excellent Daughter*, and Fox on *Divine Worship*. The boys were rewarded with books and halfpence (she does not say what books); not because they were the more intellectual sex, but because boys' clothing was so expensive.[1]

It even took time, as we have seen, to put such classics as George Burder's *Early Piety* and Janeway's *Token for Children* into readily accessible tract form. These records of the lives and deaths (which were the more stressed) of devout young persons had long been favourites among evangelicals, Janeway indeed since the seventeenth century. Once taken up by the Religious Tract Society they remained steady favourites, appearing in an 1850 list as outstandingly successful, along with the inevitable Watts' *Divine Songs* and Legh Richmond's *Annals of the Poor* which were to persist for a good many years to come.

We catch a glimpse, albeit a fictitious one, of how Janeway was received in the cottage home in *The Sunday Scholars' Magazine or Monthly Reward Book*. (This little periodical which was published in Oxford, seems to have been born and died in the one year, 1821, thus ante-dating the much more robust *Child's Companion* [which went on until 1889] by three years.) The Sunday school teacher, come to visit a cottage home, finds one of his scholars reading *A Token for Children*,

---

[1] Later it was agreed that the Brentford boys should be encouraged to dress properly by allowing twopence in the shilling to parents who bought them sturdy, sensible garments, such as carters' frocks and leather breeches.

and expresses the hope that he will become like 'those children of whose holy lives and happy deaths you read in that good book.' The mother becomes tearful at these words.

'"Ah sir! that's what I'm afraid of; for the best seem always to go first, and now my poor boy is become so good, I sometimes fear I shall lose him too, and I can't bear the thought of it: – but to be sure it is the most entertaining book that can be. Night after night, as soon as ever Tom comes home from work, he helps me turn the mangle, and then gets to his book; we be never tired of it."'

She tells the teacher too what a remarkable effect the Sunday school has had upon Tom, an almost alarming one. He does not play on the green any more, in spite of her urging; he is afraid to, for the boys say bad words, and cheat and quarrel, and he tells his mother that 'Evil communications corrupt good manners'.

This is a point which is made quite often in literature for the Sunday scholar. An unknown versifier in *The Sunday-Scholar's Gift, or, A Present for a Good Child* (published in 1814 for twopence by F. Houlston & Son of Wellington, Salop) lists it among good little Hannah's many virtues.

> *Each sabbath morn she rose betimes*
> *And dress'd her clean and neat;*
> *Nor ever utter'd naughty words,*
> *Or loiter'd in the street.*

Loitering in the street, playing on the green – both of these would put a child within reach of the unreclaimed ones. Those who had raised the Sunday scholars from tumbling in the gutters had no desire to see them return there, and they felt very strongly that if they came into contact again with their old companions all the good would be knocked out of them. There was also among some evangelicals the uneasy feeling that play was evil in itself – had not Wesley resolutely banished it from his rigidly conducted Kingswood School? But on the whole it was agreed that play of the right sort, in the right company, was harmless, though as it was so difficult for a child to discriminate, he would probably do best to steer clear of all games, especially since idleness was one of the failings that the Georgian adult most deprecated in the young.

We see an example of this in the fable about Peter Player that Jonas Hanway included in his *Comprehensive Sentimental Book*, along with the lessons in reading and in the holy scriptures. Peter 'was but two years of age when his father and mother died and poor Peter had no relations to take care of him and was thus exposed to fall into the company of the worst boys and girls in the town.' He learns to lie and swear through idling with bad companions, such as Tom Trifler, of whose family old George Goodman warns him: '"They pretend to be sober people, because they do not pick our pockets of money, but they rob us of our time which is more valuable."' Tim Trusty gives further doleful warnings. '"Dost thou think thou wert sent into the world to spend thy time, and particularly the sabbath day, in play and idleness with an idle companion?"' Happily Peter falls in with 'a number of little boys, walking two and two, with clean hands and faces, and cleanly and decently clothed, with a grave-looking man at their head'. These are the Sunday school boys, on their way to church, and the master tells Peter that a bad idle boy like Tom Trifler cannot be a good friend. Thrice warned, Peter is convinced. He joins the school, takes kindly to his book, repents the idle days lost, and becomes a sober lad.

And it is on the foundations of Peter Player, Darius Clayhanger, Charles Shaw, that the vast empire of Victorian industry and respectability was to be reared, to say nothing of the children's book trade which played no small part in promoting it.

[4]

The cottage child
and his Sunday School prize
1800–1880

'THEY can answer no end, except to depict pleasures he can never share, raise hopes it is impossible for him to realise, or awaken ambition it would be wrong for him to feel.' This was the assertion of a fictitious Mr Maynard in a collection of tales called *Rich Boys and Poor Boys*. He was deeply dismayed to see little Charles about to pass on to a farmer's son the stories of Miss Edgeworth. The author, Barbara Hofland, did not support his views. She makes little Charles point out the benefits he himself has derived from the *Parent's Assistant*, and how he expects it will do young William just as much good as manuals on husbandry and accounting, by improving his heart as well as his head.

This was 1833, and it is clear that Mrs Hofland believes herself to be enlightened and unusual in her views that a farmer's son could benefit from a little of the fiction that his betters were allowed to read. Mr Maynard combines the old-fashioned utilitarian outlook which deplored imaginative literature, with the newer attitude – to be carried to extremes by the earlier Victorians – that the two categories of children must be kept absolutely distinct, and each provided with a separate literature.

By the 1840s the two cultures were firmly established: one culture for the gentle, another for the simple, and a different code of ethics for each, until for a time the two sets of children so moved away from each other that it would have been difficult for either to derive amusement or profit from the other's books.

In the eighteenth century, as we have seen, when the production of children's books was a haphazard, happy-go-lucky affair, there was a fairly simple message that anybody could grasp, whether it was young Master Augustus in his nursery, or poor Jem scaring birds in the fields. Be diligent, be obedient, and you will get on in the world. And these precepts were put into pretty little books that could have done duty for either boy.

But when it became understood that a writer's duty was to educate his young reader poor Jem could no longer keep up. Master Augustus pulled past him, fortified with information that was considered useless for a bird-scarer. To a certain extent the evangelicals treated both boys the same. There was a feeling that earthly knowledge was vanity. Mrs Sherwood in *The Infant's Progress* had even gone so far as to say that the schoolmaster Mr Worldly Prudence and his kind 'turn aside many young persons from the right way, in order to fill them with such knowledge as only puffeth up and tendeth to destruction'. All children had to be constantly reminded of the wickedness of sin and the depravity of human nature, and though simpler tales were provided for the less literate, the message did not vary. But before going on to consider the content of the Sunday school reward book which for so many decades provided the main reading of the cottage child, it might be as well to go over its history.

The term 'reward book' is perhaps misleading. Only the later books with their gilt and pictorial covers really suggest prizes. The earlier, drab little tracts, measuring about four and one eighth by two and three-quarter inches, very often only paper-covered, may have been given as prizes, but were more frequently distributed to poor homes by parish workers. 'Reward books' in fact covers a whole category of publications bought in bulk to be given away. Chapter three has given some account of the early Sunday scholars and the books they received. It was obvious that only the more literate could make use of the printed word. Besides, the children had urgent material needs. Mrs Sherwood in *The Little Sunday-School Child's Reward* shows us little orphan Sally who begs to be admitted to the school in spite of her dirt and rags. She is equipped with a brown stuff gown, and a white apron, and a brown bonnet and tippet, 'and because she had no daddy and mammy, the lady was so kind as to give her two new shifts and a flannel petticoat, together with shoes and stockings and a blue bed-gown'.

But there was a strong feeling that these scholars rescued from a world hostile to religion should carry back with them something that could keep them faithful in days of temptation. The short-lived *Sunday Scholars' Magazine*, for instance, in June, 1821, had an article describing how one school had devised a scheme whereby their leavers should carry with them 'a testimonial of approbation from the conductors of those schools which they have attended for a number of years' which 'might be serviceable in procuring them

Train up a Child in the way he should go, and when he is old he will not depart from it. Prov. xxii. 6.

SUNDAY SCHOOLS

UNDER THE ESTABLISHMENT.

This Certificate was presented to A—— B——, late a Scholar of St. J————'s Sunday School, M————, as a Testimonial of Improvement in Learning, and Propriety of Conduct, during Years' Attendance at the said School.

C—— D——, Minister.

E—— F——,
G—— H——, } *Visitors.*
I—— J——,

St. J————'s Sunday School,

March 24, 1821.

A testimonial to be given with reward books. *The Sunday Scholars' Magazine.*

employment, or in recommending them to situations in respectable families'. The reward in short should act as a reference, as a steadying influence in the years of temptation that would follow, and there was also something in the nature of a school report handed out with the gift. Jane H— was warned against lightness and frivolity of mind, of yielding conformity to the world and falling into its delusive snares. Sarah S— however was commended for her humble and unassuming demeanour, her uniform and exemplary deportment.

We have seen in chapter three some of the titles that the Religious Tract Society suggested might be used as rewards – a hastily culled, job lot of tracts never intended for children. By 1824, however, there were enough poor children who could read for the Society to launch a little monthly magazine, *The Child's Companion*. It was a miniature version of the *Evangelical Magazine*, it contained pious examples of children who died holy deaths, awful examples where catastrophe overtook the impious, 'improved' accounts of shipwrecks and earthquakes, and a sprinkling of informative articles.

Houlston of Wellington, Shropshire, were among the first providers of penny and halfpenny booklets for Sunday scholars. They were already at work in the first decade of the nineteenth century, and published many little stories by Mrs Sherwood and Mrs Cameron. By 1828, when the firm opened a London office, the market was expanding, but could not really be called an industry until the 1840s. Not only were the Religious Tract Society and the Society for Promoting Christian Knowledge fully aware by that time of the need for religious stories, but there were plenty of commercial firms, such as Darton, Joseph Masters, Mozley, and Nisbet, competing with them as well.

The 1850s and 60s were the golden years for the amateur writer. Torrents of little books cascaded down upon the Sunday schools, advising, exhorting, and laying down the law for the cottage child. Only modest talent was needed to tell young Sally to avoid light conduct and vanity in dress, and many a clergyman's wife or daughter seems to have made pin-money in doing so. Though there was the occasional flash of professional talent, such as the stories that Charlotte Yonge wrote for her parish schoolgirls, most are monotonously drab.

In the 1870s the picture changes. The Education Acts had come into force, and there were Board Schools now as well as the church and charity schools. Publishers such as Nelson, Blackie and Warne

74

An early Victorian reward book from the S P C K, showing a
clergyman visiting a cottage. Cover from *The Raspberry Garden*,
c. 1850.

began putting out children's books to meet the vastly increased demand for rewards. The Board Schools had rather different require-
ments, they wanted informative books, perhaps with an authentic
foreign or historical setting, and uplifting manly or womanly sentiments. Authors such as Ballantyne and Fenn were just right for boys,
and for girls there were historical stories by Emma Leslie and E. S.
Holt and Emma Marshall. The Sunday school prize was smaller,
cheaper, and more heavily moral, but it was losing something of its
specifically church character. The content was increasingly less

scrutinised. It was a sad falling-off of the zealous early days. Not only did the cottage home value the books mostly for their decorative potentialities – they were the pious equivalent to the silver cups on the sideboard – but the Sunday school teachers relied on publishers' lists and prices. These quite shamelessly dwelt glowingly on how much gilt and cardboard and thickness the buyers could get for their money, and divided their wares into price categories.[1] There were shilling books and two shilling books and very handsome ones for three shillings and sixpence for the top scholars or the school with a really munificent benefactor. There is an SPCK story called *The Sunday School Prize* about Lucy who is thrown into a frenzy of grief when she misses a prize for good attendance: 'such a beautiful one, in a red cover, all over gold and a lot of pictures'. The same story shows the clergyman and his sister choosing the prizes from a boxful sent down by the publishers. Of course there is not time to read their way through these, nor do they seem to be influenced by the names of the authors. (In fact many of the books might well have been anonymous.) They are guided by the binding and the pictures.

It was to try to bring the Sunday schools and the church schools back to choosing in a more responsible way that Charlotte Yonge produced her pamphlet *What Books to Lend and What to Give* in 1887. But though it may have helped those with time to hunt out her recommendations, it was far easier, especially if you lived in the provinces, to deal with one publisher only, the tone of whose church-manship you found reliable. Besides, the books went out of print with great rapidity and were constantly being replaced with new titles. Certain ones, however, were steady favourites: *The Fairchild Family*, the works of the American author, Elizabeth Wetherell, the stern fables of A.L.O.E., the street arab stories of Hesba Stretton, Mrs O. F. Walton and Silas Hocking all persisted till after the end of the century.

But by then the cottage child was gradually drawing abreast of the nursery child. He might well be bored by the stories that amused the nursery, which in any case would not be available in the sort of cheap editions that his pastors and masters could afford to give away. Charlotte Yonge in her Hampshire parish was something of an

---

[1] By 1913 the RTS had apparently so far abandoned its high principles of a hundred years before, that it advertised a series of reward books for girls as 'good bulk, well printed, admirably illustrated, well-bound,' and gave no indication of the contents.

anachronism by 1887, when there was a huge lower middle class town population who certainly would have spurned many of the little tales she recommended, aimed at country children in church schools dominated by the local gentry. The days of a specific cottage literature were drawing to a close.

Five years later, reading through the lists of the National Society's Depository (which provided prize books of the better sort in the 1880s and 90s), books such as Charlotte Yonge's *The Cross-Roads* ('a story of domestic life at Langhope Mead') and her *Our New Mistress* ('the difficulties met with by a young trained schoolmistress in taking charge of a village school') are rarities among the mass of stories with colourful historical or foreign settings that would have been considered wholly unsuitable for the early Victorian cottage home. No fantasies or fairy tales are on the list. Though Charlotte Yonge considered that these could be read to classes as a treat, it was generally felt that only a child of the more refined sort could actually benefit from them. But the reward book was now well on its way to being secularised, and its interest as a separate category of juvenile reading had come to an end.

'A very praiseworthy series of Prize Books. Most of the stories are designed to enforce some important moral lesson, such as honesty, industry, kindness, helpfulness.' This is the *School Guardian* reporting on the firm of Blackie's prize list. And: 'to be enabled to reprove the errors of young people without severity is a very useful and happy talent,' – the smug pronouncement of George Mogridge who wrote under the name of Old Humphrey.[1] 'Lessons' and 'reproof' – here is the essence of the books doled out to the cottage home throughout most of the nineteenth century. Whereas it was recognised far earlier that the more prosperous child had a time to learn and a time to play, poor Jem and Sal had to use what time they could squeeze for books by reading to improve. And since they were coarse-fibred and thick-headed the moral must be hammered in. It is paradoxical that, making this assumption, the writers should then demand a standard of Christian behaviour from them that none but the rarest soul could achieve in any circumstances. They should bear all things with fortitude and resignation and faith, not only leaky thatch and

[1] One of the many pseudonyms of George Mogridge (1787–1854) who was a prolific writer of moral and religious books. He also called himself Peter Parley, Alan Gray, Aunt Mary, Grandfather Gregory, Grandmamma Gilbert, Ephraim Holding, The traveller, Uncle Newbury.

Precepts for the cottage home adorn the schoolroom. (*Band of Hope Review*, 1860)

grumbling belly and gross over-crowding, but the death of those very
dear to them – for to mourn was to show lack of faith. No child was so
poor that he might not give – whether it was helping a cross old
woman, or pumping the parish organ or laying out the dead. Time
was short and one's duties manifold. Play was not in itself sinful, but
association with undesirable companions presented grave moral
dangers, so that a child seen playing was probably an idle wastrel
who neglected his lessons and his Bible studies and the duties he
should be undertaking at home. He must honour his parents, of
course; every good child knew his Catechism and the fifth com-
mandment. But – here was another paradox – unlike the Victorian
mother in the drawing room tale, so good and dear and infallible –
the cottage mother was very fallible. She was often to be presented

as feckless, slatternly, obstinate, foolishly indulgent, and the cottage child was supposed to rise superior to the home influence, to avoid direct conflict if he could, but to hold steadfast to the truths that he imbibed at his Sunday school.

The ideal poor boy of the early Victorians was truthful and steady (a favourite adjective), ready to take orders from his superiors and to carry them out. Neither book-learning nor initiative were expected of him. 'The gentry did not want him to know; they did not want him to think; they only wanted him to work. To toil with the hand was what he was born into the world for, and they took precious good care to see that he did it from his youth upwards,' said Joseph Arch ferociously, remembering his own youth in the 1830s when the only schooling available to poor boys were 'parsons' schools; we call them voluntary now, but parsons' they are still, and they will remain so to the end. I should like to see them swept away from the face of the country.' The boy who from a bad background doggedly achieved a respectable situation was a great favourite, and the reports of philanthropic societies congratulated themselves on the instances of Ragged School boys who had become worthy shoeblacks, or had emigrated to be farm labourers in the dominions, while in the cottage tales a boy who was taken on as a stable boy or who had the prospects of becoming a warehouse clerk was held to have every ambition satisfied. For the more contemplative boy there was the occasional reward of a parish clerkship at the end of a long and diligent life or he might even become superintendant of a Sunday school.

The ideal girl was modest and submissive. As with her brother, quickness at lessons was not desired, and the good girl was usually one of the slowest in the class, but never failing in her application. She could not be tempted to spend her ha'pennies on ribbons, nor her time in idle play, for there was always mother to be helped and the smaller children to be supervised. In time she would be rewarded with a situation in a good household where she might rise to be head housemaid, but she must never be tempted to wish to be a lady's maid, for in that way lay, if not ruin, then the gravest temptations to vanity.

It is only fair to say that there is a discernible difference between the attitude taken towards the poor by, say, the Wesleyan Sunday schools and the Anglican ones. Hence the temptation for the donors of reward books to deal unquestioningly and uncritically with the firm they knew suited their particular variety of churchmanship.

THE SHOE-BLACK BRIGADES.

MANY of our young friends who live in London, have doubtless seen the industrious little shoe-blacks, in their bright-coloured jackets, busy at work in front of the Royal Exchange, and other places.

It is a pleasure to find that the benevolent gentlemen who have devoted so much of their valuable time to the management of these boys, have not laboured in vain, neither spent their strength for nought.

The following interesting letter from Mr. John MacGregor, (at whose suggestion the first Shoe-black Brigade was commenced in 1851,) will afford pleasure to many of our friends:—

My dear sir,—Perhaps your readers will like to hear a short account of "Corny Keane," the boy who gained the first medal in the Red Brigade of Shoe-blacks, on the occasion when his portrait and that of Mr. Joseph Payne were taken for your pages.

I found the boy at Field Lane Ragged School in May, 1855. He was then a miserable looking beggar boy. After admission to our Shoe-black corps, he speedily rose in the ranks, until in November 1856, he gained the medal for the highest earnings in "the first City division," that is, in our highest class of boys.

The amount he had earned during the previous month was £3 16s. 3¼d.

At various times during his career in the Society, he had saved up and drawn out from his "Bank" for expenditure, £8 11s. 6d., besides his usual quota from his daily earnings.

When he left us, the sum of £8 7s. 7d., still remained in his "Bank," and was paid to him. Corny Keane, (the son of an Irish Roman Catholic,) is now in a situation in a gentleman's

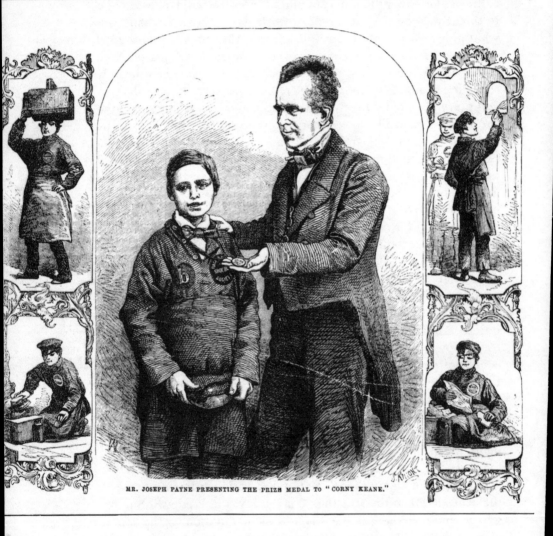

MR. JOSEPH PAYNE PRESENTING THE PRIZE MEDAL TO "CORNY KEANE."

The deserving shoe-black. (*Band of Hope Review*, 1857)

The evangelical publishers tended to cater far more for the urban poor, their message was more universal, there was not the same stress on the lowliness of the readers' station and the necessity for staying there. The melodrama of their street arab stories appealed to a wide readership, and latterly at any rate it seemed safe to put even stories of middle class families into grimy, horny hands without the fear that the owners of these would start dangerously yearning for forbidden fleshpots. A writer such as A.L.O.E., for instance, showed the same austerity and rigour and prohibition in her middle class as in her cottage home, and the evil of alcohol was preached to readers of all ranks of society.

Publishers such as the SPCK and Mozley and Joseph Masters catered more for the sort of paternalistic parish that Charlotte Yonge and her friends knew, with the squire at the top, the clergy-

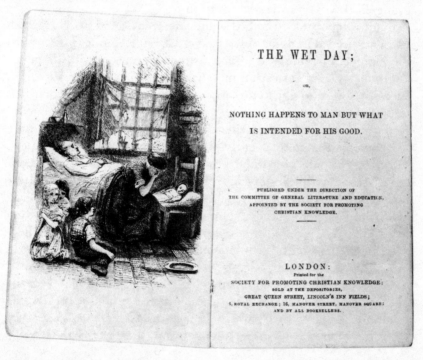

man and his devoted flock of female helpers below, and the well-ordered mass of tenantry below that – Joseph Arch's 'parsons' schools,' in fact. It is sad that the High Church never managed to produce a truly popular writer for the children in its parish schools. Their books covered every fault that the cottager might be tempted to commit, and catered for every sort of parish organisation. There were books for mothers' meetings and sewing groups, for girls' friendly societies, young servants, and pupil teachers, for thrift clubs and choir boys. Sound religious teaching was given, good advice sometimes – though on occasion it might seem misplaced, like a tale for choirboys whose moral was celibacy for the clergy, it showed a starving clergyman in a decline, the bailiffs in the house, and the children crying for bread. But there was rarely a story that rose above the didactic level, and the attitude was undeniably patronising. Mrs Ewing's stories of poor children, such as *Daddy Darwin's Dovecote* and *Lob Lie-by-the-fire*, though they used the classic plot of orphan boy attaining humble respectability, were far too difficult for any but the most literary, and minor masterpieces though they are, never achieved the universal success of the works of such evangelical writers as Hesba Stretton.

But it was possible to embed sound advice in a good story. Hannah More succeeded in doing this with her Cheap Repository Tracts. In the eighteenth-century tradition, she encouraged thrift, diligence and honesty, and instead of merely complaining, as her Victorian successors were so apt to do, about the sluttish wife who could not feed her family properly, she gave recipes for simple, nutritious food. And unlike the Victorian writers for the cottage she did not hesitate to denounce the unsatisfactory employer, particularly the farmers, of whose grasping greed and obstinacy she had had bitter experience.[1] Her descriptions of country life must have been immediately recognisable to the cottager, whether she was writing about Black Giles the Poacher's slatternly brood with their dirty faces, matted locks and naked feet, or the house-proud Mrs Wilmot's cottage where the daughter is kept hard at it 'stoning the space under the chairs in fine patterns and whim-whams'. The cottagers in her books appear as far more forthright and independent and outspoken than ever the Victorians allowed theirs to be, and it is perhaps significant that the tract most admired by Charlotte Yonge was *The Shepherd of Salisbury Plain*, one of the most famous, but not by any means typical. Here the

---

[1] *The Hubbub, or The History of Farmer Russel, the hard-hearted Overseer* opens with an account of the villagers, cheered on by Hannah More, mobbing Farmer Russel in front of the poorhouse door. 'Betty Jobbins beat the frying-pan with the key of the door, Sally Gore pounded the pestle and mortar, Nelly Shepston rang the warming pan, Dick Devonshire blew the ram's-horn, whilst Nick Stafford and the others gingled the sheeps' Bells.'

message is submission. It is one of the earliest of the efforts to convince the poor that to bring up a family of six on eight shillings a week, with a rheumaticky wife shivering beneath a leaky thatch and a single thin blanket, is richness indeed and ennobling to the character. At moments it can even seem like a parody of the genre, as when the shepherd comes home to find his wife weeping: '"O it is too much, we are too rich, I am now frightened."' – she had been given two blankets and half a crown.

It is interesting to compare two books of approximately the same period, both about poor children. Mrs Hurry's *The Faithful Contrast* was published by Harris in 1804. Harris's publications, though they could be improving like this one, were often (see page 19) merely frivolous, and he is not associated with the Sunday School trade. John in *The Faithful Contrast* has, aged ten, been abandoned with his mother and sisters by his father (an inebriate shoemaker who enlists

BE THANKFUL

Little Children's Duties, an SPCK reward book, *c.* 1853.

as a soldier). He gets work at three shillings a week and within a few years can afford to rent a cottage to which he moves mother and sisters. He cultivates his garden, he feeds a pig. 'There is no sight more pleasing than the efforts of industry, striving to overcome the hardships of poverty.' Then, when John has raised himself to be a tenant farmer, he meets a party of men dragging between them an old soldier who has just stolen a loaf. John succours him, and behold, it is his father, returned from the wars. 'He took him to his home, nourished him, and supported him; and, during the remainder of his days, cheerfully administered to all his necessities. Thus performing the various and often severe duties of life, John lived to old age, respected, beloved and happy.'

A wholesome moral tale, no doubt, but the Sunday schools did not think it wise to hold out the prospect of material rewards, or to encourage children to better themselves. *Peggy and her Mammy* by Mary Elliott (Darton, 1819) is their version. Peggy in her efforts to keep a comfortable home for the old woman who took her in as a baby is a model of thrift and prudence and loving kindness. But she aspires to no more than to earn a few extra shillings by making silk pincushions so that she can buy a comfortable armchair to ease her poor Mammy's aching limbs. Before taking a pincushion apart to study its construction, she is careful first to ask permission of the young lady who originally gave it to her. Her diligence touches the hearts of the more prosperous, and Peggy's Mammy is given not only an armchair but a load of wood and a cloak.

Ambition was greatly discouraged by the Sunday schools. Many early Victorian tales showed little girls too eager to win prizes to remember that doing one's duty steadfastly and meekly was far more important than quickness at lessons. Old Humphrey had an example, of course. In *Lessons Worth Learning for Girls* he cited Caroline Hawker who to her astonishment fails to win the coveted prize in spite of being far quicker at learning her hymns, producing Scripture texts, hemming pocket handkerchiefs, and working her sampler than slow and clumsy Susan Price who does receive it.

Far worse than a desire for prizes was the desire to move out of one's social station. *If I was a Lady* is the title of a little mid-Victorian RTS collection of picture fables. The story of the title shows Fanny and Mary window-shopping and choosing the clothes they would like to buy if they were ladies. 'Time passed, and those children grew up, not to be *ladies*, for that they could not be . . .' Lydia White is the

'As Susan rested her aged form in her new chair, and Peggy, in soft accents, read a chapter from the Bible, the snow and wind beat against the window unheeded.' (Mary Elliott [Belson] *Peggy and her Mammy*, 1819)

good girl of the fables. She 'has just left off attending the village school because she is old enough to help her parents by earning a trifle towards her own support. She has always borne a good character for truthfulness, honesty and industry, so she is likely to get on in the world if she does her best.' She is shown being interviewed by an old gentleman who needs a servant; 'getting on in the world' would be understood to finish with being a respectable upper servant and perhaps marrying a good, steady artisan.

'"I am glad you can clear-starch, Sophy,"' says one of the adult helpers in *The Sunday School Treat to Richmond* (1860). And she adds with a touching belief in the reward of merit: '"Strive to improve more and more, and do not be satisfied till you can wash and iron better than any one else you know; and who can tell, but in a few years you may have the great honour of being one of the clear-starchers to Her Majesty."'

A girl who wished to better herself in the worldly sense was an easy prey for the seducer; this perhaps was often at the back of the mind of those who lectured her on the folly of it. Even as late as 1909 the RTS was rebuking girls for such silly notions. Alfred Cooper in *Sunday School Romances* speaks of the plight of Tom Owen who has speaking eyes but a commonplace nose, thick lips, and large ears. He is an honest workman and loves Maggie Stewart. 'I believe that more young fellows would choose the manly occupations of the carpenter, the blacksmith, and the builder, but for the fact that women show preference for the man who works at something that does not soil his hands, and who can keep his collar on while he does it.' But Maggie begins to get 'notions' and looks for a frock coat, a shiny hat, an imitation pin and a walking stick instead of a blue serge suit and a cap (a bowler on Sundays).

Maggie's 'notions' are ominous, but there were very few writers indeed who could bring themselves to tell their readers where they might lead. Mrs Sherwood in a very early story, *Susan Gray*, showed what happened to Charlotte Owen who became an army officer's mistress. Mature years and possibly the Victorian climate led her later to regret the book. Hannah More a few years earlier had specified exactly what had happened to Betty Adams in *The Good Mother's Legacy*. Over-fond of clothes and smart company, she had left home to go to London as Lady Townley's waiting maid. She is seduced by the butler, and staggers home with her dying baby to die herself. 'At Mrs Adams' request, the following Sunday, the curate

preached an excellent sermon, to advise all young people to take
warning by poor Betty Adams and to learn to be content and happy
in that station of life in which Providence has placed them.'

But though the Victorians were no doubt just as aware of the fate
that lurked for the flighty girl, they could only beseech her as Mary
Modest beseeches Rose Ready in *Money and How to Spend it* (London,
William Mackintosh, n.d.) not to be 'giddy and gay, and thoughtless
and wild, and rude and bold, and free and easy, and smirking and

None is so poor that he may not give. Tom gives his services as an
organblower. (*My Sunday Friend*, 1870)

smiling, and laughing and joking'. Or to advise her, as giddy Lucy is reminded in *Lucy Page, The Young Lady's Maid* (London, the Book Society, n.d.): 'Do not be drawn into doing what you know to be wrong, and be very careful to avoid levity in your behaviour, as young persons cannot be too careful. Read attentively the sixth chapter of Ephesians, and make it the rule of your conduct; above all, remember that God's eye is upon you.'

One looks in vain for Victorian employers to be directed to the ninth verse of that chapter, and for the reminder that in heaven there is no respect of persons. The young servant was led to understand that it would be her own fault if she failed, and to this end she was warned about every conceivable misdemeanour, from pilfering to idle gossip, from pertness to sweeping the dirt under the carpet. Earlier writers allowed themselves to touch on more physical matters, like the author of *My Station and its Duties* (Seeley and Burnside, 1832) who instructed girls not to let their feet smell, and Jonas Hanway who in 1805 warned them not to be corrupted by 'a certain Chinese drug called tea'. Hanway had also added a strong caution about dancing and singing – not because they were in themselves wrong so much as 'in our station, dancing company is, I think, generally bad company . . . never conducted with perfect decency and free from danger to young women'.

Here was the rub. There was undoubtedly truth in what he said, but to read cottage literature is to become aware that there was no safe recreation. Dancing, singing, smoking, drinking – none of them morally wrong in themselves except to the teetotal evangelical, and indeed permissible to those who lived in more comfortable circumstances – must all be avoided by the poor. There were grave dangers in cheap books, so they had much better read only those that their betters handed out to them. Even playing threw a child into doubtful company. Dress and hair-style must be of the plainest, no aping the fashions of a superior class. 'If only you were to hear how foolish the gentlefolk and ladies think those girls, you would never wish to look so silly again.'

This was how the gentry saw it – an offence against good taste. It also meant that one stepped out of one's station and was dangerously tempted by the sin of pride. In *Poison in the Packet*, a Religious Tract Society story of the 1880s, a London friend sends the Beamonds a parcel of fine clothes, much too fine for a carpenter's family: a blue silk dress with flounces for Sarah, a black velvet jacket for Robert.

POISON IN THE PACKET,

An Old Story Re-told,

WITH OTHER READINGS.

"POISON!" EXCLAIMED HIS WIFE, STARTING BACK WITH AMAZEMENT.

But the disapproving man who has packed this parcel on the friend's behalf has marked the clothes POISON. The clergyman comes to the cottage and soberly warns the parents against pride; the squire tells Beamond sarcastically that at this rate *he* will have to live in the cottage and Beamond at the hall. Quarrelling and dissension split the family, the other villagers are resentful; the package has indeed proved poisonous. But nobody – neither Beamond, the squire nor the clergyman – has suggested that silk and velvet are sinful in themselves; only when worn by the lower orders.

So much when viewed with the anxious eye of the Sunday school teacher, looked as though it might later lead to great sins when the children had left the fold. More fortunate children would be carefully supervised until they were seventeen or eighteen at least; these would have to face the wicked ways of the world unprotected when they were twelve, or perhaps even younger. So the mischief and high spirits allowable in mid-Victorian nurseries, thought manly in public school boys, were the horrible prelude to a life of crime in the cottage boy.

'"Just what I should expect,"' says a farmer to a boy who has taken corn from the sheaves. '"A boy begins by idling away his time, and then steals, to hide his fault. And I tell you what, you may be very thankful this has all come out. If you had escaped this time, you might have gone on stealing until you became a confirmed thief and liar – the two faults generally go together – and you might have ended your days on the gallows; think of that. Many a boy has begun a wicked life as young as you are, by stealing apples when he ought to have been at church on the Sunday, and has gone from bad to worse, till he has been hung for some dreadful crime."'

(*The Gleaners*, SPCK, n.d.)

So we are fully prepared for a boy's jokes to end tortuously in the near death of a friend from a decline, and for larks in the schoolroom (the girls had tickled each other and cracked nuts during lessons) to bring about a fatal case of smallpox.

Occasionally a writer was struck by the sadness of the contrast: the home where childishness was encouraged, the home where it was stamped out. 'She was thirteen,' wrote Charlotte Yonge of a little nursery maid in *Cheap Jack* (1880), 'and all that she viewed as child's play had long been gone out of her; she could not understand [her charges'] fun and nonsense, or why Mrs Grey would not have them called "naughty" for getting their frocks torn, and their hands dirty, or for pulling all the chairs about, the very things that gave the most trouble.' Poor little Bessie; forbidden these pleasures in her own childhood, she was now scolded for not tolerating them in others.

[5]

The evangelical child
1818–1880

IN the 1920s Lord Frederic Hamilton, a self-styled mid-Victorian, set down his reminiscences of a long and varied life. It ran to three volumes in the end, mostly of anecdotes, for he was an accomplished raconteur and had travelled widely in a world where high English connections gave you the entrée anywhere, from the Imperial Russian Court to a French Trappist monastery. He was indeed highly connected; his father was the Marquis, later the first Duke of Abercorn, Lord Lieutenant of Ireland; his brothers achieved a fair degree of distinction in their own right; his sisters married into the most noble English families. His mother, the sister of Lord John Russell, was an intimate friend of Queen Victoria with whose grandchildren Frederic and his brothers sometimes played. But in common with all well-conducted mid-Victorians from palace, mansion, parsonage or back-street house, he had been reared on the stories of Mrs Sherwood and her sister Mrs Cameron, and particularly upon that spiritual food of the young Victorian's Sunday – *The Fairchild Family*, the first, and best-known part of which was originally published in 1818.

The works of these two ladies were a unifying force as no other children's books of the century were able to be. They cut across class and sect; they were to be found in the High Church household as well as the evangelical one, for until the High Church collected itself in the later 1830s there *were* no other religious tales for children known to the general public. And even after Harriet Mozley had made a start in 1841 with *The Fairy Bower* and Elizabeth Sewell and Charlotte Yonge were set on their course, Mrs Sherwood's *The Fairchild Family* and *Henry Milner*, and short tales more accessible to those with less leisure and less learning, like *Little Henry and his Bearer*, and *The History of Margaret Whyte* or *Memoirs of Emma and her Nurse* (the latter two by Mrs Cameron) remained far better known, and were handed out by Sunday schools to their pupils until the end

92

of the century. They were a habit; they had welded themselves to the English Sunday; they were as much a part of English childhood as *Alice* was later to become. Frederic Hamilton described how in the 1900s he had attended a Fairchild Family dinner where every guest had to appear as one of Mrs Sherwood's characters.

One has only to open any book of reminiscences of a Victorian childhood to see the names of Mrs Sherwood and Mrs Cameron. Very often they are all that the writer can recall of his nursery reading. 'All the little Sunday books in those days were Mrs Sherwood's, Mrs Cameron's and Charlotte Elizabeth's,' wrote Charlotte Yonge of her childhood in the late 1820s, 'and little did my mother guess how much Calvinism one could suck out of them, even while diligently reading the story and avoiding the lesson.' Annie Keary, born two years later, had been nourished on the same diet. Her sister Eliza writing in 1882, though she said the child of the eighties would despise them as 'goody goody', thought them preferable to the 'sensational stories of ragged London depravity' that were by that time doing duty as Sunday reading. Mrs Molesworth, born in 1839, was more dutiful than Charlotte Yonge. She recognised that the stories in *The Fairchild Family* were, though so delightful, only the chaff. The real grain, undoubtedly hard to swallow, lay in the prayers and sermons incorporated into each. So she set to work to read all these first, so she could have the undiluted enjoyment of the doings of Henry, Lucy and Emily.

Some of the Victorians enjoyed this diet, some were bored, some – like Arthur Clennam in *Little Dorrit* – execrated the whole style and its 'hiccuping references' to texts. But Frederic Hamilton's attitude was probably the most typical: 'I liked [*The Fairchild Family*] notwithstanding. There was plenty about eating and drinking; one could always skip the prayers, and there were three or four very brightly written accounts of funerals in it.'

By the 1920s the book seemed to him a quaint relic of a bygone age of pious respectability, where Sabbaths were kept strictly and sermons lasted from sixty to ninety minutes.

'Mr and Mrs Fairchild were, I regret to say it, self-righteous prigs of the deepest dye, whilst Lucy, Emily and Henry, their children, were all little prodigies of precocious piety. It was a curious *ménage*; Mr Fairchild having no apparent means of livelihood, and no recreations beyond perpetually reading the Bible under a tree in the

Pride is brought low – Henry falls into the pig swill. Illustration to a
Victorian (1875) edition of *The Fairchild Family*.

garden. Mrs Fairchild had the peculiar gift of being able to recite a
repertory of prayers off by heart applicable to every conceivable
emergency; whilst John, their man-servant, was a real "handy-
man", for he was not only gardener, but looked after the horse and
trap, cleaned out the pigsties, and waited at table. Even [he] had a
marvellous collection of texts at his command.'

Fifty years later, in the 1970s, the book is more than quaint; it is marvelled at as something unique, an extraordinary compilation of Calvinistic sentiments, cruelty, necrophily and cant. But, though undoubtedly remarkable, it is compounded of ingredients familiar to any evangelical of Mrs Sherwood's day, and to look at it in detail is to get some idea of the literature that lay behind it and of what the evangelical ideals were for children in the early years of the century.

Mary Martha Sherwood was a prolific writer in many styles. She produced school text books; witty and satirical sketches of society; missionary stories for the Hindu; many penny stories for village children which were published by Houlston in Wellington, Shropshire, and were found very useful by the early Sunday schools. She

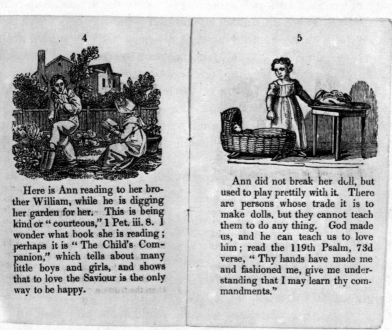

4

Here is Ann reading to her brother William, while he is digging her garden for her. This is being kind or "courteous," 1 Pet. iii. 8. I wonder what book she is reading; perhaps it is "The Child's Companion," which tells about many little boys and girls, and shows that to love the Saviour is the only way to be happy.

5

Ann did not break her doll, but used to play prettily with it. There are persons whose trade it is to make dolls, but they cannot teach them to do any thing. God made us, and he can teach us to love him; read the 119th Psalm, 73d verse, "Thy hands have made me and fashioned me, give me understanding that I may learn thy commandments."

In the Sherwood style. (*The Happy Girl, or The History of Little Ann Goodchild*, c. 1825).

re-wrote Sarah Fielding's *The Governess*; this had appeared in 1749 and she wished to bring it up to the moral standards of 1820 and exclude the fairy stories, now considered so undesirable in an age which deplored imaginative literature. She also produced one work, *The Nun*, where imagination was sanctified since it dwelt on the terrifying practices of the Roman Church in the matter of converts.

She was born in 1775, the child of George Butt, a prosperous clergyman. She was not brought up as an evangelical. To her father's religious outlook she only made guarded reference in her auto-biography, writing of it from her own very different Calvinistic viewpoint that she thought it was 'more of the heart than the head' but one of 'enlarged love and charity and confidence in divine love,' even though 'neither he nor my mother had any distinct ideas of human depravity'.

There seem to have been few restrictions or deprivations and many worldly pleasures in the childhood that she remembered as so radiantly happy. 'Some may at first be disappointed at not finding in Mrs Sherwood's early years that evangelical piety that gilds every page of her after-history,' wrote a reviewer of the autobiography in the *Christian Times*. She makes no mention of Sunday books. *Robinson Crusoe*, fairy tales, Sarah Fielding's *Governess*, and Aesop's Fables were the whole of her library, and she spent a great deal of time with her brother acting fairy tales, or else writing them herself.

It was not until she was married to her cousin Henry that her out-look became sternly evangelical. She was living in India now, and the chaplain at Berhampore, and later her friendship with the young missionary Henry Martyn, enlightened 'my total ignorance respect-ing the doctrine of human depravity'. Besides, India itself was a sobering experience with the misery and ignorance that she saw all around her, particularly among the soldiers' families whom she strove to help.

In England she had written two romantic novels, followed by *Susan Gray*, the story of a village Clarissa, told for the benefit of the girls in her Sunday School. Those days were over. She rewrote Bunyan for the young, *The Infant's Progress*, a grim little manual, composed at a time when she was watching her first born children fading and dying, and doing what she could at the same time for the soldiers' orphans in the cantonments nearby. When one reads her autobiography and sees the gentleness, the love and affection that she lavished on these babies, so far removed from the harsh austerity with which *The Infant's Progress* suggests that a child should be handled, one realises that the latter is a book written from the head, not the heart. *Little Henry and his Bearer*, an altogether gentler book about a little boy who is brought from spiritual darkness into light, and before dying brings his Indian servant to share that same light, was published in 1817, a few months after the Sherwoods' return to

England, and the first part of *The Fairchild Family*, with which her name is perhaps chiefly associated, in 1818.

The Fairchild Family is the chronicle of Lucy, Emily and Henry (named after Mrs Sherwood's own children) aged nine, eight, and six respectively, and is sub-titled *The Child's Manual, being a collection of stories calculated to show the importance and effects of a religious education.* It is part I that is generally remembered. The second and third parts were not written until 1842 and 1847 respectively and contain rather less of the Fairchilds, and more of the peripheral characters and of stories that are related to the children. The religious education is given by Mr Fairchild, and the point that he is most concerned to stress is his children's natural depravity, his great hope 'that God will give us a knowledge of the exceeding wickedness of our hearts; and we may, knowing our wretched state, look up to the dear Saviour who alone can save us from hell'. Interspersed with the prayers, hymns and homilies are accounts of the day-to-day doings of the children, which are as delightful as Frederic Hamilton and Mrs Molesworth remembered, with plenty of descriptions of delicious food, pretty toys, together with a fair degree of naughtiness.

For they were by no means ideal children, though there were traces of that 'aggressive piety' of which Frederic Hamilton complained. Six year old Henry could shake his head over his great aunts and say that he feared they had not gone to heaven, since they believed that good works, not merely faith, could get them there; but he could be wilful, disobedient and quarrelsome too. Indeed, it is because of a childish quarrel that Mr Fairchild takes his children on the famous trip to see the gibbet with the rotting corpse of a man who had murdered his brother.

The ideal child of the book is Charles Trueman, a cottager's child and 'one of the most pious little boys in all that country,' and it is he who brings Henry to a right way of thinking, after Henry's defiance of his father when ordered to learn his Latin. Mr Fairchild had whipped Henry, driven him from his presence with the terrifying words 'I stand in place of God to you, whilst you are a child,' and forbidden any of the household to speak to him. Desolate, he wanders out into the country and meets Charles who is to be such a redeeming force. Charles tells him much about hell, and the misery of the damned, about which he says his father has often talked to his children as they sit round the fire, until they have been in a quake. '"O Lord Jesus Christ," added the little boy, joining his hands and

97

looking up, "thou bleeding Lamb! Save us miserable sinners from hell."'

He tells Henry of his own conversion, how he was brought to a knowledge of his own sinful nature by going to the funeral of a child who had been burnt to death through disobedience, how subseqently he had gone down into the church vaults and examined the coffins and come to the realisation that death was a very horrible thing, sent as a punishment for sin. From this he was drawn to the conviction that his heart was desperately, horribly wicked, and he joyfully thanked God who had granted him this knowledge.

Soon after this episode, little Charles lies on his deathbed to which Henry, now fully reconciled to his family, is led, together with his sisters, by his parents. It was not the first death they had seen. They had been taken to visit the corrupting corpse of an old cottager, that they might learn the exceeding sinfulness of sin and its horrible nature, and hear Mr Fairchild's reflections. Now they all cluster round Charles, together with Mr Somers the clergyman and the Trueman family, and watch the agonies of death – 'a dreadful sight, for the sinful body struggles with it'. Mr Somers begs Charles to speak last words to comfort them, and Charles turns his dying eyes towards Mr Somers and answers '"I know that my Redeemer liveth; and though after my skin worms shall destroy this body, yet in my flesh I shall see God." (Job XIX, 25, 26).'

The young evangelical was taken to many funerals. (*Band of Hope Review*, 1855)

THE FUNERAL.

The funeral of Charles concludes this book, which was not to be resumed for twenty-four years. It is attended by the whole parish, and Mr Somers preaches an eloquent sermon, exhorting the young people present to repent, and warning them of their filthy and corrupt hearts. The last words are spoken by Mr Fairchild, when he prays with his family that his dear children and poor servants should not be condemned to everlasting fire.

From this summary will be seen what a large part death played in *The Fairchild Family*. There was undeniably a morbid streak in Mrs Sherwood's imagination which showed itself in the gloating description of the carcass on the gibbet and of how horribly the corpse of the old gardener smelt, but her emphasis on death was by no means unusual. The funerals, the holy deaths, the corpses, the gibbets had been part of the background of the evangelical child for decades. His parents had daily talked to him of the first three, perhaps threatened him with the last, since his early infancy. *The Fairchild Family* was certainly unusual for the scale on which it was written at a time when most religious writing for children was in the form of short tracts, but its real innovation lay in the combination of fiction with spiritual exhortation (fiction still being suspect among the stricter), and its unique flavour comes from the spectacle of these – on occasion – delightfully life-like children disporting themselves in a neo-Gothic stage set of graveyards and vaults and coffins, the fashion for which was already on the wane when the book was written. It was in fact the culmination of a long tradition, and it owes the fact of its survival into times that were completely ignorant of that tradition to the excellence of Mrs Sherwood's writing.

When Hatchard, the publishers of *The Fairchild Family*, requested a sequel they were sent *The History of Henry Milner*, the first part of which was published in 1823. This story of 'a little boy who was not brought up according to the fashions of this world' was almost as familiar to young Victorians as the Fairchilds, though possibly less popular. It has only one main child character, and he after a few early skirmishes with the housekeeper settles down to a career of unswerving steadiness. Mrs Sherwood too, after the first part, was moving away from her extreme evangelical position; there are no dramatic visits to gibbets, and a marked lack of corpses, vaults and lavish funerals. Instead, Mr Dalben, who would remind us of Thomas Day's worthy Mr Barlow except that he is of course of an unfailingly religious cast, gives little Henry instruction concerning the Millenium, natural history, and his sinful, proud and ambitious heart.

At eleven years old Henry is greatly improved. By that time he has spent eight years with Mr Dalben. He answers all grown people with civility, without stopping to consider whether they are rich or poor. He can read English very well, and when he comes to a hard word he always asks the meaning of it. He has found many precious things in the Bible. He has learnt Hebrew and can read the first book of Genesis. Hebrew was a safe language, since there *are* no books but the works of Scripture, for

'little Henry was not like those poor little boys, who, not being blessed with pious parents and careful teachers, are obliged to seek instruction in dictionaries, where, instead of meeting with holy lessons, they often fall upon such pieces of information as Christian children ought never to know, and thus, instead of being nourished with manna, they learn to desire the leeks and garlic and flesh pots of Egypt'.

In some ways, with its atmosphere of optimism, Henry's upbringing is more reminiscent of Harry Sandford's and Tommy Merton's than that given to the orthodox young evangelical who was reminded before all else of the punishment that awaited the unconverted. It is interesting to see that his preceptor allows him books of amusement, one at a time – fairy tales or Sindbad the sailor, which Thomas Day and the earlier Mrs Sherwood would both have frowned upon.

The serious evangelical, such as Mrs Sherwood had been during her years in India, stopped at nothing, however immediately painful to the child, to bring about a change of heart. Early piety – this was what they strove for. 'And now, dear children, I have done,' wrote Janeway at the end of his *Token for Children*.

'I have written for you; I have prayed for you. But what you will do, I cannot tell. Oh children, if you love me, if you love your parents, if you love your souls, if you would escape hell fire, and if you would live in heaven when you die, go and do as these good children. And that you may be your parents' joy, your country's honour, and live in God's fear, and die in his love, is the prayer of your dear friend, J. Janeway.'

Solemnly and persistently in tracts, sermons and hymns, writers and preachers tried to drive home to children the depravity of their nature, the inevitability of death, and the ghastliness of the punishment that awaits the unconverted.

'Could a lost soul drop but one tear, once in ten thousand years,' John Pike warned his young readers,[1] 'and do this till a sea as vast as all the seas on earth together were filled with tears, all its sufferings in that long, long period, would be but the beginning of eternal misery. All those millions of years of wretchedness would bring the unhappy soul no nearer to an end of its torments, than one poor fleeting hour. Oh, infinitely miserable creature! that when millions of years of sorrow are past, can only say, "These flames again, these tortures again."'

Some writers sought to impress their message by this sort of sombre eloquence, others tried to stir young readers to emulate children as young as themselves who, like Charles Trueman, had died holy deaths. James Janeway's *Token for Children, Being an Account of the Conversion, Holy and Exemplary Lives and Joyful Deaths of Several Young Children*, the most famous of these anthologies, was the pattern for those that followed in the eighteenth century. Originally published in two parts in 1671 and 1672 it recorded the examples of children who, as soon as they could speak, delighted to pray in secret, lament their sins, and remonstrate with their family and friends and 'put in some word to keep them from naughty talk or wicked actions.' Like Charles Trueman, they are 'frequent in spiritual ejaculations' and urgent in reminding those around them of the necessity of death. 'The axe is laid to the root of the tree,' the seven year old John Hervey would say. The same child was not content till he found an interpreter to help him convert a Turk, and would urge his mother to be careful to avoid gratifying a proud humour in his brother and sister.

Seven years old was by no means early to achieve piety. There are plenty of examples in the evangelical magazines of far younger children, of three or four perhaps, who spent their time in prayer, weeping over their sins, and exhorting those around them to greater holiness. There was John Talbot Edwards, aged three years, five months, whose example was cited in the *Child's Magazine* of 1828. He

---

[1] John Deodatus Gregory Pike, 1784–1854, Baptist pastor and author of *Persuasives to Early Piety*, a popular Religious Tract Society publication.

Then turning himself to the young people present, he said, "You see that I am a dying man, I desire you may take warning by me to remember your latter end, seeing you know not how soon it may be your turn to be in this condition."

A holy deathbed. The departing Joseph Whally exhorts his young friends. (*Examples for Youth in Remarkable Instances of Early Piety*, 1822)

was much given to the rebuke of his elders, and did not hesitate to forecast doom for those who stopped their ears. Of three men drowned when they were drunk, he said that it was too late, the blood of Jesus could not save them now. Another child rebuked some soldiers in the street for swearing. '"As you despite all that I have said," he added, "I will just mention one word more . . . the wicked shall be turned into hell."'

We have already seen in a previous chapter how one Sunday scholar enjoyed Janeway. William Godwin's comment probably reflected the feelings of many. 'I felt as if I were willing to die with them, if I could with equal success, engage the admiration of my friends and mankind.' These deaths held the starved imaginations of evangelical readers. There was the dying child lying in his chamber, surrounded by marvelling family and friends. From time to time his elders would catechise him; this was not just for the benefit of his own soul, but to inspire those around him. An assurance was required that he was aware of his sinful nature, of the nature of death and the destiny of the soul.

The dying child had been long accustomed to such catechism in the days of his health; had probably, if he was ready with his answers, enjoyed it. 'Oh that sweet catechising, unto which I always resorted with gladness, and attended without weariness,' Janeway reports the dying Susannah Bicks as saying. And one remembers the deep satisfaction that Edmund Gosse derived, in his Plymouth Brethren childhood, from his spiritual examination by two elders of the congregation: 'I sat up on the sofa in the full lamplight and testified my faith in the atonement with a fluency that surprised myself. Before I had done, Fawkes, a middle-aged man with the reputation of being a very stiff employer of labour, was weeping like a child.'

Edmund Gosse lived to write, in *Father and Son*, his own recollections of that scene. Nor was it the end of his triumph. He was to hear the elders pay tribute in the full congregation to his holiness, wisdom and humility, and then to experience the glory of baptism at ten years old, a privilege granted normally by the Brethren to adults only. 'To me it was dazzling beyond words, inexpressibly exciting, an initiation to every kind of publicity and glory.' The vast majority of children could only experience this intense excitement vicariously, through the triumphant deathbed scenes recorded in the compilations of early piety. Small wonder that Victorians reared on these in the earlier decades of the century had their appetites for deathbeds whetted, and were to introduce them into fiction over and over again, long after their religious significance had been discarded and there were other outlets for the imagination.

Death was an essential part of the evangelical education; but it did not stop at contemplation of it in print. Like the Fairchild children, the young evangelical was taken to deathbeds, saw many corpses, and regularly attended funerals. The boys of Kingswood, the school founded by Wesley, were led during a revival of 1770 to see the corpse of a neighbour, and the visit was 'improved' by an evening meeting and the singing of a hymn about death, which resulted, to quote Southey, in a scene 'worthy of Bedlam'. Days of delirium and hysteria followed, and then a mass conversion of the boys. In 1795 the children from one of Hannah and Martha More's Mendip Sunday schools were led to the funeral of a teacher. It was attended by vast crowds to whom the clergyman, almost speechless with emotion, delivered a thirty-five minute discourse. The children, drenched with tears, were led back to school as soon as the ceremony was over, and Martha then 'wrung their little hearts' as best she could, 'for I know but too well that the world and young blood would make an excellent sponge to wipe out full soon the awful business of the day.'

They were even led to prisons. Mary Milner, for instance, who wrote the life of her uncle Isaac Milner, the famous evangelical divine, in 1842, went with him to see a man in the condemned cell at Carlisle. She does not remark on this as the least unusual, but reserves comment for her uncle's compassion, and the eloquence with which he expounded the doctrine of redemption to the doomed man.

Time was so short, eternity yawned beyond the grave; the evangelicals could not bear to see their children wasting those precious moments and letting life drift by, and continually searched their minds for methods to shock them into seriousness. Annie Keary was haunted by one such tale in her childhood. Called *The Warning Clock*, it began with a picture of a little girl asleep in bed, a clock on the wall of her room, and an old nurse drawing aside the bed curtain. The child wakes and says, 'Call me again, nurse, in an hour's time, then I will get up.' Thus it goes on all day, till midnight comes. Then there was a picture of the clock pointing to twelve, in the doorway a man with a veiled face, of whom the story said that 'he would brook no delay,' and the child sitting up in bed at last, but with an expression of agony on her face.

Mrs Sherwood wrote *A Drive in the Coach through the Streets of London* (1818) with the same purpose, and sub-titled it 'a story founded on fact.' Julia is heedless and gives too much thought to things of this world. Her mother takes her on a drive through London, and allows her to choose an item from each shop that they pass, stipulating only that she promises to put all these to the use for which they were

28   A DRIVE

cannot have any thing out of that shop. Do look, mamma!"

The lady looked up, and saw a shop in which there was nothing for sale but coffins. "Why are you alarmed, Julia?" she said; "you know that this is a kind of shop to which we must all be customers, sooner or later. Shall I put down a coffin in the memorandum?"

"O no, mamma!" said Julia, laying her hand upon her mother's, "don't do any thing so shocking. I did not think of

Julia and her Mamma passing the Coffin-Maker's Shop.

c 3

Heedless Julia is taught a lesson. (Mrs Sherwood, *A Drive in the Coach through the Streets of London*, 1818)

intended, and does not omit any shop. Julia duly chooses a writing table, a pair of blue satin boots, a varnished work-box, a cap with artificial flowers, a dress and a pearl necklace. But then comes the coffin-maker's shop. '"Shall I put down a coffin in the memorandum, Julia?"'

The serious evangelical child had given much thought to his salvation. Many of the tracts began by asking him if he was saved. Only the individual soul could answer this question. It went far beyond just being a 'good' child, as John Pike's *Persuasives to Early*

Piety showed. Man is a transgressor from the womb, he urges; the imagination of his heart is evil from his youth. 'Perhaps you may have been tender and compassionate, dutiful and obliging, but will this save you? No, never.'

All that was necessary to salvation was contained in the Bible, and so on the study of the Bible the evangelicals put enormous stress. Bibles were rushed to the relief of the starving when a depression hit Paisley in 1837; they were distributed in city slums in the 1840s when a wave of cholera was expected. For this alone the early Sunday schools taught the children to read. 'Actual comprehension was not

THE RECLAIMED ONE AND HIS BIBLE.

"THE WORD OF GOD IS NOW MY DELIGHT, AND I LOVE TO READ IT TO MY FAMILY."

Band of Hope Review, 1851

necessary,' Richard Altick has written. 'Enough if the reader were able to pronounce, in a fashion, most of the words he looked upon . . . One who knew his letters, regardless of any further education, was sufficiently equipped to perform the sacred rite which lay at the very heart of religion.' Nor was the learner given any guidance as to what to read in the Bible. The commentaries used by scholars were not necessary to the simple man who had faith; the divine light would guide him to the all-important texts, and would show him which of the Mosaic laws had relevance, like the keeping of the Sabbath, and which had not, like the prohibition of pork. Hannah More's passionate conviction was that any who doubted whether the ignorant could understand the Bible without a commentary must be an infidel or a papist.

The attitude of the Roman Church towards the Bible was a further proof, if such were needed, of its utterly damnable nature. 'That wicked man – the pope of Rome,' said Rowland Hill in one of his sermons to children, delivered at Surrey Chapel on 12 December, 1824, 'forbids the people to read the Bible by peculiar decrees; but it is your mercy to obtain it. The Lord grant that you may be taught to read the Bible; and God make it a blessing to your hearts. O what a blessed thing, when, like young Timothy, you are taught to read the Scriptures.'

But the young evangelical needed no further persuasion of the devilishness of Rome. In the less partisan days of the eighteenth century the influential children's books had carried a message of tolerance towards other religions. The Unitarian Dr Aikin and his sister Mrs Barbauld had made a point of it in *Evenings at Home*; the High Church Dr John Gregory in *A Father's Legacy to his Daughters* (1774) had recommended 'an enlarged charity for all mankind, however they may differ from you in their religious opinions.' The Rousseauist Thomas Day had seen to it that Harry Sandford and Tommy Merton were taught to respect the religious beliefs of others. But to the nineteenth-century evangelical such tolerance was almost as damnable as the heresy itself, and interdenominational hatred and suspicion was to be an outstanding feature of Victorian religious life, with the greatest hatred reserved for Rome.

Edmund Gosse described how he and his father used to discuss the Roman Church during his childhood in the 1850s 'in the language of the seventeenth century such as is now no longer introduced into any species of controversy'. This was the style of Charlotte Elizabeth whose chief aim it was to counteract the errors of Popery. To her, 1829 – the year of Catholic Emancipation – was forever the 'most hateful year in the annals of England's perfidy to her bounteous Lord.' To her, Popery was the Babylon of the Apocalypse, as it was to thousands of others, and Judaism was infinitely preferable. 'The Jew possesses the fair blossom of gospel truth, which by kindly fostering is to be expanded and ripened into the rich fruit; the Papist holds in his hand an apple of Sodom, beneath the painted rind of which is a mass of ashes and corruption.'[1]

So she and many others wrote to warn children about the wiles of Rome. Mrs Sherwood's *The Nun* has been mentioned. It described the terrible fate of a nun who apostatised and became a Protestant, and it made a deep impression upon the young Keary children in their evangelical vicarage home in Hull in the 1830s. They were denied imaginative literature, of course, as a matter of principle, and they made up their own stories. One of these was that Father Render, the burly good-natured priest who was their neighbour in Hull, had so persecuted a renegade nun that she had hidden herself above the housemaid's closet in their own vicarage. It started off as play, but it became reality to them. They poked up food to her through the trapdoor, and even mobilised their friends into making an attempt to rescue the fugitive, and frightened them all into fits. As for Father Render himself – they recoiled from his pleasantries, shuddering at 'the contamination of contact with such a black-hearted son of Belial'.

Mrs Sherwood wrote other books about the dangers of Rome. They had not seemed so potent in the days of *The Infant's Progress*. Here she had followed Bunyan and shown the Giants Pagan and Pope as enfeebled and 'by reason of their age and infirmities, incapable of doing as much mischief as they had formerly done'. This was some fifteen years before the Catholic Emancipation Act which perhaps was responsible for stirring her into producing *Victoria* (1833), the Protestant child who is nearly ensnared because of the apathy of her father, and *The Flowers of the Forest* (1830), where the

---

[1] It should be said of Charlotte Elizabeth that she came to love the Irish and individual Catholic friends. She devoted much time and money to relieving distress among her husband's cottagers, and during the time of the Irish famine, when immigrants were starving in London, she went among them to combat 'starvation and popery,' and never experienced a 'disrespectful or unkind look'.

particularly attracted our attention, and we
wondered that things so beautiful should
have been formed in places where none saw

and none admired; and this led me to speak
of the infinite goodness of God, and of his
bounty towards the children of men.

At length we reached our village, and parting at the garden gate, I retired to my study
to examine the Holy Bible respecting those
passages to which my little companion had
alluded.   And in that long quiet day, a day
never to be forgotten by me, such convictions
flashed upon my mind respecting the errors
of my church, that before the evening hour I

The little Protestant converts the Roman priest.
(Mrs Sherwood, *The Flowers of the Forest*,
R T S edition, *c.* 1873).

pretty little heroine converts a French abbé from his Popish fancies.
Aimée became, in fact, the pattern for a child who was to make
repeated appearances in evangelical literature later in the century,
the little one who knows her Bible and could win over the Pope
himself, had he not in his pusillanimous way, hidden himself behind
the walls of the Vatican.

One of the great accusations the Victorian English levelled at
Rome was that its adherents desecrated the Sabbath, forgetting how
recently strict observance of the day had been generally introduced
into England. Robert Raikes, regular though he was in his attend-

ance at the cathedral and anxious to keep the urchins off the streets on Sundays, was no Sabbatarian. Sunday was probably one of the busiest days at his printing works, and the Gloucester shops in his time stayed open for the benefit of the country people who poured into the city.

From the very beginning the Wesleyans made a great issue of this as their seventeenth-century Puritan ancestors had done, and many were the accounts that we read in the *Evangelical Magazine* of fatal accidents to those who had disported themselves on a Sunday. The schoolmaster in Hannah More's *Black Giles the Poacher* noted in his pocket-book during the week any useful story in the newspaper such as boys being drowned as they were out in a pleasure boat on Sundays, so that he could relate it to his class as an awful warning.

By Victorian times the evangelical insistence on the sanctity of every moment of Sunday had become part of the national way of life. It was far more than a religious duty, it became equated with law and order and decency and respectability. Conscientious writers for the young tried to stress the positive side. Mrs Sherwood describes how the Fairchilds kept it. There was a ritual cleaning and washing and cooking on Saturday, and all was made ready for the following day. Then on Sunday after a special breakfast of bread and butter and tea, they set off quietly for church and school. They went sedately, for the children were not allowed to run on Sundays. Before the morning service they had to teach the Sunday scholars, hearing them their catechism and giving them religious instruction for two hours. Lucy and Emily had six little girls each, and Henry six boys, and they sat with these children in church to help them find their places in the Psalter and see that they behaved well. Then the family went home to dinner. It was understood that nobody would chatter idly about worldly matters, and that they would instead try to reflect on the words that they had heard in church. In summer they went to church again in the afternoon, in the winter they had prayers at home, followed by reading from Sunday books and singing of hymns.

'Now of all the days in the week, Sunday was the day the children loved best; for on this day there was no worldly business – no care about money, or clothes, or cooking dinner; no work to be done but God's work, the sweetest of all works, the work which angels delight to do.'

Elizabeth Sewell, writing in Victorian times, stressed the festive nature of the day in *Laneton Parsonage*. 'You know what it is to keep a birthday. The person whose birthday it is is the one object – the great person of the day. We are constantly thinking what he will like; how we can please him: his wishes are consulted, and if we forget for a little while, we are always meeting with something to remind us of him. Now, our feeling on a Sunday should be of the same kind.'

But it was the negative aspects of Victorian Sundays that made the most impression on those who lived through them. They obtrude in nearly every book of the period. One of Charlotte Yonge's young men so far forgets himself as to whistle on a Sunday, and instantly apologises to the clergyman by his side. In their excitement at realising that their friends, marooned on an island for several days, are still alive, two little boys in Annie Keary's *The Rival Kings* (1857) take off their hats and shout, 'though it was a Sunday'. The prohibitions reach almost Judaical rigidity in *The Children's Tabernacle* (1871) by the evangelical A.L.O.E., where a child helping to make a model of the Jewish Tabernacle for the delectation of a Ragged School, is tempted, very wrongly, to stitch at its curtains on a Sunday, and cannot sleep with an easy conscience until she has confessed.

Even by 1844 when *Laneton Parsonage* was written, the sober English Sunday had become a deeply engrained national habit. The most frivolous schoolgirl observed it, outwardly at least.

'"After church I go with Jane to have luncheon and we have great fun."

"But what fun? fun on a Sunday!" asked Jessie.

"Do you play?" inquired Ellen Hastings.

"Nonsense, children! don't interrupt. You cannot understand. I tell you we have fun."

"Yes, but is it talking?" asked Alice.

"What should it be but talking? We are not heathens."'

To keep the Sabbath became a talisman against evil. To break it, as repentant young criminals testified, was the first step on the downward path, to be followed by drinking and gambling, and then the gallows. Occasionally a lone voice was raised in protest. Baroness Bunsen, the Victorian philanthropist whose life was written by Augustus Hare, wondered 'how those who really love their Saviour, and wish to follow His precepts, can reconcile themselves to setting up the great idol of Sabbatarianism, *the* sin against which He was most eager and earnest in warning His disciples, and against which more of His teaching was directed than any other single offence.' But no doubts such as these ever ruffled the calm surface of the Sundays recorded in the children's books.

The ideal evangelical child was to change as the nineteenth century moved on. The earlier writers had thought of him as achieving salvation and then dying. Later books became less exclusively concerned with the inward child, and the message was gentler. The ministering child began to replace the dying child, and good works were more stressed, though these were always subordinate to the gospel message.

Charlotte Elizabeth's model girl in *The Simple Flower* is pious, cheerful and active, always looking out for opportunities of doing good. She says,

'There are younger girls than me buried in the churchyard, and if I am called away also, I must not be found like the foolish virgins, sleeping in idleness, without oil in my lamp. There is much for such as me to do, many poor children are ignorant of what I am made happy by knowing, that Jesus Christ is the Saviour of all who believe, and that they who name his name are required to depart from iniquity. I must assist to teach these poor children; and I must earn a little, and save a little, to give to those who are sending Bibles and missionaries to the heathen and the Jew.'

It is this sort of child who peoples the pages of Maria Louisa Charlesworth's enormously popular *Ministering Children*. Published in 1854, its sales had topped 122,000 fifteen years later, and it was still good for many years to come. It is hardly a story, but more a collection of interwoven examples (some of which were to be published separately) of good children intent upon their salvation who seek out opportunities for charity to assist them on their path to glory. None is so poor that he may not give. Little Ruth, white with hunger, takes the soup a benevolent lady has given her, to feed to a sick child. The poor shoemaker's family go without their Christmas dinner in order that they may fill the missionary box with sixpences and shillings. There is a heady excitement about such heroic giving. The characters themselves feel it: 'The flickering firelight showed the elder and the younger face, both gleaming with the glow of blessed

The ministering child. An incident from Maria Louisa Charlesworth's own childhood illustrated in *The Children's Friend*, 1881. The child had admonished the drunken poacher, 'had led him from the error of his ways, and anxiously watched over his after-course'.

charity.' So did readers, who experienced the same sort of emotional thrill that an older generation had drawn from the account of the inspiring deathbeds of young evangelical saints. We can see this from a prize winning story contributed to the *Sunday Scholar's Companion* in December, 1881 by fourteen year old Frances Ethel Canning.

Was hers a Useless Life? she called her story. Helen de Coinville, proud, in furs and tippet, with flashing though cold brown eyes and a curled upper lip, passes by a ragged beggar. Agnes Melville, on the other hand, leaps from her carriage and saves him and is doomed to livelong invalidom as a result of her heroism.

'There she lies on her couch, surrounded by a dozen boys of various ages, rough, uncouth, unmannerly, with clothes in rags, though hands and faces clean. Look at their eager faces as they bend forward to listen, to take in every word which falls from the sweet lips of "their own lady" . . . tears steal down their sunburnt cheeks and words of repentance fall from those lips which have only been accustomed to curse and swear.'

And Agnes's pale hands move tirelessly as she stitches meanwhile for the poor and needy, and distributes warm clothes, mingled with blessed words of love.

For the poor and needy themselves there was also a more practical message. The temperance movement had begun and was to be as great a force in their lives as the earlier Sunday School movement had been. Henceforward these were to walk hand in hand. The ideal

Little girls' sewing society. 'Although we are young, we think we can do *some* good; and we have agreed to form a society in which we can make our little fingers useful by sewing for the poor heathen children; and we hope thus to grow wiser and better as we grow older; more benevolent to our fellow-creatures and more pleasing to God.' (*Band of Hope Review*, 1860)

Sunday scholar was also a Band of Hope child, and had signed the pledge. We meet him in the *Band of Hope Review and Sunday Scholar's Friend* which first appeared in 1851. For a halfpenny the young reader got four well-printed three-column pages, which included some fine engravings. They contained little anecdotes of good children who resisted drink; news of Ragged School boys with the will to succeed; stories of the dreadful end of the intemperate. However, the message was mostly one of quiet, cheerful optimism – such as the hope that the seven year old Prince of Wales might one day become the Patron of the Band of Hope. It also carried anti-slavery news, and campaigned, mildly, for clean water supplies for the poor (showing in one instance, a picture of a boy lapping water from a pool in the street), and for early closing on Saturdays, so that workers could prepare themselves for the proper spending of Sundays. Smoking was discouraged, because it created thirst and led men into the company of those who drank.

Towards the teetotal children of drunken parents it was tender. They should plead gently with their elders, and very likely their example might convert, like that of little Jane, who scrounged scrap-iron to buy a twopenny orange for her sick mother when her father had spent everything on drink. Her father is moved. '"Come, let us go and see these cold water men,"' he says, '"they are carrying the whole world before them."' And he goes with her to sign the Pledge.

There is a whole literature of mid-Victorian temperance stories, many of them specifically aimed at children, and usually incorporating a gospel message as well. The dangers of drink were very real and very terrible in those days, and the writers felt that if these could be burnt into the minds of every Sunday scholar there was hope for the next generation.

It is ironical that the evangelicals, who so mistrusted works of imagination, should throughout the century produce the juvenile fiction that sold. They had the secret of the common touch; they could find the subject and the style that was able to grip both cottage and drawing room. *Jessica's First Prayer* (which first appeared in *Sunday at Home* in 1866) sold 1,500,000 copies, *Little Meg's Children* (1868) and *Alone in London* (1869) 750,000 between them. All these three were by Hesba Stretton. The American Elizabeth Wetherell, author of *Queechy* and *The Wide, Wide World* was also enormously popular. Time and again evangelical writers hit the jack-pot, and were able to bask comfortably in the warming thought, as few best-

The little pleader. An illustration from the *Band of Hope Review*, 1855. The evils of drink were much stressed in Sunday School literature.

selling writers are able to do, that they had won souls as well. There were some stricter brethren like the Salvation Army mother who in 1890 wrote an article on *How we Trained the Baby* after reading General Booth's book on the subject, and said that her boy should never be allowed to read lies under any name, whether fairy stories,

Sunday-school books or any other.[1] But this was an extreme point of view.

More remarkable still, the moralists and the young readers were in agreement – at any rate over the attractiveness of the street arab evangelist who succeeded the dying child and the ministering child as the hero of the Sunday story. Sensational stories of ragged London depravity Eliza Keary had styled them – but hers was a solitary voice of disapproval. The street arab was frequently a ministering child and a dying one too. There was high melodrama, sanctified violence, and much opportunity for tears. Flora Thompson described in *Lark Rise to Candleford* how the women and children of an Oxfordshire hamlet in the 1880s were caught up in the sufferings described by 'Brenda' (Mrs G. Castle Smith), of Froggie's little brother and longed to give him some country air and country food to bring colour into his cheeks.

The fashion for the slum background began in the 1860s, with the new interest in social conditions. (Mayhew's *London Labour and the London Poor*, which it had taken fifteen years to compile, appeared 1861–2). Some authors, such as the gifted Hesba Stretton who had worked among the poor and was one of the founders of the National Society for the Prevention of Cruelty for Children, had first-hand experience of the conditions they described, and genuinely burned, too, to bring the gospel message to their readers. Others, one suspects, wrote up their accounts of starving crossing sweepers, waifs whose only shelter was the railway arches, and cruelly used children of drunken parents, from the abundant journalism of the 70s and 80s, because it was so profitable and so enjoyable to harrow the readers. Even Ballantyne tried his hand at the genre with a story that he called *My Doggie and I*, and May Wynne, who later kept to schoolgirl fantasies, must have been writing from memories of the stories of forty years before when she produced in 1903 *Mollie's Adventures*: about little slaves gumming matchboxes in a Hoxton cellar, and conditions that belonged to the days before the Education Act and school attendance officers.

The street arab story usually followed much the same pattern. A

[1] This same mother, incidentally, echoed Mrs Sherwood in her feeling that parents possessed Divine authority. 'You stand in God's place to him,' she tells her husband. 'It's a tremendous thing to stand in His place to a little soul.' (From *All the World*, vol. VI, 1890)

destitute or a neglected child is brought into contact with a Bible story, such as the parable of the Good Shepherd, or a text – 'Wash me and I shall be whiter than snow' was a favourite – and we are shown how it has the power to redeem him, to strengthen him against the temptations that surround him, and to sustain and comfort him when the utter wretchedness of his miserable earthly life seems to offer no hope whatever. Sometimes the story is made to end happily, such as in Hesba Stretton's *Little Meg's Children* where the long-lost father comes home to cherish what survives of his family, or on a muted note of optimism, such as in *Froggie's Little Brother*, where Froggie, having lost father, mother, and adored brother, is accepted by an orphanage. But more often he dies, radiant and joyful in the thought that his earthly woes are over and his heavenly reward beginning.

One of the very earliest examples, which anticipated *Jessica's First Prayer* by three years, is also one of the best. Mary Howitt published *The Story of Little Cristal* in 1863 as 'a freewill offering from all who are concerned in producing it . . . on behalf of their distressed and suffering brethren and sisters of the cotton districts'. Mary Howitt was not an evangelical, she was a Quaker who had discarded the strict practices of the Society of Friends, and was later to become a member of the Roman church. Her unobtrusive talent and quiet style of writing kept her in the background when her more showy contemporaries succeeded in holding public attention, but this account of a waif's redemption is one of the most convincing and poignant of the thousands that were to succeed it.

Too many of the writers of the street arab school who succeeded her were to endow a single gospel text with a seemingly magic force that could infuse into a totally ignorant child, who had no previous contact with Christianity, a grasp of the Christian ethic so that he foreswore all dishonest practices and became as scrupulous as the young Edmund Gosse. But Cristal remains convincing. Like the small Sunday scholar, Charles Shaw, who has been mentioned in a previous chapter, he holds fast to the only beautiful things in his darkened life. At first it is the snatches of hymns or texts from the Bible told to him by an old man who takes him on never to be forgotten journeys into the country outside London. Then it is the memory of the wonderful colours of a stained glass window, representing Christ blessing the children, which he sees with the sun behind them one day when he ventures into a church.

THE SUNDAY FAIRY

2d

A CHARMING NEW WEEKLY PAPER FOR BOYS AND GIRLS TO READ ON SUNDAYS.

Helen Jacobs

The Coming of the Sunday Fairy.

No. 1. Vol. 1.   PRICE TWOPENCE.   May 10, 1919.

1919: the twentieth century resolves to try to brighten Sundays for the young.

'As he so knelt and so yearned towards the Divine Saviour and Friend, all at once, he saw that his little dirty hands, his breast and all his poor clothes, were covered with a glorious light as of rubies and emeralds and transparent topaz, all purple and red and green and gold.'

The thought of this lightens his last moments as he lies dying from exposure in the wintry London streets.

The evangelical child lost his power as the nineteenth century waned. Living conditions improved and the street arab hero was discarded. The temperance movement had brought a tremendous change in drinking habits, and tracts dwindled to a trickle. In *Brave and True*, for instance (sub-titled *An Illustrated Weekly Paper for the Sons and Daughters of the Church*), the 1893 argument against drink is given by a doctor, who shows an alcoholic naval officer kidneys in various stages of rot. The eloquent pleadings of such children as Alice in *Alice Leigh's Mission* of whom the publican said 'the sight of that child was enough to make any man sober,' are finished. In the 1933 descendant of the *Band of Hope Review* we find many medical arguments, and only occasional reminders of the Victorian heroism such as the anecdote of a child who, with limbs horribly mangled from some accident, refuses brandy saying, 'I can't drink it, I'm a Rechabite.'

Sabbatarianism was to vanish. Perhaps it was the memory of Victorian prohibitions that made the publishers resolve to brighten young lives in the twentieth century with *The Sunday Fairy* whose first number appeared in 1919 and brought a message from the Sunday fairy herself:

'But now, having once arrived, I shall come to you EVERY WEEK, and tell you all about fairies, and gnomes, and little brownie men in Fairyland, and many other things you love to read about. I shall tell you all the best stories I know, and I shall give you pictures of fairy folk, and quaint animals in Ever-so-far-away-land.

'Best of all, I shall tell you those sweet stories we read of in the Bible – the best book in the world, that tells us of Jesus, the Friend of little children, and His great love. These are the stories we like best to read on Sundays.'

A fairy to preach the Gospel! The Bible second to fairyland!

[6]

The happy family
1830–1880

'WHAT a merry party always came round to claim a kiss when we came out of church,' wrote Catherine Tait, as she pieced together in her great sorrow a memoir of the five little daughters who had died of scarlet fever at the Deanery in Carlisle in the spring of 1856. Catty, May, Chatty, Frances, and Susan; the oldest nine, the youngest not two – their mother's account of their short sweet lives reads like one of the family tales that were such a notable contribution to children's literature in the middle years of the nineteenth century. She described the 'exceeding brightness of that home,' where the children learned with their mother and prepared their lessons in their father's study, repeated their psalms and hymns to him, conducted their own Sunday School – 'we from our room could hear their sweet voices' – and were to be seen on summer Sundays by passers-by, sitting clustered in the Deanery garden, examining their Sunday pictures and reading *The Pilgrim's Progress*.

Perhaps there never has been a time when the behaviour of real children might conform so nearly to the ideals set down by the writers of their books. The doings of the pasteboard little Miss Sprightlys of the late Georgian tales bear no resemblance to the experiences of Elizabeth Grant of Rothiemurchus who described so vividly the tomboyish high spirits, the ferocious battles with the governess, the worldliness and the savagery of a Regency upbringing. And very few of us who were brought up in the 1930s would recognise Arthur Ransome's John, Susan, Titty or Roger as sharing the same hopes or fears or aspirations as ourselves; with their calm efficiency and capacity for coping without adults they were infinitely remote from our staid lives. But if we read *Dulce Domum*, the record of Bishop Moberly's family, we find there the same girls who fill Charlotte Yonge's novels with their ardent dutifulness, their self-sacrificing devotion to parents, and the happiness they feel in the companionship of their brothers and sisters.

See Chap 2nd

A happy family gathering, Mamma with her younger children, the older sisters at their music, baby playing with his cart, the middle children preoccupied with their books. Lithograph from *Christmas Improvement, or Hunting Mrs P.* (1834)

Archbishop Tait's family have their counterparts in scores of tales designed to guide and also to amuse the Victorian child. The moralists now accepted that writers for the young had a duty to entertain as well as to teach. 'A good book for young people,' wrote Old Humphrey 'should afford them amusement; for otherwise they can be hardly expected to like it. It should impart useful information, thereby making them wiser. It should impress their minds with some important truth. It should correct their errors in judgement and practice. It should reprove vice and encourage virtue; and it should increase their love for mankind, and establish them in the fear of the Lord.' These were the ideals of 1851, and there were plenty of writers who strove to abide by them.

Gentleness and affection are the keynotes of their products, and many of the authors possessed considerable talent: Annie Keary (1825–79), Elizabeth Sewell (1815–1906), Juliana Horatia Ewing (1841–85), Charlotte Yonge (1823–1901) and Mary Louisa Molesworth (1839–1921) who carried the tradition into the twentieth

122

century. The Victorian middle class family circle was a close one. The younger children and the girls were taught within it and rarely moved outside it. It was therefore important that family virtues should be inculcated: toleration, forbearance, generosity, patience. A great deal was exacted of these children, a selflessness amounting to heroism, and it says much for these domestic writers that they could make their characters so attractive and present virtue so convincingly.

Though they achieved much prestige with a discriminating public, these authors cannot be said, any of them, to have been truly popular. Only Elizabeth Sewell's *Tales and Stories* (in nine volumes) which sold 68,000 copies between 1858 and 1863 is listed as a best-seller in Richard Altick's *The English Common Reader*. They were essentially books for the educated middle classes; the situations and backgrounds they described would have held no interest to the average cottage reader, the literary style was too difficult and – of great importance in the eyes of those who like Charlotte Yonge sifted and recommended children's reading – the moral was not slanted towards their needs. For we are still in an epoch where the ways are very much divided, and cottage and drawing-room needs were reckoned to be poles apart. Not for the cottage child the difficulty of deciding how best to reconcile home and outside duties, how to allocate pocket money, the best use to make of leisure.

But even over the educated classes their hold was not strong, with the exception of Mrs Molesworth who wrote more specifically to entertain, and of Charlotte Yonge who, though her influence later diminished, in the mid-Victorian years commanded a large band of devoted followers. They appealed to the thoughtful parent rather than to the common run of young readers who wanted a more sensational or a more sentimental type of story.

There was no English equivalent of Louisa Alcott's *Little Women* (1867) which endeared itself to so many millions by the warmth and informality of its family life, or of Susan Coolidge's *What Katy Did* (1872). Both these American authors succeeded in showing simple, kindly goodness without directly advocating any particular code of conduct, and their huge public loved them for it. Charlotte Yonge invented plausible families, but their lofty ideals, their seriousness, their intellectual interests, their upper class fastidiousness, set them apart from the ordinary reader. Nor could Mrs Ewing, with her greater gaiety, achieve that contact with the reader that the Americans seemed to slip into with such ease. Undoubtedly the lack of emphasis by the latter on class differences had something to do with it, and perhaps the lesser deference to the proprieties.

American children too had a sturdy self-reliance that their English contemporaries lacked, and immigrants apparently gained this the moment they arrived. It is interesting to compare Mary Howitt's account of her own children, *The Children's Year* (1847) with *Our*

The Bright family gardening. Page for painting from the *Children's Friend*, 1881. The ideal family shared all their recreations.

Cousins in Ohio – the record of her little nieces' and nephews' lives which she put together in 1849 from her sister's letters. Herbert and Meggy Howitt in England seem very childlike beside their Alderson cousins newly settled in America, and already having to take on their full share of responsibility in a household where there was no time for a separate nursery life.

The writings of Elizabeth Sewell, less known today than those of her more prolific and successful contemporary Miss Yonge, are worth some consideration as an extreme example of the seriousness of some of the early Victorian writers for the young. Like Miss Yonge, she lived a quiet retired life, in the Isle of Wight, devoted to the orphan nieces and nephews whom she helped to bring up and to the girl pupils taken in to make a livelihood. Like Miss Yonge she had been profoundly stirred by the Tractarian movement in her youth, and was moved to write stories from the High Church viewpoint. The need for them was much felt at the time. 'I am sure we shall do nothing till we get some ladies to work to poison the rising generation,' Newman had flippantly written in 1836 to a female correspondent who had proposed writing such a story. By the mid 1840s the ladies were hard at work, and Elizabeth Sewell referred herself to the many tales 'illustrative of the Oxford teaching . . . which were hailed with special satisfaction by young people, who turned from the texts, and prayers, and hymns, which Mrs Sherwood had introduced into her stories, and yet needed something higher in tone than Miss Edgeworth's morality'. It was not just the young who now rejected Mrs Sherwood; the High Church early Victorian parent realised that her writings were hardly suitable for any except the extreme Calvinist.

Elizabeth Sewell's output was small. She wrote nine novels for the older girl, and two – *Amy Herbert* (1844) and *Laneton Parsonage* (1846) for the schoolroom child. Her writings have often been mistakenly equated with those of Charlotte Yonge who aimed, as Eleanor Sewell pointed out in her appendix to her aunt's autobiography, at 'the harmless novel and innocent amusement with an equally religious tone and the same school of thought,' whereas each of Miss Sewell's tales had its own point of instruction in some part of the faith and practice of the English Church. An Anglican clergyman[1] paid a touching tribute to *Laneton Parsonage* in a letter to the author

[1] The Rev J. J. Lias, Chancellor of Llandafff Cathedral. Quoted by Eleanor Sewell.

in 1889. He had been roused, he said, from 'a sentimental evangelicalism in which the reading of good works and thinking of (perhaps) good thoughts was to me the whole of religion,' and turned to 'a Catholic Christianity which holds fast the Word of God and the Creeds and honours the Sacraments'. Elizabeth Sewell's exposition of her faith had provided the foundation stone of his subsequent religious life.

Miss Sewell had suffered herself under the Sherwood and Cameron tales; no decently religious household of her generation could have escaped them. The style had always offended her with their description of children 'quoting texts, and talking of their feelings in an unnatural way, or what seemed to me unnatural,' and she had writhed at the cant evangelical phrases that seemed to flow so glibly from her school teachers. The teaching in her own books is conveyed with dignity and restraint, in the form of conversation between the children and their parents, and discussion among themselves, and is combined with an acute observation of character and insight into the feelings of adolescent girls. But essentially her books are for the conscientious reader prepared to give them much time and thought.

Laneton Parsonage, which Mr Lias had valued so highly, was designed to give practical illustration of the Church's Catechism. Published originally in three parts, there are some 800 pages describing quiet domestic life. We see Madeline and Ruth Clifford in their parsonage home, blessed with tender and loving parents who teach them, watch over them, guard them from evil, and the orphan Alice Lennox at the neighbouring manor, brought up by Lady Catharine Hyde, a close friend of Alice's dead mother. The characters of the three girls are analysed in great detail, the temptations that each has to face, the advice that is given to them. We follow them to school – Mrs Carter's establishment of fifteen young ladies – and see the new moral predicaments that confront them there, and how each child in a different way falls from grace. Finally they are shown to us at home again with the great responsibility of confirmation approaching them.

Events in these quiet lives are not many, and even the smallest creates high drama. In the first part there is the episode of Alice Lennox's dishonesty and disobedience. Her guardian has expressly forbidden her to set foot in certain rooms in the manor. They had been used by Lady Catharine's dead husband, and she regards them

Hymn-singing round the piano. (*Children's Friend*, 1883)

as peculiarly sacred, and maintains them as a shrine to his memory into which only she and her maid may set foot. Inevitably Alice finds herself drawn to them, and then becomes enmeshed in a web of deceit in which she flounders helplessly, terrified of the severe Lady Catharine.

In the second part we are more concerned with Ruth and Madeline's consciences. At home their parents had shielded them from contamination by the world. At school they encounter for the first time undesirable companions. Clara, giddy and empty-headed, draws her friends into habits of idle, silly chatter; worse still, she

127

incites them to read French novels from a circulating library, knowing that such literature is absolutely forbidden. Madeline and Alice are nearly drawn into this wrongdoing against their will, but it is Ruth, whom everybody thinks so good, so proud of her own rectitude, who is the one who reads two chapters secretly and is gnawed with fearful remorse. She admits nothing, however, until the moment when her companions vote that she should, being morally the best, become their leader, and then collapses in penitence and shame at her teacher's feet.

By the third part, Ruth and Madeline are restored to the tranquillity of their parsonage, happily surrounded by loving parental care. Alice at the manor is not so lucky. She has the emotional crises of adolescence to endure with only a parent substitute – Lady Catharine, who, though an excellent woman and devoted to the girl, has not a manner which invites confidence. However, all is put right by the end, and Alice, Ruth and Madeline together kneel to receive their first Communion, watched by the parents 'who then saw themselves bound to their precious children by the most hallowed of all ties,' and by Lady Catharine 'who read in that solemn act the pledge that the one treasure of her life should be hers for ever in heaven'.

The representation of affection within the family circle was a

An early representation of affectionate parents. Greeting the little boy on his return from school. Lithograph by Denis Dighton from *Early Impressions*, 1828.

relatively new development in the children's book. We get glimpses of a loving, tender mother in the poems of Ann and Jane Taylor in 1804.

> *That dear little face that I like so to kiss*
> *How altered and sad it appears!*
> *Do you think I can love you so naughty as this,*
> *Or kiss you, all wetted with tears?*

But the parents of the pre-Victorian books are more often presented as chillingly reasonable like Rosamond's mother in *Early Lessons* who with enviable detachment presents the child with the choices and leaves her with the ultimate decision; or ready with the lecture and the whip like Mr Fairchild; or distressingly silly and ruining their children with false indulgence.

In contrast, the parents of the Victorian family story are presented as always anxious to have the confidence of their children. The home influence is the all-important one.

'A quiet, methodical, religious home,' wrote the author of *Boys and Their Ways* (1880), 'in which the parents are actuated by a high sense of duty, in which all the members are linked together by love's golden chain, in which a place is found for everything and everything is in its place, so that the mind is insensibly trained in habits of discipline and order, in which happiness constantly prevails, because tempers are subdued and wills controlled by the very spirit of the scene; such a home exercises an influence which lasts till death.'

It was only such a home and such parental influence that could protect a boy from corruption and the evils that he inevitably met as soon as he was plunged into school, and many a mother's heart quailed within her, as in Dean Farrar's *Eric, or Little by Little,* as she looked at 'the small shining flower-like faces – the trustful loving arms folded round each brother's neck,' and wondered whether the twelve years of tender protection and gentle guidance would be armour enough to withstand what he was about to encounter.

The ideal mother gave all the religious instruction herself. She expected that her children, and certainly her daughters, would reveal all their thoughts, doubts and difficulties to her. And in a son's willingness to do this lay his best hope of keeping himself untarnished by the school world.

'If he go to her knees with all his confessions, all his little secrets, all his fancied wrongs, all his real sufferings, all his misdeeds, if he never fail in his tenderness towards her, in his deep love and reverence; then – whatever may be his follies or faults, I shall not despair of him.'

This is the ideal boy of *Boys and their Ways*, and plenty of other writers, Thomas Hughes and Dean Farrar among them, would have agreed that a boy's love for his mother was 'a talisman, a guardian angel.' She did not scold or punish, she grieved at her children's misdoings. The author of *A Whisper for the Nursery* (1847) described the agony of the first and only lie she ever told to her mother.

'The pale, sweet face, sad and grave, turned upon the little culprit, the big, unbidden tears, which rolled over her soft cheek, as for the first time she sent her child unblest to bed! Oh! it was an hour of agony – never to be forgotten – never to be endured again. Sleep had fled from the eye of childhood . . . Henceforth, the truth was identified with a *mother's* happiness, and it was sedulously sought and sacredly preserved.'

Similarly, in *Laneton Parsonage*, it is the thought of her mother which so haunts Ruth in her agonies of guilt at the contamination she feels she has derived from her illicit reading: 'before her mind's eye there floated a fair, gentle, shadowy image; a face of beauty, purity, holiness'.

The storybook father is not often invoked in this way as a talisman against evil. While he is usually presented as affectionate and kind, there is a quality of remoteness about him, as there was in real life. Archbishop Benson, so devoted to his children, so passionately interested in their intellectual and moral development, 'had no idea what awe and fear his displeasure cast over them.' Even his adored eldest son, Martin, would write from school to his mother when he was in trouble over a lost railway ticket; his letters to her are far more intimate than to his father, for whom he reserved grave matters such as discussion of classical texts. The author of *Boys and their Ways* admitted the difficulty, and while he insisted that a boy should try to be on good terms with his father, he implied it was by no means easy. A son, he said, should be forgiving and remember the laws of filial duty and bear in mind that a father is often fretted and irritable

The sacred rôle of the Victorian mother: 'Golden hair drawn back from the broad white forehead, and the calm blue eye meeting his so deep and open . . . the lovely tender mouth that trembled while he looked.' Tom Brown meets Arthur's mother. Illustration by Arthur Hughes to *Tom Brown's School days*, 1869.

because of the fatigue of his work and responsibility and 'onerous daily duties'.

It is worth noting too that while storybook fathers might be pushed to the background, or conceded to be hasty and over-severe, as Mrs Molesworth (no doubt with the violent temper of her own husband in mind) makes Captain Desart in *Carrots*, where the mother always tries to stand between her husband and the nursery children whom he terrifies – the attitude of reverence to the mother and her rôle never seems to vary. To the modern eye she may appear unreasonable in the demands she makes on her daughters (especially is this true of the Charlotte Yonge mother), but even the most irreverent do not question her motives or quarrel with the counsel she gives. To do so would seem to be sacriligious. It would be impossible to write such a story as F. Anstey's *Vice-Versa*, with a mother in the rôle of the comic domestic tyrant.

Perhaps the most sympathetic and completely drawn picture of a Victorian father is Charlotte Yonge's Dr May in *The Daisy Chain* (1856), the chronicle of a large motherless family (the oldest of the eleven is an undergraduate, the baby only six weeks old when the story opens). Here we have the authority which can unnerve even the eldest on occasion, mingled with freely acknowledged failings. Miss Yonge had venerated and reverenced her own father, but even in the youth of his fatherhood (he was twenty-eight when she was born) he preserved an awful distance from his little daughter. She spoke about his eyes with 'the most wonderful power both for sweetness and for sternness . . . I dreaded their displeasure more than anything else'.

Dr May, however, had a boyish impetuosity about him that clearly never afflicted William Yonge. In the opening chapter he seems as boisterous as his own sons, heedless, incautious, and indiscreet; it is Mrs May who brings order to the deafening babel and scramble of a family meal, and she who shields her children from his hasty impatience. But when she is killed in a carriage accident which occurs as a result of her husband's headlong driving, Dr May has to try to take her place.

He is clumsy at first, and the sons who would have readily gone to their mother with their troubles are slow to give him their confidence, endearingly anxious and tender for them though he is. He is humble about his failings, remorseful about his inadequacies, but in moments of crisis neither he nor anybody else in the family doubts that his is the ultimate authority, in spiritual as well as temporal matters. Thus when Harry dresses up and frightens his invalid sister, Dr May decrees, to the consternation of the whole family, that he may not present himself for Confirmation. Everybody, Harry included, pleads that the doctor should relent, for the boy is about to

ı the Navy and is terribly cast down at the thought of being de-
·rred from Communion for an indefinite period. But Dr May is
adamant. '"I cannot be certain whether it is right to bring you to
such solemn privileges, while you do not seem to me to retain steadily
any grave or deep feelings."'

Charlotte Yonge here vests the father with the authority of a priest.
She was often to depict a father with many failings – far more frequently than she was to concede the smallest fault in a mother. Some
are despotic and try to interfere with their daughters' wishes about
church-going; Frank Willoughby's father in *The Castle Builders* insists on his son entering the Guards instead of the Church; Mr
Egremont in *Nuttie's Father* is disreputable and hard-drinking. But
she never for one moment doubted that, however morally inferior
the man might be, it was into his hands that the direction of the
family had been committed. 'I stand in place of God to you, whilst
you are a child,' Mr Fairchild had said to Henry. Charlotte Yonge
would have considered this assertion blasphemous, but she and many
of her contemporaries were still influenced by its spirit.

As the image of the parent, as shown by the Victorian writers, had
become more attractive, so had the child. The ideal child was no
longer the one ready with his texts to rebuke, exhort and convert, the
sort that Elizabeth Sewell had shrunk from in her own youth; he
was the child who listened to his conscience. And since his wise and
devoted parents had instilled the highest principles into him from his
earliest infancy, his conscience could readily tell him, if only he
would give up the time to examine it, what was right and what was
wrong and where his duty lay. He might be high-spirited and up to
all sorts of mischief; very likely he was since the Victorians on the
whole found this attractive, but fundamentally he was serious.
Madeline Clifford is the ideal child of *Laneton Parsonage* – 'as unlike I
was as light is to darkness' her creator said of her deprecatingly – gay,
joyful, thoughtless sometimes and led into mischief, but quick to
acknowledge her faults when these are pointed out, and deeply
penitent. Ruth too, though she finds it hard to wrestle with her sin
of moral pride, is ready for Confirmation when the time comes. But
over Alice Lennox the clergyman is uncertain, not because she
behaves badly, but because her attitude does not seem serious
enough.

The ideal Victorian child *wanted* to be good, and the best writers,
and a large proportion of the lesser ones too, had the gift of making

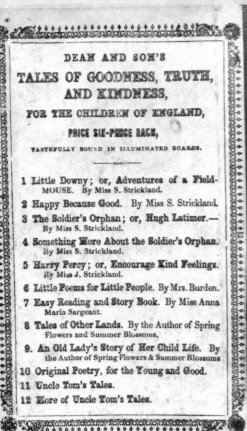

simple goodness seem extraordinarily attractive and credible too, without necessarily having to resort to such devices as early deaths to draw attention to their characters' holiness.

Take *Father's Coming Home* (1871) by 'The author of *The Copsley Annals*'. The children's father is returning from India after long years of separation, and they debate how they can best please him. Hugh decides to try to win the conduct prize at school – he knows he could get the prize for work too easily. Maggie gives up her leisure to make clothes for little Alice Donald whose own father has been drowned, so that she will be fit to go to school.

'"And you hate needlework!" said Jamie.

"God is giving our father back to us, Jamie," she answered; "and even if I hated it worse, there oughtn't to be anything we wouldn't do for him."'

134

Jamie agrees to tend the front garden and get it beautiful with flowers to greet his father, and Nannie says she will learn to read properly, because she only knows 'Tom was a good lad,' and 'The cat ate a rat' and that sort of thing in the spelling book.

' "I wonder what sort of rat was eaten and dished up in a spelling-book," said Hugh; "but listen to my plan. We'll help you, Nannie, every day after play-time, or at home, and if you try very much, you'll be able to read a chapter in the Bible for father the night he comes home." '

The writers of these family stories tried to persuade children into wanting to improve, sometimes by presenting improvement as an exciting game. The author of *Christmas Improvement* (1834) hit on the device of calling Pride 'Mrs P' and the children of the story gleefully devote their holidays to searching her out within themselves, and detecting her in their behaviour. ' "Oh, hunting Mrs P! that will be capital fun; how we will rout out the nasty old thing from all her holes and corners! Hunting Mrs P. Oh! famous, famous! capital!" ' And Mrs S. C. Hall supplied a story called *The Whisperer* (1850) in which Cousin Jacob talks mysteriously of the friend of his youth called by this name, who is subsequently revealed to be Conscience.[1]

The standards of selflessness expected of children within the family circle were always high and sometimes amounted to heroism. It was assumed without comment, for instance, that they would never tell tales. This was always of course the code for school life, but tale bearing was equally taboo in the home circle; plenty of older brothers and sisters silently and stoically endured their parents' grieved displeasure when they were accused of some piece of wrong-doing to which the child responsible was too frightened to own up. Armar in Mrs Molesworth's *Story of a Spring Morning* (1890) is an

[1] The story is, however, more interesting to the modern reader for the attitude of the writer (born in 1800) towards the new generation. Aunt Tart is 'of "the old school", which, however clever, and brilliant, and "off-hand" the new may be, had certainly the advantage of better manners, better English and more graceful deportment.' She is appalled by her nephew's slovenly speech, his 'ain'ts' and 'don'ts' and 'won'ts', and his slang; 'the very best fellows in our form,' 'up to that sort of thing,' 'I have more tin to sport,' 'I thrashed Joe Finch and no mistake.' When his aunt asks if there is no language which he can speak correctly, Edward replies, 'I'm booked if I know, Aunt. I have worked at the languages; but they floor me so!'

extreme example. He is very severely handled by his father for his supposed disobedience in taking the younger children out of the grounds, but never says a word to explain that it was his naughty little sister who had run away in spite of his warnings, and he had only gone after her to bring her back. The truth is not known until Carrie herself tells the full story.

Perhaps the most famous example of the unselfish child occurs in Mrs Ewing's short story *Madam Liberality*. The little girl called by this name spends her childhood scrimping and saving to contrive treats and presents for the rest of the family. It is a household where there is not much money, and sweet things and plum-cakes do not often appear. The other children gobble up their share, but Madam Liberality carefully extracts the currants and raisins from her slice of cake so that she can give dolls' tea-parties with her brothers and sisters as guests. One memorable Christmas she presents herself at the dentist and allows his assistant to hack out the broken fangs of a tooth from her jaw so that she can get the traditional family reward of a shilling for a fanged tooth. Tragedy follows – the money is lost, and she has so desperately needed it to decorate a Christmas tree for the others. But at the last moment an anonymous stranger comes to the rescue, and sends her a magnificent present of dolls' furniture, a box of beasts, and a toy tea-service which supplies her with gifts for everybody more splendid than she has ever been able to provide before.

It says much for Mrs Ewing that the reader is entirely convinced by this child's generosity, and is never tempted to dismiss the story as mawkish. She writes as though such acts of self-denial are commonplace in the ethos of the Victorian nursery, and indeed it is fairly clear that they were. Angela Brazil, for instance, in her memoir *My Own Schooldays*, describes how when she was six she saved up enough money to buy a tiny horse which she had coveted for a long time. She had just triumphantly brought it home when her mother came in with a story of a little boy who did not possess a single toy. The horse was the only object in the nursery which could be given to a boy. Her mother did not urge or insist, but looked at her with a disappointed face. 'I crammed the horse into her arms, bolted upstairs, crawled under the spare-room bed, and indulged in a thoroughly good private howl.'

Most difficult of all, writers considered, was to learn to give way to other members of the family. Mrs Ewing called one of her stories

A Very Ill-Tempered Family (though by most people's standards these family quarrels would not be exceptional), and presented the sort of situation in which it would be difficult for the mildest to keep calm: family theatricals which are disrupted by an overbearing older

PART I. JANUARY, 1874. PRICE THREEPENCE.

CHATTERBOX.

CHATTER BOX

PUBLISHED FOR THE PROPRIETORS BY W. W. GARDNER, 2 PATERNOSTER BUILDINGS.

Chatterbox, founded in 1866, tried to convey on its cover (but not so successfully in its contents) the new spirit of happy, high-spirited goodness.

brother who insists on intervening at the last moment and ruining the play at which the others have been labouring. One of them manages with supreme self-control to swallow her pride and give way and thus saves the situation. Mrs Ewing is realistic; the family temper does not instantly improve, the old Adam peeps out even during the subsequent reconciliation. The little brother is remorseful at having misjudged the bullying elder Philip. '"I was going to have eaten raw meat, and dumb-belled, to have made myself strong enough to thrash you,"' he says. '"Eat a whole butcher's shop full, if you like," replied Philip with contempt.'

Annie Keary made an extraordinarily compelling story of two self-willed boys in *The Rival Kings* (1857) where the Lloyd children, faced with the three children whom their father has adopted, realise that sharing toys is easy; real self-denial comes with the far more difficult task of enduring the undoubted tiresomeness of these strangers. They have to learn, not to give away, but to give in. The point that Annie Keary and Mrs Ewing tried to make was not a popular one, and too subtle for the common taste. Readers preferred *Ministering Children*, with its dreamworld of children gracefully distributing largesse to an ever-grateful, uncritical poor.

When it came to the rating of misbehaviour there was no question whatever which was the gravest sin, and what defect in a child's character a parent dreaded most. 'She had told a lie;' Elizabeth Sewell had written of Alice Lennox in *Laneton Parsonage*, 'firmly, openly, without hesitation; she had spoken words which were utterly false. A deadly sin, perhaps the greatest a child can commit.'

It is the most dramatic episode in the whole book. Appalled, incredulous horror seizes the adult characters when it is realised that one of the three children in the two households must have lied about who was responsible for entering the forbidden rooms. A thunderstorm heightens the tension, and Mr Clifford and Lady Catharine gallop to and fro between the two houses to disentangle the truth and unmask the real culprit. When Alice Lennox, trembling with fear, at last confesses to the act, she is regarded as so depraved that she is, on Lady Catharine's orders, ostracised by the whole household, and isolated from her former companions in case she con-taminates them. After many weeks of solitude and without any word as to her destination she is dispatched to boarding school where at last life can begin again with the slate wiped clean.

On this point of lying Miss Sewell and Charlotte Elizabeth – poles

BE TRUTHFUL.

From *Little Children's Duties* (SPCK, *c.* 1853)

apart though they might be in temperament and churchmanship –
were at one. Charlotte Elizabeth in *Personal Recollections* recalled her
emotions as a child after she had told a lie at the bidding of a servant.

'My terrors of conscience were insupportable; I could ill bear my
father's steady eye fixed on mine, still less the anxious, wondering,
incredulous expression of my brother's innocent face, who could not
for a moment fancy me guilty. I confessed at once; and with a heavy
sigh my father sent to borrow from a neighbour an instrument of
chastisement never before needed in his own house. He took me to
another room, and said, "Child, it will pain me more to punish you
thus, than any blow I can inflict will pain you; but I must do it; you
have told a lie; a dreadful sin, and a base, mean, cowardly action. If
I let you grow up you will reproach me for it one day; if I now spared
the rod I should hate the child." I took the punishment in a most
extraordinary spirit; I wished every stroke had been a stab; I wept
because the pain was not great enough; and I loved my father at that
moment better than even I, who almost idolised him, had ever loved
him before.'

This episode had taken place at the turn of the eighteenth century. Some seventy years later, when methods with children were much milder, it is still a flogging sin, the ultimate depravity. In *Geoffry's Great Fault* by Emilia Marryat Norris (1873) the hero, though well-meaning, persistently forgets to obey orders. Overwhelmed by the magnitude of the disaster that follows one of his pieces of thought-lessness, he suggests that his father ought to beat him.

'"My dear child," said Mr Lisle, "I trust I shall never have to flog you as long as I live, as I never have yet. Flogging is for liars, Geoffry; and my boy, thank God, was never that. I would not degrade an honest boy like you by flogging him."'

It would seem to be the evangelicals who stressed the enormity of this particular sin, which remained, long after their hold on public morals had slackened, the most abhorrent to the average Englishman. In the eighteenth century, before the evangelical movement had gathered itself up to full strength, there were plenty of Georgian moralists who, as we have seen in chapter two, shrugged off lying as a socially disadvantageous habit which might be the prelude to a life of crime in the lower classes. Under Wesley's influence the general attitude hardened. Lying was no longer merely imprudent; it was recognised to have the terrifying consequences that Isaac Watts had indicated.

The Lord delights in them that speak
The words of truth; but every liar
Must have his portion in the lake
That burns with brimstone and with fire.

Then let me always watch my lips,
Lest I be struck to death and hell,
Since God a book of reckoning keeps
For every lie that children tell.

Nor did it merely include the obvious forms of deceit, but the social white lie too. The *Evangelical Magazine* in the 1800s records plenty of examples of martyrdom to the cause, where gentlemen's servants had left good places because they were ordered to deny that their masters were at home.

Indeed lying came to evoke such emotion, such horror, that the later Victorians could not bring themselves to create a central child character who lied. It was so obviously a mortal sin that there was no point in constructing a moral tale round it; one did not moralise to children about murder. The very word 'lie' became an obscenity; 'untruth', 'story', 'fib', 'whopper', 'crammer' were substituted for it. It became a crime that only foreigners or the lower classes could commit, parents might worry that their children showed 'want of openness,' but never that they were liars. A child who was not 'open' was one who did not readily own up, who concealed his faults. To own up, however great the enormity, was to gain instant absolution. But a child who seemed to the outside eye to be the best-behaved and most diligent member of a turbulent, trouble-making family was often watched with anxious foreboding by his parents, who suspected in him that fatal want of openness.

Between this and the lie direct, however, lay a world of difference. Moral tales were constructed around the former failing long after the child of gentle birth had apparently ceased even to be tempted to lie. It was something that no English gentleman could possibly contemplate, since he acquired a love of truth as a birthright. Most writers who tacitly assumed this (it was a sentiment that came into vogue in the 1880s and 90s with the slackening of the evangelical influence over children's books) did not actually state it in as many words. Frances Hodgson Burnett, however, in that as in other matters, had no inhibitions. Sara Crewe in *A Little Princess* (1905) rebukes Ermengarde for her lack of breeding.

'"That's almost like telling lies," she said. "And lies – well, you see, they are not only wicked – they're *vulgar*. Sometimes" – reflectively – "I've thought that perhaps I might do something wicked – I might suddenly fly into a rage and kill Miss Minchin, you know, when she was ill-treating me – but I *wouldn't* be vulgar."'

The hero might not lie, but he could be falsely accused of lying, and this was to become a popular plot. In story after story the child who has been wild, disobedient, even insolent, the despair of the authorities, faces up to the charge of lying with brave fearless eyes. He is a *gentleman's* son, and the implication is that his accusers must by their very suspicions be inferior both morally and socially. Meanwhile the real villain skulks nearby, and we have been prepared for his character defects in the first chapter by learning that he has, if a boy, some foreign blood, or if a girl, that she is over-dressed – since even more damning than a foreign upbringing is to be wealthy and connected with trade. But the falsely accused child is not, on the whole, a mid-Victorian type, he belongs to the sinless pickles of a later age.

[7]

The innocents
1880–1930

THERE had been mischievous pickles before the last Victorians took them up and dolloped them so lavishly over the pages of their juvenile books. There had been, for example, Harry and Laura Graham in Catherine Sinclair's *Holiday House* as long ago as 1839.

We have seen in the chapter on the rational child, what Miss Sinclair thought of the early nineteenth-century fashion for cramming children, 'stuffing the memory, like a cricket ball, with well-known facts and ready-made opinions [so that] no room is left for the vigour of natural feeling, the glow of natural genius, and the ardour of natural enthusiasm'. To register her protest, she wrote *Holiday House* in which she 'endeavoured to paint that species of noisy, frolicsome, mischievous children, now almost extinct, wishing to preserve a sort of fabulous remembrance of days long past, when young people were like wild horses on the prairie, rather than like well-broken hacks on the road'.

Noisy and frolicsome Harry and Laura certainly are, on a scale that would only be possible in a wealthy upper class home. The trail of devastation that they leave behind them would do credit to a pack of university bloods in the grand old days. No window pane, glass or porcelain is safe if they are near it; their clothes cannot be kept clean or whole from one meal to the next; if they see a ladder or a tree they must swarm up it; they fall into every pond and down every hill they find. Their grandmother mildly expostulates, and their Uncle David just laughs.

'"I am not so seriously angry at the sort of scrapes Laura and you get into, because you would not willingly and deliberately do wrong. If any children commit a mean action, or get into a passion, or quarrel with each other, or omit saying their prayers and reading their Bibles, or tell a lie, or take what does not belong to them, then it

From S. R. Crockett: *The Surprising Adventures of Sir Toady Lion*, 1897

might be seen how extremely angry I could be, but while you continue merely thoughtless and forgetful, I mean to have patience a little longer before turning into a cross old uncle with a pair of tawse.'''

There is, by way of a counterbalance, a good boy – their brother Frank. But he plays so little part initially in the action that we are uncertain whether the author believes in him herself. She certainly hardly troubles to give him much life.

'Never was there a more amiable, pious, excellent boy than Frank, who read his Bible so attentively, and said his prayers so regularly every morning and evening, that he soon learned both to know his duty and to do it.' At school, 'he gradually became so clever that the masters all praised his extraordinary attention, and covered him with medals, while Major Graham often filled his pockets with a reward of money, after which he ran towards the nearest shop to spend his little fortune in buying a present for somebody.'

As literary characters, Harry and Laura seem fifty years in advance of their time, but Frank seems fifty years behind his – the sort of pasteboard Master Diligent with which the Georgian authors filled their little tales. But old type and new were united in the last three chapters of *Holiday House* which is perfectly in the evangelical mood of the day, and shows Harry and Laura being jolted into sobriety by the slow and lingering death of Frank. With its sudden swing of mood from the boisterous to the deeply serious, and the promotion of the shadowy Frank to the central figure, it does not make for a well-balanced whole, nor are the naughty Laura and Harry more credible than the amiable and excellent Frank. Historically, though, it is interesting, for Miss Sinclair took much the same attitude to naughtiness as her successors in the 80s and 90s – that it was loveable, always provided the children came from the upper strata of society, and rigorously toed the ethical line that had been drawn for them. Thoughtlessness and destruction was one thing; lying, quarrelling, unkindness – all commonplace enough among real children – was quite another matter, and completely foreign to the nature of the literary pickle.

Holiday House, however, stood isolated. It was much enjoyed by children of the educated sort. (It was not, naturally, given to the cottage home, whose children might have drawn inflammatory ideas from it.) It was not taken amiss by serious parents, for after all Lady Harriet did try to subdue her grandchildren with gentle sermonising, and the book did conclude with a very uplifting death scene. But it attracted no immediate imitations. For thirty years the children's stories continued sober records of children who really tried to be good, or children with a precocious moral sense.

And then, thirty years later, in 1869, came *Misunderstood*. Florence Montgomery did not intend this story for children; the preface states the fact quite clearly; it claims to be 'for those who are willing to stoop to view life as it appears to a child,' and her *Moral Tales for Children* (1886) are quite different, of an almost anachronistic severity. But although it was to have a compulsive influence on the adult reader too, it was widely regarded as a children's book. From the start it seized the public imagination. It went into four editions in 1870, two in each of the following three years, and was continuously reprinted during the next thirty years. It satisfied a deep need in readers who had reacted against the demands that early Victorians had made on children; not the intellectual demands that Catherine Sinclair had complained about, but the moral demands. Most adults did not attempt to understand child nature, Florence Montgomery insisted, and she set out to expound Humphrey Duncombe's to them.

Humphrey is a handsome, manly little fellow; seven years old, loving and full of high spirits, but somehow spurned by his father whose anxieties are all for the delicate four year old Miles, the image of his dead mother, so gentle and trusting, and constantly led into trouble by his elder brother. His mother had understood Humphrey, that went without saying in 1869. But when the book opens she has been dead for several years. She is just a portrait on the wall to whom Humphrey steals, weeping, when his loneliness becomes unbearable. To the ordinary eye, and to his father, he is noisy and heedless and full of mischief. Only the author can tell us how he yearns for the loving kiss, responsive voice, ever-ready ear to listen and sympathise, and for the caresses that his father lavishes on his little brother Miles. They do not make him jealous, of course; he adores the child.

As with Mr Dombey, Sir Everard Duncombe comes late to appreciate his eldest child . . . too late, for Humphrey is now on his deathbed. An arrant act of disobedience has brought him to it. He had been told not to climb on the rotten branch but he defies his father. Thirty years before such disobedience might too have brought death, but as a punishment – the fitting end to an unsatisfactory life. Here the punishment is meted out to the father, who suffers bitter remorse for having failed to understand. Humphrey goes to a heavenly reward and the arms of the mother he has so sorely needed.

Not all the responsibility for the cult of childish innocence that followed can be laid on Florence Montgomery. The infection was also spread by 'sweet, old-fashioned Paul Dombey, with his strange fancies, and his thoughtful dreamy nature; Little Nell with her wistful looks and patient devotion; lonely David Copperfield, a small and solitary pilgrim; the child of charity, Oliver Twist; gentle Little Dorrit; poor Joe, always moving on; motherless, severely-brought-up Esther Dennison; Agnes, David's guardian angel' – to quote Theodora Elmslie who also contributed her offering of tender child spirits – and the children's writers came belatedly to realise how misunderstood the child nature had been, and what a gold mine lay in interpreting their feelings to their elders, and, since it was now permissible, in revealing these to the children themselves.

The stories about the innocents can be divided into three main types: those about the nursery children; the tales about their older brothers and sisters – scamps, pickles, torments, madcaps; and the

Merry pickles: the Scamp children enjoying nursery tea. From L. T. Meade: *The Scamp family*, serialised in *Jabberwocky*, 1906.

portrayal of the little sunshines who bring light and warmth to aging, ice-bound hearts. Mrs Molesworth provided a link between the mid-Victorian family story and the new style. She wrote understandingly of the nursery child; she could be sentimental if they were dreamy, sensitive little boys, but she could also correct their faults sharply (particularly if they were girls).

There were not many stories about nursery children before the

1870s. The fairy tale had been restored; there were picture books, alphabets, short fables telling them how good children behaved and what happened to bad ones. But there were few authors who wrote, as Marie Edgeworth and Mrs Barbauld had, of simple everyday things in a simple style, and many who assumed a vocabulary and a mastery of syntax and of ethical and religious truths far beyond the reach of any five year old. When Mrs Sherwood, for instance, had adapted Bunyan for infants, she peopled it with characters like Inbred Sin (i.e., the children's corrupt human nature), and Mr Worldly Prudence the schoolmaster, who teaches the little pilgrim from the writings of the ancient authors, dangerously deflecting him from his path to heaven (Henry Fairchild, who had been flogged for not learning his Latin, would surely have found this most confusing), and the Old Interpreter and the New Interpreter of Holy Writ.

Even when the story to amuse became acceptable, there were not many that the nursery could easily absorb. What was needed was an uninvolved plot about matters within a small child's own experience, preferably told in short episodes that could be read aloud at a single sitting. This Mrs Molesworth perfectly understood, and with *Carrots, Just a Little Boy*, produced in 1876 one of the earliest nursery tales.

Such plot as there is concerns a nursery misunderstanding. Carrots picks up a half-sovereign. He has never heard of such a coin; to him 'sovereigns' are the kings and queens that his sister talks about. He thinks he has found a 'fairy sixpenny' and he hides it so that he can buy his sister a doll, and quite truthfully denies knowing anything about the missing money which has thrown the household into such a turmoil. His officious elder brother drags the bewildered, tear-sodden child to the stern father, and it needs all his gentle sister's understanding and his mother's patience to sort out the trouble. Within this small teacup Mrs Molesworth with her gift for convincing characterisation and her powers of story telling managed to create quite a dramatic storm.

She was to produce other dramas on this minuscule scale, about children who get lost, children with worries and fears, children who try to replace something that they break, who wander away from Nurse. She understood the excitement of going out for a drive with Mamma, of having a visitor to the nursery, the anxiety of being bidden to a meal downstairs with the grownups when you are used to bread and milk in the nursery. She knew that it is the nature of most children to grumble, squabble and sulk, but she treated these as

"What are you thinking about, my poor old man?" said auntie,
fondly.

Concern for the nursery child and his small needs. Illustration by Walter
Crane for Mrs Molesworth's *Carrots*, 1876

social failings rather than sins which imperilled their mortal souls.

The late Victorians wanted to make the child feel secure in his nursery world; cocooned in loving understanding. Many of them, brought up in sterner times, had been tormented by hideous fears of God's wrath, of eternal damnation – this is recalled frequently in the memoirs of the period. Eleanor Acland, author of *Goodbye for the Present*, wrote of two childhoods: her own (she was born in 1878), darkened by a cruel and oppressive nurse and her own unrevealed fears of hell, and that of her daughter (1913–24) whom she brought up in a totally different fashion, telling her only of God's loving kindness, trying to shield her from all that was not joyful and happy. Mrs Molesworth knew how the small child craved stability and affection, but she would not tolerate bad behaviour, and she made him fully aware of the misery that it caused both himself and the people round him.

Other writers lost their sense of proportion. Stella Austin in *Stumps* (1873) – a nursery classic, many times reprinted – created a child who is the darling of the nursery, all curls and dimples and huge brown eyes, four years old and not able to speak plainly. But Stumps is stubborn and passionate; she has a naughty temper, and is determined to resent the new stable boy with all her tiny baby power – though he idolises her – because she thinks her favourite brother likes him too much. She glowers at him, and sulks, and turns her back on him. Then on a picnic he sees her in great danger and calls to her.

'Shall Peter tell her to go back? Stumps' little teeth press one against the other, her eyebrows wrinkle, and her brown eyes look hard defiance at Peter as she says scornfully: "I s'an't."' Peter saves her, but cripples himself for life. He will never walk again. Gravely but lovingly Mother tells Stumps about his sacrifice. Tears well up in Stumps' eyes. '"Tumps is derry, derry sorry, Peter. Now you've talked to Tumps, won't you make it up wid Tumps?"' Mother kisses Stumps. '"I like an untidy crumpled *good* Stumps better than a clean, starched, *naughty* Stumps. Come and let me put you upon the sofa, darling, and you will have a nice rest before dinner."' All is well with the world; Peter lies on his bed where he is to spend the rest of his life, and dear, kind, good Stumps gives him her share of the strawberry jam that she so loves.

'Ah! the children, how the thought of them spans life from end to end, as with a rainbow. Little ones, remain children as long as you can. Soon enough you will have to come out of your cloud-land, to take up what we "grown-ups" call the serious business of life; but I ask myself, if in your innocence, your joy, your trust, you are not nearer than we are to the inner truth of things.'

'A very small boy' – illustration from Theodora Elmslie's *Black Puppy*, 1894.

This sentiment, taken from an article contributed to *The Girl's Realm* in 1899 reflected the mood of many of the writers of the times.

'It is a quaint and pretty little figure. A very small boy – almost a baby – attired in a white frock and a sash. A small boy, with chubby legs cased in tan socks and shoes. A small boy whose eyes are blue as a summer's sky, and who, with his fair, curly head, and sweet infantine face, might well be some cherub child stepped straight from the canvas of a Raphael or a Corregio . . .
' "isn't this place Heaven please? Me thinked it was . . . me thinked as you was an angel, cos your dress is white, and you's kite buful, like the picture of the angel in daddy's Bible at home. Is you an angel, please?" '   (Theodora Elmslie: *Black Puppy*, 1894)

Innocence and a loving, trustful manner are the key attributes of the late Victorian and the Edwardian ideal child. And prettiness had become of great importance. To the Georgian moralists it had been a positive blemish in a child; the early Victorians had forborne to comment, but their descendants adulated it – 'dainty' was one of their favourite adjectives. To see all these qualities in their most extravagant form we have only to turn to Mrs Hodgson Burnett. In *Little Lord Fauntleroy* (1886) we meet Cedric Erroll of whose innocence and manliness and grace and loving heart we are assured on every page. He has a 'graceful, strong little body, and pretty manners and bright curly hair which waved over his forehead and fell in charming love-locks on his shoulders'. Like so many of his literary contemporaries, he is a little friend of all, and there is not a cross-grained dog, earl, or grocery man who can resist him.

Little Saint Elizabeth, in the story of that title, is much the same, though frailer and less of this world. Her face is pure and pale; her eyes large and dark, and when she walks down the village street in her miniature nun's habit, the cottagers 'adore her, almost worship her, as if she had been, indeed a sacred child'. Editha in *Editha's Burglar* has the same purity and innocence. She disturbs a burglar who is removing the household silver, begs him to be as quiet as he can so that he will not disturb her mamma's sleep, and refrains from troubling her parents next morning by telling them of the incident.

Even the evangelical writers took up this ideal. The Religious Tract Society who, eighty years before, had been urging its child readers to consider the horrible depravity of their natures, by the

The later evangelical writers used artless prattle to win their readers' hearts.
Page from *All the World*, 1890, a Salvation Army journal.

Golden curls and blue eyes were used to pluck brands from the burning.
From Amy le Feuvre: *Probable Sons*, 1905.

1900s was publishing the prolific writings of Amy le Feuvre[1] whose children convert as much by the beauty of their golden hair and calm, trusting brown eyes, as by their artless talk. '"I was just waving to God, Uncle Edward, I thought I saw him looking down at me from the sky."' And '"Do you know what I think about the stars? They're angels' eyes, and they look down at me and blink so kindly, and then I look up and blink back."' This is Milly in *Probable Sons* (1905). Betty in *Odd* is another of the lonely little girls that Amy le Feuvre delighted in creating. Nurse says of her that she is 'sometimes naughtier and more contrary-like than all the others put together, and sometimes so angel-like that I wonder if she won't have an early death'. Betty, 'a dainty little white figure,' treads through the pages of *Odd*, falling into mischief certainly, but, far more important, thawing the ice in her elders' hearts. For the Edwardians could even use mischief as an evangelical tool.

Madcaps, tomboys, pickles and scamps – these are the children who are to bound through the juvenile lists for the next thirty years or more: *The Madcap of the Family*, *The Taming of Tamzin*, *Mixed Pickles*, their titles as monotonously predictable as their contents. At home high-spirited children fall in and out of trouble; at school wild Irish girls who have never known a curb are tamed but not cowed. Usually they are all mere machines for mischief, but occasionally in the hands of a really good writer, they have survived the age for which they were written. E. Nesbit's Bastable children, in *The Story of the Treasure Seekers* and *The Would-be-Goods*, bring high imagination to their exploits, in a style which young readers of later generations have always found attractive. The Indian uncle, asked to schoolroom dinner, finds himself helping pretend that the stewed rabbit is a deer and must be roasted on sticks over the fire, and that the suet pudding is a wild boar to be killed on the floor with forks. He enters into it wholeheartedly and is reckoned to be a true gentleman by the children.

Elaborate games of this sort, though perhaps less boisterous, had played a large part in the older Victorian nurseries and schoolrooms when imaginative literature had been frowned upon. The Keary children, who had created the apostate nun (page 108), had acted

---

[1] Under their twentieth-century style, the Lutterworth Press, they still keep her works in print. Her popularity is maintained overseas, if not at home.

out scenes from Greek history, for instance. Now, in the 1890
games featured in the books of writers who drew on men
their own childhood; they even became a sort of cult with t
intellectual. 'They were unaware of Indians,' Kenneth (
makes his narrator in *The Golden Age* say scornfully of
around him, 'nor recked they anything of bisons, or of pi.
pistols!) . . . They cared not to explore for robbers' caves, nor dig for
buried treasure.' And the Bastable children are caustic about any of
their contemporaries who fail, like Albert-next-door, to appreciate
the privilege of being a pretend prisoner in dog-chains under the
nursery table.

Mischievous children without any responsibilities became so
much the accepted pattern that even the Sunday School magazines
took them up. In 1844 the *Child's Companion* had showed its readers
the dreadful example of a Sabbath scholar who, though spoken of by
his teacher 'with peculiar pleasure as a hopeful character' was
tempted to stroll in the fields one Sunday when school was done. He
broke his leg and suffered great mental anguish as well as physical
pain. In 1923 this same magazine was carrying a serial about two
children known by their mother as the Torments, and their cat
Torrid (he is 'hot stuff'), whose desperate deeds result in stolen
diamonds being restored to their owner.

Of course the Torments have to disobey orders; they would never
have found themselves in that fateful boat listening to the criminals
otherwise. But by the twentieth century disobedience had become
attractive – in gentlemen's children, of course. Catherine Sinclair
had countenanced it in *Holiday House*, implying that Harry and
Laura would grow out of it, and repentance and remorse would
come in the fullness of time. But writers such as L. T. Meade, a great
favourite with the children who grew up during the First World War,
gloried in it. It showed spirit and character; the tomboy who dis-
regards her elders and the boy who is careless and forgetful about
obeying are both infinitely to be preferred to the nagging elder sister
and the superficially well-behaved boy who might be suspected of
'want of openness'.

'"I want to have a great big glorious bit of naughtiness – I don't
mind if I have to repent afterwards and have a punishment. I do so
desperately, badly need to be naughty."

. . . Babs felt excited – she did not know why. That sweet voice seemed to lure her on to be naughty. All of a sudden she felt quite sure that she also wanted a desperate downright spree.

"I say," she cried, rising to her feet. "If we do this thing, we'll do it fair. It would be horribly mean on the little mother to do wild, rebellious, naughty things when she is away – that is, without telling her. I don't mind doing it a bit if we may tell all about it afterwards."

"'fess, you mean?" said Jackdaw, looking with considerable awe, and almost fear, at his sister.

"Well – yes," said Baby, "confess, make a clean breast of it – tell her out plain that we had to be naughty, and we were naughty, and that, of course, we'll take our punishment. I'll go on those terms; I won't go on any other.'" (L. T. Meade: *The Scamp Family*, 1906)

Here is L. T. Meade's ethical boundary – honour. 'They were honourable children', she had said in *The Autocrat of the Nursery* (1884), 'and I don't think any of them would have stooped to tell a lie. They were also brave, and had no small meannesses – one small boy would never screen himself from a well-merited punishment at the expense of another, and the three boys were chivalrous and tender to the one girl . . . They were not in reality anything remarkable; they were just like other thousands and tens of thousands of tenderly cared-for little ones.'

This hazy word, 'honour,' with all its emotional overtones, was to dominate the childish code of ethics from the later years of the 1890s all through the first four decades of the twentieth century. It was never exactly defined, but to everybody of gentle birth it was assumed to have both meaning and force. 'I put you on your honour not to talk while I am out of the room,' our schoolmistresses said to us in the 1930s, and those who did whisper were made to feel by the silent hostility of the rest that we were in some way tainted. We were put on our honour not to read unsuitable books, and to be caught doing so by a friend was humiliating. 'Honour bright,' we promised, a sacred oath we would never have broken. 'Honour' was part of the birthright that all writers of children's books assumed their characters to have. They were gentlemen's children; they played fair. In *The Story of the Treasure Seekers* the Bastables, who are trying to restore the family fortunes, encourage their dog to attack an elderly man, blithely hoping that when they rescue the victim he will in his warm gratitude offer to bring them up as his own children, as in the story books. The unfortunate victim does not, alas, play up as

Jack Carew, cool, self-reliant, daring, well-built, handsome – the very picture
of what a healthy English lad should be, shows up the cringing, mean and
miserly Murdstone. Illustration to *Jack Carew of Castlemoor* (*Boys of England*,
vol. LXVI, 1899)

expected. He describes their conduct as ungentlemanly, and finishes
his admonishment: '"Always remember never to do a dishonourable
thing, for money or for anything else in the world." And we
promised we would remember. Then he took off his hat, and we took
off ours, and he went away, and we went home. I never felt so cheap
in all my life! . . . It was what Lord Tottenham had said about
ungentlemanly.'

It was indeed wounding, for the Bastables, though the family
fortunes might be at a low ebb and though the silver had had to be
sold and policemen came to the door with summons for debts, never
doubted for one instant that they were gentleman's children. Indeed
it is one of the few stories where the characters are admitted to have

behaved contrary to the code. The mistaken accusation, the wrong-
ful rebuke, was far more common, when a child's honour was
impugned by a hasty coarse-grained adult who doubted his word.
In this case the blundering fool would be confronted by a brave
fearless face, steady eyes, a tilt of the chin, perhaps a stamp of the foot.
It might take a good many chapters, but in the end honour was
vindicated. Everybody agreed that honour meant telling the truth,
and not betraying one's friends and schoolfellows. After that it
became more nebulous. L. T. Meade, as we have seen, stretched it to
include chivalry to one's sister, but here one suspects she was hoping
by the emotional force of the word to shame boys into treating girls
kindly.

A good many people felt that not only friends but enemies too
must be shielded, if they were one's own age. In Samuel Rutherford
Crockett's *Sir Toady Lion*, a bloodthirsty, fast-moving account of
warfare between the laird's children and the local louts over the
ownership of a ruined castle, where no holds are barred and blood
really spurts, the children resolutely refuse to identify the boy who
has beaten them up, even when the chief constable himself comes to
question Hugh John as he lies in bed, bruised and battered. It is
what the laird had hoped of his children, and he glows with pride.

'Honour' is not derived from any religious belief; it is connected
with being English and a gentleman. As the evangelicals had implicit
faith in the power of the individual soul to recognise the moment of
salvation, so descendants of Victorians reared on this system knew
that their children would hear the clarion call of honour and obey
it. 'Whenever a little thing tugged down in his stomach and told him
"not to" Hugh John said "Hang it! I won't be dasht-mean." And
wasn't. Grown-ups call these things conscience and religion; but this
is how it felt to Hugh John, and it answered just as well – or even
better.'

One writer only demurred. Kenneth Grahame in *The Golden Age*
(1895) and *Dream Days* (1898), essays originally written for adults,
but treated as children's books, though in fact their archly ponderous
style makes them quite unsuitable, created children not only without
any sense of sin, but without a sense of honour either. They have no
ethical boundary. As long as they are undetected they have no
scruples about what they do. They live in a permanent state of
antagonism with the adult world – the Olympians, they call its
inhabitants, whom they regard as born directly into middle age

THE SURPRISING ADVENTURES OF SIR TOADY LION WITH THOSE OF GENERAL NAPOLEON SMITH

AN IMPROVING HISTORY FOR OLD BOYS, YOUNG BOYS, GOOD BOYS, BAD BOYS, BIG BOYS, LITTLE BOYS, COW BOYS, AND TOM-BOYS

BY S. R. CROCKETT

AUTHOR OF "SWEETHEART TRAVELLERS", "THE RAIDERS", &c

ILLUSTRATED BY GORDON BROWNE

London

GARDNER, DARTON AND CO.

The independent child untrammelled by adults.

through their own choice. They are wild, destructive and disobedient, of course, but they also outrage the gentlemanly code by stealing, lying, and ill-treating animals. But Kenneth Grahame evades the issue of direct defiance of parents. 'To children with a proper equipment of parents,' he says at the outset, 'these things would have worn a different aspect. To those whose nearest were aunts and uncles, a special attitude of mind may be allowed.' Even Kennth Grahame would hardly have dared imply that a mother could be a natural enemy like the rest of the adult world.

He had no imitators. The urge to provide security and loving understanding and safely exciting adventures was the main pre-occupation of the featureless years of juvenile publishing that stretched between 1910 and the 1940s. The world was reduced to child proportions to please them. There was nothing to frighten them, nothing ugly. The Great War passed with hardly a comment. 'What shall the children read today?' asked the writer of a pamphlet called *A Child's Bookshelf* in 1917. She thought that they should certainly be told of the heroism and the sacrifice that war involved, but that the terrible realities should not be glossed over. 'When a child with his frank and fearless eyes asks us hard questions about war and Christianity, we must answer truly and humbly as best we may ... But our greatest service will be to surround him with worthy material from which he can learn to build his own Utopia.'

But very little worthy material came to him in the way of fiction. F. S. Brereton, the successor of Henty (who had died in 1902) and G. M. Fenn (died 1909), produced the expected crop of stories about soldiering adventures: *With French at the Front, At Grips with the Turks*. Angela Brazil contributed *A Patriotic Schoolgirl*, where the heroine decks her dormitory cubicle with V C portraits in bijou frames, and the girls suspect a headmistress of being a German spy, but it is Chrissie Lang (wickedly anglicised from Lange) all the time who is sending heliograph signals to the enemy by bicycle lamp. In the end she runs away leaving a list of gun and tank emplacements behind in her hurry. '"Is it right to forgive the enemies of our country?"' her friend asks the headmistress. '"When they are dead,"' pronounces that grim oracle.

The oracle also warns the girls that they must be very careful not to overstep the mark when it comes to one's own side. '"Knit and sew for the soldiers, get up concerts for them, and speak kindly to them in the hospitals, but never for a moment forget in your conduct what is due both to yourself and to them,"' she says in stern rebuke after there has been a snowball fight between the girls and some convalescent Tommies. It is safest just to send comforts and feel warmly disposed.

'They went to a cafe for tea, and as they sat looking at the Allies' flags, which draped the walls, and listening to the military marches played by a ladies' orchestra in khaki uniforms, patriotism seemed uppermost.

"It's grand to do anything for one's country!" sighed Marjorie.

"So it is," answered Elaine, pulling her knitting from her pocket and rapidly going on with a sock. "Those poor fellows in the trenches deserve everything we can send out to them – socks, toffee, cakes, cigarettes, scented soap, and other comforts."'

But this stirring message came too late for the girls of England to respond, for the book did not appear until 1919.

Wars, in fact make very little impact on children's books, and one might read one's way through the two World Wars without realising there was anything amiss. The natural instinct of adults at such times is to reassure and to protect, and the temptation to escape into a world where everything goes on as in happier years is very strong. While their fathers and uncles and older brothers were struggling through the mud of Flanders, the children at home were reading about happy, safe family life in the stories of Evelyn Everett-Green, or crying a little at the pathos of Amy le Feuvre, or envying the exploits of the dashing girls in the school stories which during the last ten years had become all the rage.

The cosiness did not diminish in the years that followed. The 1920s was the era of pixies and brownies and bunnies, of winky-wonky birds, and pippities who find ponkles. Enid Blyton was writing her 'sunny stories for little folks', and, at a higher level, A. A. Milne was creating a nursery dominion where a little boy reigned over his animals and no adult ever set foot. There was no question now about the respectability of imaginative literature. Children were being urged to escape into a fantasy world where only the young could unmask diamond smugglers, track down spies, and dig out buried treasure. And as with Christopher Robin, they were untrammelled by grown-ups – except right at the end of the stories, when their elders clustered round to applaud. ' "What adventures these children did have to be sure, and how well they managed everything,"' says the father of one of Enid Blyton's Famous Five gang at the end of the umpteenth episode of intrepid daring in which his daughter has been a ring-leader.

The storybook child was now one who acted alone, requiring no adults for his achievements. For the time being the educational pundits were silent and allowed the readers to enjoy his adventures.

[8]

The manly boy
1800–1914

I

Boys before Arnold

'"To you who are leaving Harrow, poised for flight into the great world of which this school is the microcosm, I commend the memory of Henry Desmond. It stands in our records for all we venerate and strive for; loyalty, honour, purity, strenuousness, faithfulness in friendship. When temptation assails you, think of that gallant boy running swiftly uphill, leaving craven fear behind, and drawing with him the others who, led by him to the heights, made victory possible. You cannot all be leaders, but you can follow leaders; only see to it that they lead you, as Henry Desmond led the men of Beauregard's Horse, onward and upward."'

So the headmaster in Horace Annesley Vachell's *The Hill* (1905) addressed the school upon the death in the South African War of one of their former companions. When we survey the cohorts of Victorian boys as they swing past us in their splendour – the heroes of Henty and Kingston and Brereton, of Thomas Hughes, Talbot Baines Reed and Ascott Hope – we marvel at their radiance. Those well-knit and vigorous forms that bear themselves with such pride, those clear faces, joyous mouths, the golden hair, the honest kindly blue eyes that look at you so frankly, that aura of manliness and authority that rallies the sinking spirits of followers, strikes terror into the hearts of rogue and dastard, before whom the foreigner quails – that image, in fact, of the British boy so potent that an illustrator of the Bible even depicted Christ as one. How does all this tally with the beefy dolts described by Taine[1] when he visited England in the 1860s, with the slouching, shambling adolescents that most of us know? K. M. Peyton's schoolboy of 1970, Pennington, surly, truculent, unco-opera-

[1] Hippolyte Taine: *Notes on England*, 1872.

*'Suffer little children to come unto me, and forbid them not:
for of such is the kingdom of God.'*

Christ as an English public school boy. Drawing by Marjorie Whittington from
The Children's Bible, Cambridge University Press, 1928.

tive, loathing in his heart for all institutions, all authority, is a type we can recognise. Public opinion no longer expects, perhaps has even ceased to desire, the Tom Brown boy and his traditions of manliness.

But for the best part of a century it was a word that rallied the young male, and not just him either. Girls devoured those adventure stories and tales of public school life. They longed to be considered 'men' and 'good sports' by their brothers, to be allowed to play cricket with them, and to be recognised by their friends. Indignantly the heroines of the girls' story spurned the notion that they would sneak or split on a fellow; they winked back the tears when they were hit by the cricket ball, forebore to scream when a toad was put into their pocket. They soaked themselves in all the shibboleths and tabus and traditions of their brothers' schools and were ready to impose the whole system and its customs upon their own very different establishments, with the ludicrous results that we see in the next chapter.

'Womanliness' had nothing like the same emotional force. There were times when the ideal of the 'womanly woman' was preached to the adolescent girl emerging from the schoolroom. Charlotte Yonge and her successors did their best with a generation that was frighteningly anxious to be 'modern girls' and forgetful of their duties to the home. But in general the moralists recognised the word's lack of appeal and tried other avenues of approach.

Indeed, girls have always had much more to endure in the way of nagging. It was early realised that boys had far less patience and to get them to read at all was a triumph. So, long before girls were allowed amusing books, boys had their Marryat and Ballantyne – books of high adventure with the occasional pious sentiment slipped in as an afterthought, but with no continuous moral message. Charlotte Yonge, when she made suggestions for boys' reading in *What Books to Give and What to Lend*, said ruefully that she had had to omit many well-intentioned books 'because they do not seem to hit off the peculiar taste of that large class'. Her recommendations were almost exclusively adventure stories: *Robinson Crusoe, Masterman Ready, Treasure Island*, the works of Ballantyne, Kingston, Jules Verne, Mayne Reid and Henty, and *Tom Brown*, though not *Eric*.

Miss Yonge based her remarks on her experiences in her own Hampshire parish, and fifty years later Christine Chaundler discussing in *The Children's Author* (1934) the sort of books that appealed to boys, had the same observations to offer: adventure stories were the most popular, and then, a long way after, school and sport stories. One might hazard a guess that the reason for this is 'the absence of any appeal to a dogmatic religious belief, or any *open* theory of conduct or education' in adventure stories. This had made, as Harvey Darton remarked, books such as the Mayne Reid stories, Kingston's *Peter the Whaler* and Ballantyne's *The Young Fur Traders* such novelties in the 1840s and 50s. The heroes put their trust in God, and fought the elements and the savages like good stout Britons, but it is their adventures that matter, not their characters. They were 'manly', that went without saying, they were also patriotic, but manliness here only meant that they were brave and looked danger square in the eye. To study the boy as the moral writers have wanted him to be we have to look elsewhere.

We take it for granted now that fearlessness has always been desired for boys. But the Georgians certainly did not think of it as a cardinal virtue. They wanted an old head on young shoulders. This was the object that Dr Arnold also strove for, though his conception of mature thinking was to be so very different. The little books of Newbery and Darton counsel prudence, diligence and industry. They recount the horrible consequences of deeds of boldness; boys are dashed to pieces while birds-nesting, drown in the mill-pool while bathing, have their bowels torn out through venturing too near a horse. Darton's *A Present for a Little Boy* (1797) contains several of these instances, and from *Dangerous Sports*, *The Dangers of the Streets*, and *The Second Chapter of Accidents* the moral emerges that everything in life is so fraught with danger that the prudent boy should avoid tops, marbles, horses, penknives and, safer still, all amusement, if he wishes to live to manhood.

As for fighting for one's country – the boy who joined the army was a fool, probably a rogue. So far as the eighteenth and early nineteenth century book went there is not a hint that a boy is doing his country a service by going off with the recruiting sergeant; he has been gulled while sodden with drink, or he is a neer-do-well who has fallen foul of his employer, and when he limps back with a wooden leg years later then it serves him right.

> *A canvas house, with wooden top,*
> *Far off from any church or shop;*
> *A room, where two can scarcely pass,*
> *A carpet made of weeds and grass,*

At length, of swimming grown so fond,

He ventur'd in a deep Mill-pond,

   Where rushes grew around :

But while he sported in the stream,

He caught the cramp, and with a scream,

   He sunk—and so was drown'd.

The Georgians desired prudence, not fearlessness, in their boys. From *Peter Brown*, a chapbook published in Otley, Yorks, *c.* 1820.

A bed expos'd to midnight air,
Of sheets and blankets rather bare,
A smoking fire of new cut wood,
A table made of turf or mud,
A cloth with human blood besmear'd,
A foe hard by, who never fear'd,
A wife forsaken and alone,
Hearing her husband's dying groan;
An orphan child, for victuals crying,
Crawling amongst the dead and dying –
Its infant moaning and imploring
Drown'd amidst the cannon's roaring;
These are the comforts war doth yield,
Or in the tent, or in the field;
Then if you relish things like these,
Go for a soldier if you please.

This was how *Moral Tales in Verse* (Hodgson & Co., *c* 1830) sought to deter young readers. This was prudent realism, but Dr Aikin and Mrs Barbauld took a more high-minded line in *Evenings at Home*, when Charles, asking Papa for 'a very pretty story . . . about a bloody murder' is given one about a battle: '"I do not know of any *murders* half so bloody."'

It was not until the Crimean War and the Indian Mutiny that patriotic feeling surged into the boy's book. Early efforts to handle this new element were rather apprehensive, like Hain Friswell's in *Out and About* (1860)

'"I mean to be an engineer," [said Flook], "and go amongst the Indians and beat them and blow them up . . . I don't care about punching another boy's head, but I would fight for my country like – like a Briton."

"You're a philosopher, old Flook."

"I try to be so; but I say, Ned, who would not strike out for the old land? Who would not try to carry her laws and glorious religion and her institutions?"'

It was going to take a little more time and practice for writers to handle this theme with ease.

Manliness, like honour, was whatever one chose it to mean – the juvenile writers soon discovered that – but it did not come into its own until the Victorian period. Basically it meant courage and independence, though by the end of the century it had gathered an enormous accretion of other virtues. Maria Edgeworth showed in 1801 the difference between the moralist's conception of manliness and the Georgian public schoolboy's when she contrasted Charles Howard with Augustus Holloway in a story about Westminster.[1] Charles champions a little boy whom Augustus is bullying and fights the aggressor (who in the style of the times has learnt his stuff by associating with pugilists). There are six pitched battles and Charles only achieves victory in the last. He is not manly merely because of these Homeric encounters, but because of his independent and active mind; he loves learning for its own sake, unlike Augustus who, though clever, spurns school and longs for adult dissipation. Augustus' particular ambition is to set up a curricle and to drive a four-in-hand: 'he had very manly ideas – if those ideas be manly which most young men have'. Miss Edgeworth here is beating down some of the brambles for Dr Arnold. Boys had to be taught that manliness did not just consist of hard drinking and racing stage coaches against post chaises.

Manliness is what little Hugh Proctor has to learn when, aged only eight, he is sent to Mr Tooke's school in *The Crofton Boys* (1841). Hugh is an eager, naïve, sturdy little fellow who has become too much of a handful for a household where females predominate. '"When a child makes God his friend,"' his mother tells him the morning he leaves home, '"God puts into the youngest and weakest the spirit of a man."' She means that he should be brave and steady in his conduct. But there are schoolboy ethics to be learnt as well. Hugh comes to grasp that while he must always keep his mother's ideals of behaviour in mind he must also, to be liked by his school-fellows, abide by their code of conduct which is necessarily quite different from home. Harriet Martineau gives her advice through the person of Frith, a wise older boy.

'"You will find in every school in England, that it is not the way of boys to talk about feelings – about anybody's feelings. That is the reason why they do not mention their sisters or their mothers – except when two confidential friends are together, in a tree, or by themselves

---

[1] *The Good Aunt (Moral Tales)*.

in the meadows. But, as sure as ever a boy is full of action – if he tops the rest at play – holds his tongue, or helps others generously – or shows a manly spirit without being proud of it, the whole school is his friend."'

An early moral tale about a boys' school. Gustavus is sociable. Christopher is quarrelsome and is shunned by all. Lithograph from *Early Impressions*, 1828.

Hugh absorbs this lesson, he wins the boys' respect for his courage and his resolution not to betray the name of a boy who has seriously injured him. *The Crofton Boys* belongs to the moral tale category rather than the school story, but Miss Martineau does in fact anticipate something of the Tom Brown spirit. The private school, however, was certainly not considered the repository of the manly traditions. A handful of boys over whom presided perhaps a clerical headmaster who ran the establishment to augment an inadequate income, aided by ill-educated, ill-paid ushers, hardly more than boys themselves and regarded with contempt by the pupils – many Victorians remembered them with loathing as hot-beds of vice where the ushers and the older boys tyrannised over the small and weak. The luckier boy left to go to a public school; others might stay on till eighteen or nineteen, idle louts with whom the prudent usher did not attempt to interfere. Augustus Hare spoke of the 'little monsters' he found at the Rev Robert Kilvert's school where 'all infantine immoralities were highly popular'. George Melly found much the same at his first school; 'perhaps that feeling of holding by one another, of treating the masters as an inimical race, and of never telling tales . . . was the one vital spark'. It was hardly a spark which the moralists would choose to puff into flame.

II
The Spirit of the Public Schools

The whole literature of the school story sprang out of Thomas Hughes and *Tom Brown's School Days*. This was published in 1856, but written of his own experiences at Rugby in the 1830s soon after Thomas Arnold had become its headmaster. Arnold died fourteen years before the book was published. It was fortunate for him that he did so, so deeply would he have been saddened to find how few of his ideals had seeped down to the ordinary schoolboy, however much that boy had hero-worshipped him.

What Arnold wanted was a school of Christian gentlemen, morally responsible beings, who would each strive, as he was striving, to sustain the character and reputation of the institution to which they all belonged. The private schools relied on the gaoler-like supervision of ushers to maintain discipline; the unreformed public schools of the old days kept order by flogging the boys who saw themselves in consequence as in a constant state of warfare with authority. He on the contrary wished to inculcate in each boy 'a true manly sense of the degradation of guilt or faults' which would make him of his own free will behave in an upright and honourable way without any threat of punishment. It was the 'moral childishness' which he thought was the great curse of public schools, and to him it seemed to lie in the spirit of combination and companionship that they encouraged, and in excessive deference to public opinion. This was fatal to free and manly feeling in individual boys. Stanley in his *Life of Arnold* records that the sight of a knot of vicious or careless boys

Lawless ornamenting Frank's Writing-Desk.

The ways of the private school – the moral childishness which Dr Arnold
strove to eliminate in boys. Illustration by George Cruikshank to F. E. Smedley:
Frank Fairlegh, or Scenes from the Life of a Private Pupil, 1850.

gathered round the great school-house fire gave him intense pain.
'"It makes me think that I see the Devil in the midst of them."'
This problem of the rule of the mob was an ever-burning issue with
him; it was the master fault, and one on which he preached many
times. 'Fear not, nor heed one another's voices, but fear and heed the
voice of God alone.' It was in his efforts to counteract this evil that he
used his Sixth Form to introduce good examples among the boys
themselves, taking over and developing the prefectorial system that
was already established at Winchester when he was there as a boy.

Certain boys did set themselves to try to attain the Arnoldian
ideals. There was Dean Stanley who wrote the life of his master, and
Clough is the famous example of one whose life was maimed by the
over-scrupulous, precociously adult conscience that such teaching
could produce in a sensitive boy. But the way that it washed over the
average boy is seen in *Tom Brown*.

Thomas Hughes paid moving tribute to what his old master's
sermons had meant to him . . . 'the tall, gallant form, the kindling eye,
the voice of him who stood there Sunday after Sunday, witnessing
and pleading for his Lord'. But he confessed that the majority of boys
listened uncomprehending.

'True, there always were boys scattered up and down the School,
who in heart and hand were worthy to hear and able to carry away
the deepest and wisest words there spoken. But these were a minority
always . . . often so small a one as to be countable on the fingers of
your hand. What was it that moved and held us, the rest of the three
hundred reckless and childish boys, who feared the Doctor with all
our hearts, and very little besides in heaven or earth; who thought
more of our sets in the School than of the Church of Christ, and put
the traditions of Rugby and the public opinion of boys in our daily
life above the laws of God?'

It was, he held, the warmth of the pleading that held the boys'
attention, the sense that here was another human being, a fellow-
soldier, urging them all, even the youngest, to fight beside him and
to fight bravely.

'It was this quality above all others which moved such boys as [Tom
Brown], who had nothing whatever remarkable about him except
excess of boyishness; by which I mean animal life in its fullest

measure, good nature and honest impulses, hatred of injustice and meanness, and thoughtlessness enough to sink a three-decker.'

And so Tom Brown roisters away his first couple of years, punching heads, poaching duck, fighting the local gamekeepers, avoiding work as craftily as he knows how, hurling himself up and down the playing fields, following the herd always. The turning point comes when he is given the charge of Arthur, a shrinking new boy, and is obliged to cast off his old careless ways to watch over him. But it is Arthur – the nearest that Hughes came to portraying one of the Arnold Sixth Form élite – who has the stronger character of the two, and Arthur who persuades him to give up the habit of using a crib to prepare his lessons. Tom gives way, not because he is himself convinced that it is morally wrong, but because he is shamed by Arthur's gentle comments into feeling that 'the Doctor' might not approve of translations to help one, however difficult the choruses in the *Agamemnon.* Thus though in one sense he has the courage to take up a minority stand, in that he is following the lead of a stronger will, he is still far from achieving the independent moral sense that the Doctor so greatly desired.

His ambitions are simple, the code of the average English boy of his class.

'"I want to be A1 at cricket and football, and all the other games, and to make my hands keep my head against any fellow, lout or gentleman. I want to get into the Sixth before I leave, and to please the Doctor, and I want to carry away just as much Latin and Greek as will take me through Oxford respectably . . . I want to leave behind me the name of a fellow who never bullied a little boy or turned his back on a big one.'

Our last sight of him as a schoolboy is in his glory as captain of the school cricket, looking back over his career. He is still quite unconscious of Arnold's influence over the school, and totally ignorant of the Arnoldian aims.

'He was wont to boast that he had fought his own way fairly up the School, and had never made up to, or been taken up by, any big fellow or master, and that it was now quite a different place from what it was when he first came. And, indeed, though he didn't actually boast of it, yet in his secret soul he did to a great extent believe that the great reform in the School had been owing quite as much to himself as to anyone else . . . As for the Doctor, he was a splendid master, but everyone knew the masters could do very little out of school hours.'

One of the masters, before Tom leaves, tries to open his eyes a little to the ways a headmaster can influence the course of events, and tells him that it was by Arnold's own desire that Tom was given charge of Arthur. At this revelation of the Doctor's deep interest in and knowledge of every one of his pupils, Tom's admiration for the man turns into blind hero worship. 'Had he returned to School again, and the Doctor begun the half-year by abolishing fagging and football, and the Saturday half-holiday, or all or any of the most cherished School institutions, Tom would have supported him with the blindest faith.' He is still in fact in that state of 'moral childishness' which Dr Arnold had for fourteen years striven to eradicate.

The author understood a little more of the Arnoldian aims than Tom Brown. He saw, for instance, that Arnold wanted to make boys fight the rule of the mob and to think for themselves. But his notion of 'manliness' was quite different from his master's. He stood for the sturdy, straightforward, spirited boy who looked you straight in the eye, and who would defend the institution to which he belonged with the last drop of his blood.

This was the torch that was to be handed on through the succeeding ages of boys' books. It was not the Arnoldian torch, whose light was too rare and strange for most, though, since it came from Rugby, it was often thought to be his. And as the Arnold ideals had suffered at the hands of Thomas Hughes so his version was to suffer again through the course of the next fifty years, until all that is left by the time we reach the school stories of the *Gem* and the *Magnet* is high spirits and prefects and organised games and not sneaking – Arnold's 'moral childishness,' in fact.

The Hughes manliness in any case was much nearer the spirit of the public schools than ever Arnold's was. There was a great body of men who had experienced the system themselves and chose to remember their schooldays as a happy and innocent time. Boys might have been rather rough and careless, perhaps, but at heart they were sound. An old Wykehamist, Frederick Gale, spoke for all those men, middle-aged in the mid-Victorian period, when he

Tom Brown, now a man, revisits Rugby School Chapel and remembers Dr Arnold's
sermons there. Illustration by Arthur Hughes to *Tom Brown's School Days*, 1869.

rhapsodised about the boys watching the Eton–Winchester cricket match:

'Look at those open-hearted generous boys, Lord Flummery, and ask yourself when you were one of them, would you have had a hand in the chicanery and perjury which you have set to work at Rottenborough?

'And would you, Doctor Swamp, thou ubiquitous ecclesiastic, have sat down to dinner enough for twenty when you were a boy, and not have given nineteen parts away?

'And would you, Lord Scamp, have done an underhand action to make sure of winning the toss for your pottle of strawberries or mould of ice at school? Not a bit of it; you were all of you once, as generous and open-hearted as they are, but the world has spoilt you all.'

Gale and his kind thought that it was a mistake to put too much emphasis on religion or to encourage its practice, since piety, if sincere, would be all the stronger for having to stand fire. They dreaded that boys might be turned into sneaks, prigs or muffs, and be diverted from what they most admired, a high confident tone and the courage to stand out and stand firm. The Rev Henry Cadwallader Adams, author of *Wiccamica*, recalled a Winchester incident which made a deep impression on him. A boy had a tendon in his leg broken by a prefect who was punishing him with a cricket stump. By an error he was flogged for the same offence next day by the headmaster and took it without a single word that might put headmaster or prefect in the wrong. This was to Adams and to many others true manliness.

But there was one author whose vision was the same as Arnold's. This was Frederic Farrar, later Dean of Westminster, and author of three school stories of which *Eric, or Little by Little* has won itself lasting notoriety, the others, *St Winifred's* and *The Three Homes* being remembered hardly at all. It is in many ways a preposterous book, in which boys' behaviour is represented either as hideously black or radiantly white, written in a frenzy of emotion, without any attempt to keep the restraints that the English gentleman usually imposes on talk about the feelings – the restraint that Harriet Martineau had thought was one of the most useful lessons little Hugh could learn. To appreciate how it came to be written and why it outraged the public schools we should look at the author and his background.

Farrar himself was not at a public school,[1] nor did he come from the sort of family that was associated with them. His father was a missionary of the strictest evangelical beliefs, and he was sent to King William College on the Isle of Man because it was cheap and because its tone too was evangelical. This was the school that was to appear as Roslyn in *Eric*. It seems to have been a repellent place. We have not only Farrar's account of its evils, which he largely attributed to lack of a monitorial system – but of young George Clough who was there in 1834 and wrote miserably to his brother Arthur at Rugby. From there Farrar went to King's College, London – an institution then completely outside the experience of any public school man to whom there only would be two universities – and finally to Trinity College, Cambridge as a sizar, a socially inferior status which would cut him off from wealthier undergraduates.

In 1852 he began his teaching career at Marlborough, which being new at that time by no means had the position it now holds as one of the 'establishment' schools. It was also completely untouched by the new seriousness, which, independent of Arnold, was creeping over the public schools. It had been founded in 1843 to provide a cheap education for clergymen's sons. Nine years later it was toppling not only on the edge of financial collapse but also of complete disintegration from the pressure of its rebellious and violent inmates. There had been a Great Rebellion in 1851 against a headmaster who, with no monitorial system to help him, tried to keep the school in hand by curtailing more and more of its liberties. There were no organised games to deflect energy from fighting, bullying, hard drinking, and poaching, and serious work was almost impossible. A boy who went there just before the rebellion found that the school's hero was not the scholar (this was hardly to be expected), nor the sportsman: 'It was the hero of the last fight, who had battered a bigger antagonist into temporary blindness, and had himself lost so much blood that he was too weak to cut his own meat at dinner!'

Farrar was later to become Master (i.e., headmaster) of Marlborough, which by then had considerably sobered down. But between his two Marlborough periods intervened sixteen years at Harrow, a very different place indeed, an establishment which drew its boys not from the modest squirearchy and commercial upper

---

[1] Only eight or nine schools were thus classified in the nineteenth century, of which Eton, Harrow and Winchester were pre-eminent.

middle classes who patronised Rugby, nor from the country clergy who sent boys to Marlborough, but largely from the aristocracy. It too, of course, had had its wild unregenerate days in the 1830s – orgies of heavy drinking, wild larking, hare and hounds over the Middlesex countryside at dead of night.[1] But all this was supposed to have changed when the great Dr Vaughan swept into the school as headmaster in 1844 at the age of twenty-eight, eleven years before Farrar's time. One of Arnold's most cherished pupils, he breathed into the school, according to the histories, a new spirit which cleansed and purified.

There was however another aspect which cheerful Victorian Harrovians did not usually record in their autobiographies. Most of them had no doubt come from private schools where they had been hardened. But John Addington Symonds who entered the school at the age of thirteen in 1854, straight from a loving and protected home, was stunned.

'The combination of brutality and lust,' wrote Dr Phyllis Grosskurth in her life of Symonds, 'made him fear that he had stumbled into the land of the Yahoos . . . It was the common practice for every good-looking boy to be addressed by a female name; he was regarded either as public property or as the "bitch" of an older boy.'

But this was not all. In 1859 the great Vaughan left Harrow suddenly and unexpectedly. For over a hundred years no explanation was produced, and then in 1964 Phyllis Grosskurth, preparing her life of Symonds, had access to the poet's unpublished memoirs. Here it was revealed that the headmaster had been writing passionate love letters to one of his pupils, that Symonds himself had received approaches from him, and that Dr Symonds had stepped in and forced him to resign. *Eric* was published in 1858, the year before Vaughan departed. Whether Farrar suspected the reason is not known. It is indeed extraordinary that such a scandal which involved so many people should have been successfully hushed up for over a century, and hard to imagine that the masters, at least, did not hear rumours of the truth.

[1] On one occasion the headmaster was even hauled up to a window in a basket by a group of boys who thought they were handling a load of provisions. Episodes such as these were said to be heard rather wistfully by Rugbeians who by that time were in Arnold's iron grasp.

Eric was certainly written while the author was in the grip of strong emotion. The theme is the one of corruption. Eric, 'truthful, ingenuous, quick,' his mind seemingly 'cast in such a mould of stainless honour that he avoided most of the weaknesses to which children are prone,' goes to Roslyn School and is gradually sucked down into the mire of schoolboy vice. His pride – his besetting sin – his

'*Miserable* coward,' said Mr. Rose, throwing into the word such ringing scorn that no one who heard it ever forgot it. He indignantly shook the boy off, and caned him till he rolled on the floor, losing every particle of self-control, and calling out, 'The devil —the devil—the devil!' ('invoking his patron saint,' as Wildney maliciously observed).

'There! cease to blaspheme, and get up,' said the master, blowing out a cloud of fiery indignation. 'There, sir. Retribution comes at last, leaden-footed but iron-handed. A long catalogue of sins is visited on you to-

Illustration by Gordon Browne to Dean Farrar's *Eric*, 1896.

fear of being unpopular, of being thought a muff, drags him back to the rule of the mob just when it looks as though he might free himself. When his little brother Vernon joins him at Roslyn the same thing happens. For want of protection and a good example set by his brother he too sinks. Vernon dies; Eric, now repentant, is wrongly accused of theft, and unable to stand this last charge, runs away to sea. He returns, broken in health, to be lovingly received by his former schoolfellows, but when he hears that his mother has died, broken-hearted at the news of her sons, he has no further will to live.

It might have been written to illustrate one of Arnold's own sermons. It hammers home in an atmosphere of mounting doom, the fearful consequences to the soul of one who courts easy popularity and stifles the voice of his own conscience. Farrar's conception of manliness is the Arnoldian one. Of one of Eric's worthier school-friends he says that the boy had been laying aside the careless sins of school life,

'and his tone was nobler and manlier than it had ever been. Montagu had never known or heard much about godliness; his father, a gentleman, a scholar, and a man of the world, had trained him in the principles of refinement and good taste, and given him a high standard of conventional honour; but he passed through life lightly and had taught his son to do the same.'

Farrar here rejects the gentlemanly conception of honour which he must have encountered all too often at Harrow. Like Arnold, he felt that manliness and honour must be Christian. Freddy Gale's adulation of the boyish boy would have appalled him, for he had observed just how vicious boys could be at his own school, at Marlborough and at Harrow. *Eric* is one of the very few boy's books that tries to warn about sexual vice. Eric begins with obscene talk in the dormitory, he goes on to an association with a little Wildney – ' "a very nice little fellow – a regular devil," ' who more than anybody else is responsible for Eric's degradation. But Farrar's impassioned pleas to Eric and to his readers to uphold purity, to abjure corruption, are never very explicit and must have puzzled younger readers.

'Kibroth-Hattaavah![1] Many and many a young Englishman has perished there! Many and many a happy English boy, the jewel of his mother's heart – brave, and beautiful and strong – lies buried there. Very pale their shadows rise before us – the shadows of our young brothers who have sinned and suffered. From the sea and the sod, from foreign graves and English churchyards, they start up and throng around us in the paleness of their fall. May every schoolboy who reads this page be warned by the waving of their wasted hands, from that burning marle of passion where they found nothing but shame and ruin, polluted affections, and an early grave.'

[1]Hebrew: 'the graves of desire', though not necessarily sexual desire. *Numbers*, ch. 11, v. 34: 'And he called the name of that place Kibroth Hattaavah: because there they buried the people that lusted.'

He wrote as he preached, and as he spoke, 'with sesquipedalian grandiloquence' as one of his old pupils described his manner, a style very different from the moderate and measured phrases of Arnold's and Vaughan's sermons. And the public schools did not, on the whole, like it. Some thought *Eric* ludicrous (this went for the boys at Harrow); some, like King William College, were offended; others, such as the critic in the *Saturday Review* (6 November, 1858) thought it unwise and most unhealthy, liable to produce priggishness and conceit in boys.

The fact was that English boys of the upper classes were not used to moral tales. There was no male equivalent of Charlotte Yonge and Elizabeth Sewell. Thomas Hughes knew what he was about when he begged his readers to forgive his few words of exhortation and hold back before they started throwing his poor book around the room. Public school boys expected sermons to be confined to chapel; they preferred a flogging to pi-jaw. It was not so much the display of feeling in *Eric* that outraged the mid-Victorian schoolboy, for the cult of the stiff upper-lip did not become an unquestioned part of the manly code until the 70s and 80s. The early and the mid-Victorians were emotional and saw no shame in it. In *Tom Brown* East breaks down and cries when he tells the Doctor that he wants to be confirmed and the Doctor soothes him and strokes his head. And when Arthur is affected to tears by the beauty of a passage in Homer, the boys are certainly taken aback that anybody could work up feeling for a boring lesson, but their strongest reaction is that somebody else will now have to construe in his place and each numskull, conscious of his inadequacy, dreads that he may be called.

But to express one's feelings in words was a different matter. When Arthur pleads with Tom to abjure cribbing it is in the simplest language, and when he sees the point is made he is silent. Farrar was never silent; he loved words, he felt passionately, he was intoxicated by imagery. His writing was like his sermons – summarised by Jowett as 'all flowers and figures' – full of reminders of the beauties of nature, the sanctity of the innocent home, the sacred influence of the mother. Boys distrusted his poetical allusions (his range of reading and his literary sympathies were immense), and disapproved of book characters who quoted hymns at each other. Farrar the self-made man, from his Gissing-like background, had none of these gentlemanly inhibitions. He had been brought up as an evangelical, and though he put this behind him and emerged a Broad Churchman, he still kept the evangelical style – the call to the feelings, the drama, the lacrimosity, the dwelling on sin.

But this touch was exactly right for the non-public school classes. They admired the purple passages, they were far more accustomed to evangelical literature than their betters and were not affronted by the lack of reticence. It was their enthusiasm that was responsible for *Eric*'s enormous sales (thirty-six editions by 1904), and it is notable that in the letters of appreciation quoted by Reginald Farrar in his life of his father, many of the warmest come from such bodies as working men's literary clubs. A curate wrote to him of his experiences in Leeds and East London that he had repeatedly noticed among both the very poor and the better sort of working class the enormous enthusiasm of the boys for *Eric*. Reginald Farrar, comparing *Tom Brown* and *Eric*, likened them respectively to Frith and Fra Angelico. The one, he said had certainly an excellent, healthy tone, but the other 'touched to finer issues'; it was the work of an idealist, and of one who never wrote without a definite moral purpose.

One never knows, of course, what the child reader derives from a book. But it seems unlikely that the poor boys who read *Eric* with such breathless attention were gripped by the moral. They were probably hanging on the melodrama; will he, won't he, repent in time? In any case Farrar's moral issues are far from clear. Why is it so unwholesome for Eric as a young boy to be 'taken up' by an older boy, when an older boy in *St Winifred's* is urged to befriend a little one, give him the run of his study, talk to him alone? Where is the dividing line between working hard, and mistakenly so overdoing this that you die as Daubeny, the conscientious, dull plodder, does in *St Winifred's*? The trouble is that Farrar is preaching so many sermons at the same time that the threads become inextricably confused. He is telling the headmasters to have monitorial systems, the masters to be tolerant and understanding, the boys to be obedient and hardworking and independent of the mob. In these circumstances the schoolboy might well feel that if he gets at cross-purposes with the masters then it is the fault of the system, and the moral that emerges clear-cut from the tangle is one that Farrar certainly did not intend – never send your son to a boarding school. But above all, the mainspring of *Eric*, the theme of impurity, is awry. How can the inexperienced possibly tell, amid all the rhetoric and emotion, which is an improper and dangerous association and which is a warm and fruitful friendship? Some of the later editors of the text were more worldly-wise and cut out references to kisses and embraces, however chastely given.

The truth was that emotional friendship between boys is a frequent element in the public school story. Admittedly it occurs more often in the book *about* boys such as Horace Annesley Vachell's *The Hill* (1905) and E. F. Benson's *David Blaize* than the formula school tale, but even so steady a writer as Talbot Baines Reed put passages which would now be considered extravagant into his books.

'Oh! the happiness of that precious quarter of an hour, when the veil that has divided two faithful friends is suddenly dashed aside, and they rush one to the other, calling themselves every imaginable bad name in the dictionary, insisting to the verge of quarrelling that it was all their fault, and no fault of the other, far too rapturous to talk ordinary common sense.'

The Hill, which is an account of the jealous love that one Harrow school boy feels for another and the efforts of a third to step between them, was styled by the publishers 'a fine, wholesome, manly novel,' and recommended by the *Boy's Own Paper* in 1913 for its portrayal of an ideal friendship. The same would have been felt about *David Blaize*, which is built round the love of two boys, one a senior, the other a junior. Few would have seen harm in either; on the contrary, in that they set before the reader an ideal of loyal, devoted friendship they would have been considered excellent models for boys. But the modern reader views them quite differently. Ernest Raymond, re-reading his own best-seller *Tell England* in 1968 after the lapse of some fifty years had this to say:

'Another thing that is a wonder to me . . . is the indubitable but wholly unconscious homosexuality in it. The earlier part was written when I was eighteen or nineteen, and in those early days "homosexuality" was a word which – absurd as this may seem now – I had never heard . . . I did not know that homosexuality could exist in embryo without even knowing its evil for what it was, or desiring the least physical satisfaction.'

The success of *Tom Brown* and *Eric* started the boom in public school stories. They were found to be the answer of how to inject, or try to inject, sound manly principles into boys. They poured off the

presses and were given away in their millions as Sunday School and
Board School prizes. They were beloved by girls, who continued to
read them even after they had their own female versions by Angela
Brazil and her kind. Nobody attempted to imitate Dean Farrar.
Eric was left, a monstrous curiosity washed up by the floodwater of
evangelical feeling, and stared at with respect, or with ribaldry. Nor
did any imitations of *Tom Brown* appear, for there was too much feeling even in that for the late Victorians. To the writers of the 80s and
90s manliness meant keeping one's emotions well under control.
' "Not a bad sermon tonight," ' says one boy huskily to another in *The
Bending of a Twig* (which Desmond Coke wrote to counteract what he
considered were the excesses of *Tom Brown* and *Eric*). ' "Not half
bad," ' says his friend. And as the hero takes leave of his housemaster
with much emotion at the end of his school career, ' "Whatever was
the Dook jawing about?" ' he is asked. 'Lycidas forced back the two
tears that had sprung to the corner of his eyes. "Oh rot of every sort,"
he answered.'

The atmosphere in the late school stories, so far as work is concerned, is of light-hearted shirking. The really serious matter is
sport, the manly ideals are *esprit de corps*, truth-telling, and standing
by one's fellows. The obsession with sport creeps in somewhere in the
early 1850s. Arnold had never promoted games. Certainly he had
suggested them as a substitute when he put down some of the more
unruly Rugby pastimes, but his lack of interest is shown in *Tom
Brown* when the key match of the year is played after the end of term,
after he has gone off to the Lake District, leaving just the team and
any town boys who care to drift along to watch. Games in those early
days were quite outside the school curriculum, and regarded sus-
piciously by masters who saw them as a temptation to idle boys.
Canon Firth in his history of Winchester, commenting on the
solemnity with which a committee of 1854 discussed the Eton–
Harrow–Winchester match, remarked:

'The claims of athleticism have since become so deeply engrained in
the Public School system and mentality that it is hard to realise how
new they were then. It was claimed that games were a preparation
for the battle of life, and the prestige of the school depended in great
part, it was held, on their successes in these important contests; the
fortunes of our country, even apparently of its religion, rested upon
an unfailing supply of these youthful heroes. All the statesmen,

divines and educationists, and the soldiers and gentry too, of every preceding age, would have thought such language inconceivably childish; and the boys who had earlier founded these matches as a merry lark, and thought themselves lucky not to get flogged for it, would have been amazed to find themselves exalted thus.'

Canon Firth did not exaggerate. In 1895 Harold Avery was writing in *An Old Boy's Yarns* of the archetypal English boy, tiresome, reckless, and danger-loving, but redeemed by his devotion to games,

Pluck and team spirit – the ordinary view of the public school ethos.
Illustration to *My First Football Match*, in the first number of the *Boy's Own Paper*, 1879.

where he 'unwittingly acquires a grounding in those qualities so dear to the men of his nation – Fortitude and Endurance, and as the autumn afternoon closes in, and we stand and watch him pulling his tired self together in a hard fight to save his goal, we see in those grey eyes the first kindling of that light which will some day be burning brightly in them as he stands face to face with danger and perhaps with death'.

The Bending of a Twig resounds with calls to leave the desk and come out on the games field. '"He won't believe me when I say he will never have any influence without games,"' says the housemaster sadly, for 'to be a "sap" comes second in the list of Shrewsbury vices,' and any decent boy indignantly denies that he is interested in his lessons. So Lycidas in his anxiety to get power in the House plods up and down the playing fields and gyrates wildly in the gymnasium.

'But the real thing was the House matches! You didn't want a coat or grub then! You kept pushing forward, to the linesman's anger, so as to miss nothing, shouting and jumping, drowning the cries of the other House, and even running up and down the line, behind. Cheering and excitement kept you warm. And when your House was in the final — !'

And running up and down the line now would be the housemaster, an over-grown version of his pupils. Gone was the Olympian aura that we noticed in the mid-Victorian period, when a schoolmaster's sorrowful words could set boys weeping, his anger bring them to their knees, his sympathy or interest evoke lifelong devotion. Talbot Baines Reed went so far as to write a story, *The Master of the Shell*, from the master's point of view, a man with such ordinary human impulses that he is even engaged – to the sister of one of the boys in his form. The masters were to descend lower than this, below the level of their pupils, in fact, and become the pompous hypocrites of *Stalky* and *Vice-Versa*, or the well-meaning nincompoops of Frank Richards' Greyfriars stories.

The message of the late Victorian schoolmaster was *esprit de corps*. '"I want your School to be a kind of minor religion with you,"' says the housemaster in *The Bending of a Twig*, 'ranked by the side of patriotism'. Just how far this minor religion could be carried can be seen in *The Hill*. Here is The Manor, a House that is decaying because of its ineffectual housemaster (he is not a public school man;

he has prestige as a scholar and he doesn't wash). The headmaster is at a loss to know how to regenerate this once fine house. Inspired, he appeals to the best Old Harrovians to sacrifice their sons to Dirty Dick's for the good of the School. They rally round, their fine boys restore the tone, Dirty Dick retreats in ignominy to become 'professor of Greek at a Scotch university'. He is replaced by Warde – 'one of the Wardes of Warde-Pomeroy, the real old stuff'. The Manor soars to its former glory.

Pounding up and down the touchline, straining every sinew to achieve that winning goal, looking your accusers straight in the eye, refusing to sneak, striving to restore the fortunes of your House, upholding your form against another, carrying your head high in misfortune – these were to be the pegs on which so many plots were hung for at least three decades of school prizes. Even when they seemed to have lost their force to shape the character; when the Tom Brown ethic was no longer preached, the public school setting was not wholly abandoned. You found it in the *Gem* and the *Magnet*, in St Jim's, Greyfriars, and Rookwood – the schools created by Charles Hamilton (alias Frank Richards and other names). You even found it in 1956 in the *Rocket* where William Temple presented 'St Rockets – the Science College of tomorrow where anything can happen.' The cadets and cadettes are the pick of the world's youthful scientists from the thousands of United Nations schools. Who leads them? Ron Crowther, of course. His hair is combed and, being British, he looks keen and alert. He keeps an eye on things when the addle-pated Professor Poppenjay is absent; he replaces the fuses when Cadet Fermi, the young Italian electrical wizard, short-circuits half the lighting system.

There was still glamour in old stone walls, school colours, and daring deeds – even in the traditional punishments (Professor Poppenjay makes obstreperous cadets write out Einstein's 'relativity formula' a thousand times). There was humour to be found in the masters, who blundered around like the old-fashioned giants of the chapbooks, perpetually outwitted by cheeky small boys. Tom Brown's ringing call had become very faint in the school stories of the *Gem* and the *Magnet*, but the occasional reader heard it. In Cork Frank O'Connor, growing up just before the First War, his father a drink-sodden ex-soldier, his mother a charwoman,

'adored education from afar and strove to be worthy of it . . . I played cricket with a raggy ball and an old board hacked into shape for a bat before a wicket chalked on some dead wall. I kept in training by shadow boxing before the mirror in the kitchen, and practised the deadly straight left with which the hero knocked out the bully of the school. I even adopted the public-school code for my own, and did not tell lies, or inform on other boys, or yell when I was beaten. It wasn't easy, because the other fellows did tell lies, and told on one another in the most shameless way, and, when they were beaten, yelled that their wrists were broken, and even boasted later of their own cleverness, and when I behaved in the simple, manly way recommended in the school stories, they said I was mad or that I was "shaping" (the Cork word for swanking), and even the teacher seemed to regard it as an impertinence.'

III
The Wage Slaves

The problem of how to influence boys like Frank O'Connor was in fact one that had exercised educationists and moralists for many years. How could they tempt them to lift their heads from the penny dreadfuls which all were agreed would get them, if not to the gallows, then to the reformatory? How to persuade them into the good fresh air, instead of the billiards saloon or the public house? How could they learn those valuable lessons which a more privileged class absorbed on the games field – team spirit, grit, determination, fair play?

The Religious Tract Society found the answer in the *Boy's Own Paper*. Its first number appeared on 18 January, 1879. It was a remarkable change of outlook. Only thirty-five years before the Society was mournfully telling boys, in the pages of *The Child's Companion*, about dying youths who regretted misspent Sabbaths, and disobedient ones who had been mangled under passing wagons. And a few years before that their ideal boy, if not a dead one, was at least dying. Now they wanted a strong, healthy boy, *mens sana in corpore sano*, and with a complete reversal of all their earlier policy they were to dwell far more on his bodily health in the confident expectation that once this was established the health of his soul would follow.

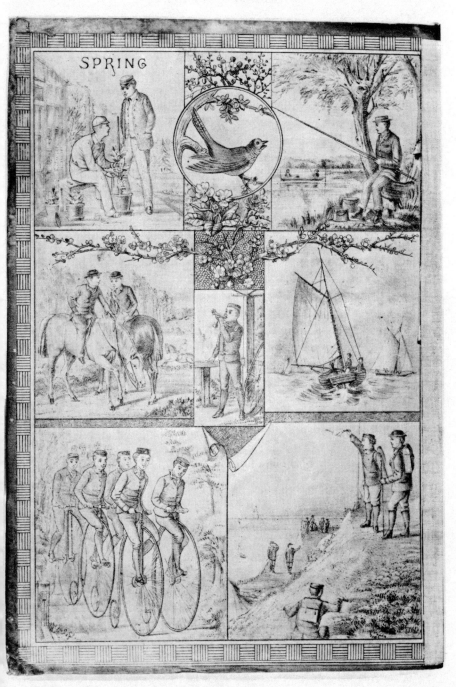

Endpaper from the first *Boy's Own Annual*, 1879.

They were not in fact aiming at the very poorest boys, who would hardly have been able to afford the sixpence a week that was asked (Frank O'Connor was envious of boys who could), but at the grammar schools and the lower middle classes, town boys probably, who might spend the week standing behind a counter, or perched on an office stool, working long hours in bad conditions, inadequately fed. Lists of prizewinners suggest that a lot of their readers came from industrial cities in the north, and that many of them were what would now be considered rather elderly for such a paper – between sixteen and twenty-one, in fact. That many of them were worried about their health is clear from the answers to correspondents (the queries were not printed); and from the frequent advice to take Virol, cold tubs, see the doctor about their chests, go on to a fattening diet, we get an impression of undersized, puny, wage slaves.[1] A host of articles and stories were provided to encourage them to take up healthy pursuits. The first issue packed in information about natural history, the uses of a jack-knife, and skating. Captain Webb wrote on How I Swam the Channel, there were anecdotes about brave boys who rescued people from drowning, W. H. Kingston started a serial *From Powder Monkey to Admiral* which startlingly suggested that poor boys might after all rise in the world. There was a poem which epitomised the spirit of the BOP through the ninety-odd years of its life.

> *Whatever you are, be brave, boys!*
> *The liar's a coward and slave, boys!*
>   *Though clever at ruses*
>   *And sharp at excuses,*
> *He's a sneaking and pitiful knave, boys.*

> *Whatever you are, be frank, boys!*
> *'tis better than money and rank, boys!*
>   *Still cleave to the right,*
>   *Be lovers of light,*
> *Be open, above board, and frank, boys.*

---

[1] The girl, however, who wrote apparently asking for suggestions as to how she might grow taller since her ambition was to become a lamplighter, was discouraged and told to be grateful for her lack of inches.

Whatever you are, be kind, boys!
Be gentle in manners and mind, boys!
The man gentle in mien,
Words and temper, I ween,
Is the gentleman truly refined, boys.

But, whatever you are, be true, boys!
Be visible through and through, boys!
Leave to others the shamming,
The 'greening' and 'cramming,'
In fun and in earnest, be true, boys!

This was the only exhortation. In Harvey Darton's words, the editorial policy was 'to combat evil by treating goodness as ordinary unemphasised decency and honesty, which knew and avoided vice spontaneously, and rejected it also with vigour, but without loud chords of moral triumph'. Clearly many of the readers were used to a much more obtrusive moral. This becomes evident when we look at the report of the adjudicators on the first competition that appeared in the paper. Entrants were asked to provide a story to fit a picture of a boy standing outside a cottage marked 'To let.' The stories were very moral indeed. 'Generally the lad was one who had disobeyed his parents and come up to London, or been self-willed and run away to sea . . . Father was, perhaps, dead, broken-hearted; and the widowed mother had had to give up her once happy home . . . Numberless writers describe the lad of the picture as having been led astray by bad literature, gambling, bad companions, or drunkenness.'

And doom-laden finales of this style were not uncommon.

'He had killed his mother, and the fatal words ring loudly and solemnly in his ears. Many a time he steals away, unobserved, to the quiet village churchyard, and there "beneath those rugged elms, that yew-tree's shade, where heaves the turf in many a mould'ring heap," he weeps bitter tears of repentance over his parent's grave.'

This was the style of bygone days, and one that the BOP had turned its back upon. Its tone was to remain remarkably consistent. The heroes on the whole were not public school boys, they went to grammar schools, or private academies, they had bright sensible eyes, merry-looking faces. They were good-natured, pleasant and frank, with a way of making friends wherever they went. Or they were figures from the past, Crusaders perhaps, or Cavaliers, or explorers, or pioneers who swooped into battle against the Indians with a ringing shout of 'Hurrah for Old England' (the motif of patriotism was now handled with far more skill than poor Hain Friswell had been able to muster). There was bloodshed, of course, but it was not gloatingly dwelt upon. Nobody could complain that the BOP was muffish, but neither was it violent. It commanded immense loyalty from bishops to elementary school boys, and in 1963, when it was approaching its demise, its earliest readers would have noticed very little difference in its contents. There were still the serials about explorers, the emphasis on healthy, outdoor pursuits. Boys still swapped information about stamps and coin-collecting, and wanted to know how to get into the Merchant Navy. Advertisements showed chest expanders and pointed out the advantages of youth hostelling. The BOP and Baden Powell between them had done perhaps more than anybody else to bring the ethos of the public schools to the elementary schools, but now those days were over. If the public schools retained any distinctive ethos in the post-war world, those outside their orbit were no longer interested in acquiring it.

There were plenty of publishers who cashed in on the late Victorian vogue for manly boys, and who saw that not all who aspired to be considered such had the sixpences in their pockets for the BOP. They turned out papers for a penny or twopence. Only the most diligent enthusiast could keep track of all their names, their sudden disappearance and re-emergence under a new title. Their aims were a watered-down version of the BOP's. They all denounced the penny-dreadful – 'blood-curdling tales of pirates, of highwaymen . . . which conveyed no lesson of manliness and honour, encouraged no patriotism, and taught nothing that was permanently useful' – and sought to provide a paper that nobody need read surreptitiously. *Cheer Boys Cheer* was indeed sub-titled 'the paper every boy can show his parents.' It offered good clean patriotic violence from the fist of a full-blooded English boy. The following extracts from the first number, 25 May, 1912 are representative.

'With scarlet cheeks and blazing eyes, Jim swung round and hit out right and left. Baker went down with a blow between the eyes; Horton staggered back with a bleeding nose.

'Lifting one dangling foot, Dick brought it down with a thud on the policeman's helmet. Completely bonneted, the unhappy man dropped to the cold, hard flagstones.

'"Lemme up – lemme up!" bellowed the headmaster's son. "I'll smash you – I'll smash you to pulp! Let go of my wrists." "Certainly," drawled the Lancashire lad, "When Ah'm ready."'

'"You dare to touch Mother!" cried Dickie in defiance. And doubling his fists, he lashed out wildly as the villain rushed at him.'

And, from a story called *Playing the Game* – 'Blind with rage, Bradly lifted his bat and struck at the captain's head. The poor fellow gave a cry and fell prone to the ground.'

'Pluck' was the new version of manliness.[1] 'I think there is no boy in the world like the British boy,' asserted the editor of *British Boys* in 1896. 'Where will you find another boy so full of pluck and daring? To call him a coward or a sneak is the worst thing you can possibly do, and I trust that none of our British boys will ever have applied to them any of these undesirable names.' Pluck was a word that had often been on Tom Brown's lips, and was a virtue so far as Thomas Hughes was concerned, though Dean Farrar had lamented the hold that it had over school boys: 'it's made the excuse for everything that's wrong, base and unmanly'. But manliness had taken a nasty knock since Arnold's day. In 1903 the *Boys' Herald*, directly under its sub-title 'A Healthy Paper for Manly Boys' showed a picture of one of the masters at St Basil's falling through the floor of a cab to the ecstacy of the pupil who had devised this prank.[2]

Like manliness, there was uncertainty about what pluck really did mean, though the boys' papers tried to attach all their moral teaching

[1] It is the exact equivalent of the modern 'guts'. Originally referring to the viscera of animals, it was taken up by pugilists and their supporters. Though it had become standard English by late Victorian times, women who used the term during the Crimean War were regarded as rather daring.

[2] This number also contained an advertisement for the promotion of moustaches by the use of Mr Dalmet's Pomade. 'Gives moustaches to all! Age no object! No more boys! No more smooth faces at thirty years of age! Send at once, as Mr Dalmet could die with his secret!'

The Boys' Herald 1d.

A Healthy Paper for Manly Boys · EVERY FRIDAY

No. 1. Vol. I.   EVERY FRIDAY—ONE PENNY.   Week Ending August 1st, 1903.

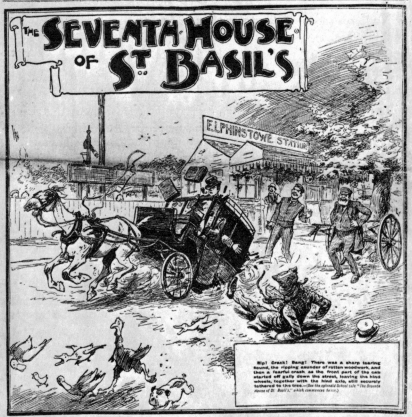

THE SEVENTH HOUSE OF St. BASIL'S

E.LPHINSTOWE STATION

Rip! Crack! Bang! There was a sharp tearing sound, the ripping asunder of rotten woodwork, and then a fearful crash as the front part of the cab started off gaily down the street, leaving the hind wheels, together with the hind axle, still securely tethered to the tree.—(*See the splendid School tale "The Seventh House of St. Basil's," which commences below.*)

THE 1st CHAPTER

Off to St. Basil's—Drugged—The Awakening—The Finding of the Red Crystal.

"Off in a minute, Harry," said Mr. Wilding, putting his head in at the carriage window.

The boy nodded. Now that it had come to the actual moment of parting he felt a lump rise in his throat; yet it had been his own wish, ever since he could remember. He had wanted to go to school and take his luck, good and bad, with other boys.

It was only a year ago that he had left India for England. His father had been a distinguished officer in the Indian service. His mother he scarcely remembered, for she had died years ago, when he was quite a little chap. The accidental discharge of a gun while hunting had robbed Sir Richard Belton of his life, and

Harry of his father and given him his title. And the boy had come to England to share the home of his only living relative, his uncle, Tom Wilding, a warm-hearted, good-natured, and easy-going man, between whom and Harry a close friendship had sprung up.

For a year Mr. Wilding himself had taken Harry's education in hand. He taught the boy to ride, to shoot, and to use his fists, accomplishments which Mr. Wilding set far above those of a more intellectual nature. But the time had come when Mr. Wilding realised that there was something for Harry to learn that he himself could not teach him.

"You'll have to go to school, Harry," he said. "It's that or a tutor. Which shall it be?"

And Harry had at once decided enthusiastically in favour of school.

to it. In 1901 the editor of the *Boys' Friend* spoke on the subject from his den in answer to a correspondent who wanted to know whether it just meant being dashing and jolly and high spirited:

'Pluck, as I think I have defined before, is the doing of a necessary action which must result in good without thought for the consequences. In fact the highest form of pluck is that shown when a man does an action resulting in good knowing that the consequences may prove disastrous to himself.'

Not very explicit, perhaps, but these modern editors did not like to embarrass their readers by discussing feelings that all decent English boys were now assumed to understand without definition. Most of the messages that came weekly from the editorial dens were very matter of fact, like the warning in *Boys' Life* (1907) that the editor would not wade through twelve pages of foreign notepaper written in violet ink, neither did he care for dead animals to dissect.

The editor of the *Boys' Herald* did, however, have a word for the boy who wanted to rise in the world; he wanted to be his chum, he said. The poor boy who today was reading those lines might become in twenty years a Carnegie or a Lipton; every boy had in him the possibilities of success. He counselled ambition – 'aim a little higher than you ever hope to reach' – punctuality, civility, cheerfulness, industry, alertness, and lastly devotion to parents who have sacrificed much for their sakes. ('Bear this in mind, boys, and don't kick against the pricks.')

The hero of many of these early twentieth-century boys' papers was Admiral Lord Charles Beresford. There were innumerable pictures of him, and sometimes messages from him urging readers to keep up the credit of the British race. At top-level, opinions of him varied. J. L. Garvin, for instance, called him 'the biggest of all recorded gasbags,' and Churchill said of him in the House of Commons that before he got up to speak he did not know what he was going to say, that when he was on his feet he did not know what he was saying, and that when he sat down he did not know what he had said. But the man in the street loved him because he was frank, open, dashing and impulsive. People remembered his exploit at the bombardment of Alexandria in 1882 when he took a gunboat up to the Egyptian guns at Fort Marabout and withstood the fire for ninety minutes. This was the sort of man for the *British Boy*, the *Boys of the Empire.* They were not interested in his brains. They knew that he could stand his ground and knock the stuffing out of any dirty foreigner who dared oppose Old England, and rouse his men to do the same. He exemplified pluck and patriotism to a generation that was to die in its hundreds of thousands in the Great War.

'Modern girls' and schoolgirls
1880–1940

THE Oxford Dictionary gives 1809 for the first usage of the term
'schoolgirl'. By 1820 it seemed to be common enough for Darton to
publish a pretty little book by William Upton called *The School Girl*
(companion to a similar book, *The School Boy*), and in fact there had
been a sprinkling of tales about her life and doings for years before
that. Sarah Fielding, Mary Jane Kilner, her sister Dorothy, had all
written tales which are well-known to book collectors and historians
if to no one else.

But these establishments are hardly recognisable as schools as we
would know them. Twelve pupils, perhaps, from eight to sixteen
years old, clustered in a single classroom, and the sole *raison d'être* of
the place the fact that its promoter had to make a living somehow,
had a tiny amount of capital and chose to take young females as
boarders, the young females being promised access to drawing
masters and French masters and music masters who presumably
were not available near their own homes. Charles Dickens' mother
tried her hand at it, but despite the brass plate and the circulars that
her children delivered, the pupils never came. Such establishments
were not held in high repute and even the children's books denounced them for turning girls into worldly and frivolous women.
Farmer Sandford of *Sandford and Merton* was only one of their many
critics. Nor, from the child's point of view, would they have seemed
particularly tempting to read about. Very few girls, however much
they detested their own governess, could have wanted to dream
about young Lucy or Sophia at one of these hot-house establishments – where the only break in the monotonous routine seemed to
be in whispered plots behind a laurel bush in the meagre garden, or
a brouhaha over a threatened elopement by one of the older pupils –
as a hundred years later they liked to dream about a world of feasts
in the dorm and ragging Mademoiselle.

The Victorians did not encourage schools for girls either. 'The selfish, inconsiderate, frivolous world of schoolgirls,' said Charlotte Yonge, who distrusted them, and favoured home education wherever it was possible. The Victorian boarding school seemed to be very little different from its earlier nineteenth-century counterpart, if we compare the latter with, say, Bush House in Mrs Ewing's *Six to Sixteen* (1875) with its 'well-filled schoolroom,' its 'meddlesome discipline,' and pallid girls drooping over lessons. School was a thing to escape *from*, not as it became later, an escape in itself.

But by the 1880's the mood was changing. The girls were growing restive, feeling fettered by the demands of home. Charlotte Yonge's message to the upper-class mid-Victorian girl had been one of ardent yielding to the home and family. 'For her the newest, *youngest* thing was to do home and family duties more perfectly. What greater happiness can be given to youth?' wrote Christabel Coleridge in her memoir of Miss Yonge in 1903, recognising that times had changed so much and that her work would have to be explained to a new and even sceptical generation. A generous, unquestioning giving of oneself was what Miss Yonge had urged, rather than cold submission to the seemingly inexhaustible demands that the Victorian family made on its unmarried daughters. The womanly woman was her ideal. And it was the ideal of many others of her time. The anonymous author of *Girls and their Ways* (his *Boys and their Ways* has already been mentioned) had this to say in 1881.

'She reads to the father, and chats with him in his hour of leisure; she assists the mother in her housekeeping duties; she receives the brother's confidences, and accompanies him in his walks and rambles; she joins the sisters at the piano or the easel; she is ever ready to partake or promote the merry games of the little ones. Her innocent laughter is home's sweetest music; her simple jest is welcomed as the most exquisite humour. There are of course,' he added darkly, '"Girls and Girls."'

By these he might have meant the empty-headed, given up to 'novel-reading, love of drama, and a too great fondness for fancy-work;' the sort of daughter that a Mrs Reaney complained of in *English Girls: Their Place and Power* (1881). This was a modest version of 'the girl of the period', bitterly attacked by an anonymous writer (later identified as the novelist Mrs Lynn Linton) in the *Saturday Review* in 1868. 'The girl of the period' was apparently a creature who

'A graceful maiden with a gentle brow.' Frontispiece to *Girls and their Ways*, 1881.

dyed her hair and painted her face, whose sole idea was plenty of fun and luxury, and whose dress was the object of such thought and intellect as she possessed. It was all part of the baneful effect that emancipation had had upon the female sex.

The 'modern girl' was another offshoot of emancipation. Most of the writers who discussed her in the journals and magazines of the day clearly disliked her or were unnerved by her, though they strained to be fair and tolerant. 'I think they are rather dreading you as a "modern girl",' said an aunt to her niece in 1887[1] welcoming her for the holidays, but warning her of the great distance between a London upbringing and family life in Cornwall. The 'modern girl' might be expected to ride a bicycle, travel on the top of a bus, go in for mixed bathing and to have forthright and independent views on topics which the old-fashioned girl would never have tackled. In Molly's case she was suspected of the blight because she was a pupil at the North London Collegiate School and was about to enter a teacher's training college at Cambridge. She had decided, with the full encouragement of her widowed mother and her brothers, to be independent. She had been offered the choice between that, and a pleasant, easy, lady's life in her beloved Cornwall, and had struck out boldly for independence.

In her case there was no moral dilemma, since nobody had tried to dissuade her. But plenty of girls were confronted with one, and a whole literature sprang up in the 80s and 90s to try to cope with their problems. It was one-sided advice that they offered, since the invariable ideal was the womanly woman, and the girl was told that home duties came first. Sometimes they sought to appeal to her self-interest.

'They would never need to worry about money; their rôle in life for the next few years would consist in being pretty and agreeable, wearing charming frocks, visiting at friends' houses, travelling in summer, hunting in winter, and, finally making suitable marriages, settling down as mistresses of other luxurious houses, and living happily ever after!

'She herself would study and cram for examination after examination; go through agonies of suspense waiting for results, and as she passed or failed, obtain a good or second-rate appointment in a suburban school. Henceforth work, work, work – teaching by day, correcting exercises by night, in a deserted schoolroom, with three months' holiday a year spent at home among brothers and sisters whose interests had necessarily drifted apart from her own. As the years passed by she would become staid and prim; schoolmistressy; the girls would speak of her by derisive nicknames . . .'

[1] M. V. Hughes: *A London Girl of the Eighties*, 1936.

'Because, Dessie, you are not free to follow your own bent.' Illustration to a serial by Agnes Giberne: *Decima's Promise* in the *Girl's Own Annual*, 1881. This story emphasised a girl's duties to her family.

This was how Mrs George de Horne Vaizey (herself, one infers, a Cambridge girl) put her heroine's choice in *A College Girl* in 1913. Darsie goes to Newnham, but the author wanted to give her readers the brutal facts.

May Wynne, later to abandon her youthful highmindedness and for forty years to flog her imagination to invent madder and madder schoolgirl 'scrapes,' reproved.

'We hear it is said that the tender womanly woman of fifty years ago is fading away, and her place is filled all too inadequately by the brisk, business, or masculine female of the end of the nineteenth century . . .

'Nowadays many girls throw their superabundant energy into games of an athletic sort, and hockey, cricket, tennis, golf, etc., take the place of the more languid amusements of a previous generation; but surely this is only selfishness cropping up again in another form? – more healthy, perhaps, but threatening to rob us of the tender womanly woman, so dear to all, but alas! so rarely seen.'

(Life's Object, or Some Thoughts for Young Girls, 1899)

There were stories of staunch girls who put the dizzy temptations of Girton behind them, and nobly took up chicken farming to prop up the sinking family fortunes – to be told by their erstwhile head-mistress that it was all a character test and, the girls having won through, they could go to college with a scholarship. Other stories showed girls who did yield to temptation and study away at their Euclid and algebra while overworked mothers wasted away into a decline and little brothers developed brain fever unheeded.

Some girls contrived to have a career and yet sacrificed nothing of their womanliness, as in Ellinor Davenport Adams' *Miss Secretary Ethel* (1898). Ethel has had a boy's education and knows Greek *and* shorthand. She goes off to be secretary to Sir Edgar, a slow-witted baronet (Eton and Christ Church). He resents Ethel, who reminds him of his dead daughter, but she makes herself necessary to him. Not only does she speak in his place at an important political meeting, she also saves his reputation as a bird watcher by contributing under his name a skilfully written article (with classical allusions) to the local paper, when despite her advice, he has made a frightful howler about the migratory habits of birds. Still he resents her, and it is only when she rescues him from a nasty accident that he takes her to his heart and adopts her as a daughter. After that her secretarial days are over. She devotes herself to filial duties, scribbles a little in her spare time, but not primarily to please herself, of course. 'No pains could be too great which could win for her the reward of Sir Edgar's proud glance and word of approval.'

But however much their elders did try to gloss over the fact and persuade them how happy they were as daughters, girls were chafing to escape from home. If they could not in fact, then they could vicariously, and one of the new ways to do so was through school fiction.

Even in the 1880s, with Charlotte Yonge still firmly in the saddle, it was generally felt that the fiction that was deemed safe for growing girls was limp and lacked 'go' – as Edward Salmon, writing in the *Nineteenth Century* on *What Girls Read* complained in 1886. 'The teaching which comes of girls' books amounts to this. If you are wicked you

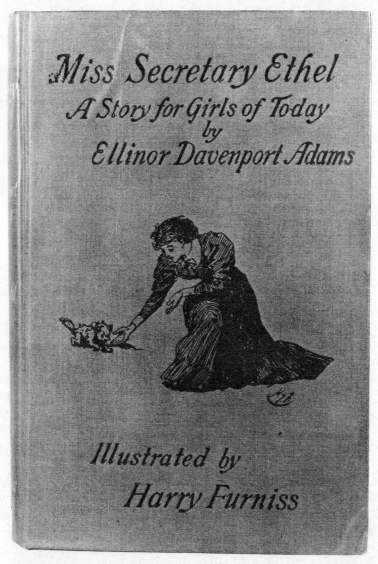

The yielding femininity of Ethel, ever subservient to the male, was stressed throughout this book.

must reform, and when you have reformed you will die! Good young people are not allowed to see many years of life.' And he quoted as an example a tale by Sarah Doudney where the heroine, once she had conquered her great sin of conceit, rushed off to nurse a step-sister with smallpox, caught the disease, was so disfigured that the man she loved deserted her, rushed off again, to nurse cholera this time and to die a noble death.

This was the sort of story which was put into the hands, in the jargon of the time, 'of growing maidens who are beyond the child story and need to have their ideal of love and courtship elevated and refined'. Maidens in those days grew for a long time, and the *Girl's Own Paper*, which was founded in 1880 to provide them with wholesome reading, catered for an age range of twelve to twenty-five. It is hardly surprising that the fiction that was supposed to cover the needs of them all should have pleased very few of them. The younger girls in particular wanted something with more life, and turned to their brothers' school and adventure stories. The author of *Girls and their Ways* was one of the many who noticed this, and remarked what a pity it was that they had not their own school stories.

'There is plenty of material. I have heard of exciting snow-ball matches at the ghostly midnight hour, of surreptitious suppers, of generous acts of self-denial, of undaunted courage in the midst of danger, of sturdy championship of the weak and timid.'

He spoke prophetically; forty years on and he would have been hard put to it to find a girl's book that did not contain one of those ingredients. But in 1881 the girls' schools had still to absorb all the boys' public school ethos – the prefect system and the organised games and the house system – which was to make them such fascinating places to those who read about them. M. V. Hughes' account of the North London Collegiate in the 1880s, dominated by obsessive counting of marks, the myriads of rules, the girls' terror of Miss Buss, would hardly provide the right sort of background. Nor would Ellerslie, the select private school in Manchester where Angela Brazil was sent. She described it in *My Own Schooldays* (1925). It was a place where 'education was combined with refinement,' where manners were carefully attended to, the surroundings were civilised and dignified, and a high standard of work and of ordered behaviour was exacted and received. Prettily dressed, they trod the highly polished floors in dainty shoes; they were expected to look, behave and think like ladies. Angela Brazil spoke of the good teaching she received there, the intense loyalty felt by its pupils, and yet there was something lacking. There were no games, no exercise beyond weekly drill, no acting, no lending library, and above all, no prefects. In short, Ellerslie was a collection of individuals, whereas she yearned to be welded into a community.

'When I go to see modern girls' schools and know what jolly times they have with games and clubs and acting, I feel I have missed a very great deal . . . If we had had prefects, and had ever been taught the elements of citizenship and social service, and that our school was a world in miniature where we might help one another, it would, I think, have brought in a totally different element. I should have been proud to know those wonderful elder girls who never noticed me, and to have some excuse for mingling with the little ones . . . How I should have adored the privileges of the modern head-girl!'

Apparently multitudes felt the same; not only girls who wanted to read about such miniature worlds, but writers who delighted in evoking a way of life that they had missed. It was to meet this need that the Girl Guide movement was started in 1911, and it is significant that the years of its greatest popularity in the 1920s and 30s coincided with an apparently inexhaustible craving for school stories. What girls seemed to want then was organisation, strenuous group activities, an appearance of self-government, and institutions which commanded *esprit de corps*. They delighted in codes of laws and in uniforms, and if they could not belong to such a body then they would read about it.

Angela Brazil is usually credited with creating the school story as it is parodied by its detractors; larky and slangy accounts of whoops in the dorm and tussles on the hockey pitch.

'"What's the matter? Zepps?" [Irene asks as her friends wake her.]
"No, no; it's your birthday party. Look!" beamed the others.

On a chair by her bedside stood the cake, resplendent with its sixteen little lighted candles and also the tin of condensed milk. Irene blinked at them in amazement.

"Jubilate! What a frolicsome joke!" she exclaimed. "I say, this is awfully decent of you!"

"We told you you'd wake up in better spirits, old sport," purred Marjorie.'[1]

[1] *A Patriotic Schoolgirl* (1919).

'Drawing herself up to her full height, the head girl assumed her most prefectorial air. "Please remember that you are speaking to a prefect."'
A school story of the 1930s, when authority was a favourite topic. Illustration from the British Girls' Annual, Amalgamated Press.

But this did not come all at once. In her first book, *The Fortunes of Philippa* (1906) school only plays a small part in Philippa's life, and is as unpleasant an experience as Bush House was to the narrator in *Six to Sixteen*. (The book in fact is very reminiscent of Mrs Ewing, whom Angela Brazil greatly admired.) The girls are over-governessed in their strict seminary and Philippa eventually collapses from overwork. There is, however, an interesting account of the sort of girls' schools available then and the attitude taken towards them.

'"I wish we went to Ecclestone, where our cousins go; it's exactly like a boys' public school; they have a matron to do all the mending, and the girls play football."

"I know they do," said Millicent, "and Mother says it is *most* unladylike. We know several girls who go there, and they behave so badly, sitting on the edges of the drawing-room tables, and gulping their tea, and bolting their cake, and talking the most atrocious slang."

"My sister goes to St Chad's," said Ellinor Graham, "and they weigh the girls every time they go back. They won't let them do any work if they're not 'up to standard,' and Patty's so thin that she's always 'turned out to grass' as they call it, for at least a fortnight at the beginning of each term. I think she has a lovely time."

"Yes, but you have to wear the school costume at St Chad's, even in church," put in Doris. "And it's ever so ugly – a frightful blue serge gym costume sort of arrangement, and a cricket-cap."'

It seems that in 1906 the ladylike ideal still lingered, and the 'modern girl' did not – in the eyes of her elders at least – yet hanker for a boisterous, gregarious life where everybody lived and dressed uniformly. Mrs George de Horne Vaizey,[1] who was writing school stories at this time, created establishments like Angela Brazil's own Ellerslie, where femininity and daintiness reigned. The school party in *Pixie O'Shaughnessy* (1903) sets the thirty pupils (the only guests) in a flutter. The floor has been sponged with milk until it is slippery, there are tables supplied with lemonade, gingerbeer and sweet biscuits, and the violin pupils take it in turn to accompany the piano. Everybody has a pretty little programme, pink for the ladies, blue for the 'gentlemen', and between dances the couples promenade, con-

[1] She began writing under the name of Jessie Mansergh.

'Pixie brought it right round the neck of Mademoiselle.' As long as
girls were 'straight', boisterous frolics were condoned. Illustration
by W. H. C. Groome from *Pixie O'Shaughnessy* by
Mrs George de Horne Vaizey (1903)

versing sedately 'and tabooing the affairs of ordinary school life'.
It is still at that date perfectly proper to introduce a romantic
situation between a young man and an older girl into the school
story, 'elevating and refining', of course, and ending in marriage, but
twenty years later a banished ingredient. Not that romance was

abandoned, far from it, but the love was female for female and thus apparently, in the eyes of those who wrote for girls, far more proper. One must assume that these authors, like Ernest Raymond in the previous chapter, had not the faintest idea in this instance what they

Jacket design for *The Honour of the School*, by May Wynne (Nisbet, 1919). This jacket was not intended to suggest romantic adventure to girl readers; Thelma and the young soldier were only 'chums'.

were writing about. '"I have fallen in love,"' announces a girl, but adds as she sees the adult's scandalised face, "'with a girl so it doesn't matter."'

L. T. Meade, who wrote this, was an extreme example. Most of the pre-1930 books recorded the adoration of girls for mistresses, the petting of pretty, smaller girls, the hero-worshipping of prefects, the devotion between friends who swore deathless fidelity, went round arm in arm, wrote each other sentimental notes, suffered furious jealousy when an attachment was waning. Marjorie's passion for Chrissie could 'flame at red heat' with perfect propriety. A book by Elsie J. Oxenham, whose Abbey Girls series was very popular in the 1930s, even opened: 'Con and Norah were a recognised couple. Con . . . was the wife and home-maker, Norah . . . the husband.' But most of them stopped short of the extravagances of L. T. Meade, who made the whole of *The School Favourite* (1908) turn on the intense relationship between two girls. They kiss and fondle each other – '"I want you! I want you!" Poppy said with a sob' – and climb into bed together, 'Elizabeth's arm flung round Peggy's neck, their cheeks touching, their young figures close together'.

Her school books are interesting in the way they show the emotional turmoil of adolescent girls as one of these might herself have written of it. The time for directing this towards religious experience was past – so far as fashions in juvenile books went – and the pop singer had not yet arrived. But to canalise adolescent emotions into a *moral* crisis seemed very proper, and so in at least two of her stories we get a public confession in front of the whole school, which takes on the appearance of the Bedlam that Kingswood School experienced in 1770 after its revival meeting (see page 104).

'No one quite knew what happened next. Some of the girls went off into violent hysterics; others rushed out of the great hall half-fainting; while others controlled themselves and listened as best they could. The scene was vivid and picturesque. Mrs Naylor [a governor] sobbed quite audibly, and took hold of Ruth's hand and even kissed it. But as she did so Kathleen herself came near and flung her arm round Ruth's neck.

"If you mean to expel Ruth you will expel me," she said . . .'

Although some of the books of the Vaizey epoch had certainly finished with marriage, these were sagas where the reader pursued a girlhood into womanhood; the courtship, of course, did not take place while the heroine was *in statu pupillari*. But the later books were to banish such incidents altogether. When males appeared it was only as 'chums'. Girls – at least the sensible ones who are the heroines, of course – treated boys as no different from themselves. If a cousin or a brother wanders into the story he is immediately snapped up by a girl to help in some jolly lark. ' "He knows of a topping farm where we can pay a shilling each and go and eat and pick as many apples as we can carry without a basket." ' And the sensible girl, looking with unuttered contempt at the gigglers and sniggerers, would treat men as she treated boys. ' "There was a man on board – a jolly fellow, about thirty – He and I were good chums." '

So in May Wynne's *The Honour of the School* (1919) fifteen year old Thelma can treat Robert aged nineteen (he strays into Polgrath School to discover the secret that will restore the house to its rightful owner) as just another 'chum'. 'Having been "comrade" all her life with Dad and Dad's many friends, who were her friends too, she really regarded this khaki-clad young hero far more as a boy than most girls of her age would have done.' (With 'a boy' of course there was no sexual attraction at all.) Thelma helps Robert in and out of secret panels and hidden chambers without any feeling that her behaviour could be misunderstood. Her heart throbs with romance, certainly, but because of the thought of the nobility of his actions. He on his part 'did not think of her at all except as a necessary guide. His whole soul was intent on this task – to cleanse a black stain from Pol-grath Manor.' The sight of Thelma's school friends appalls him. ' "Snakes, what a bunch of girls! No fear of their coming out, is there? or I shall scoot!" ' It was worse than a charge against the Huns, he tells Thelma afterwards, or being pounded in a first line of trenches.

Schoolmistresses had changed from the pre-war type, too. Then they had been drooping and feminine. 'Kiss me!' they murmured, lifting dark eyes to favourite pupils who adoringly sponged their aching heads with eau de cologne – a prelude to melting into the arms of the pupils' elder brothers. By the 1920s they were de-sexed. Angela Brazil's Miss Duckworth 'had no tolerance for slackness. She was a breezy, cheery, interesting personality, an inspiring teacher, and excellent at games, taking a prominent part in all matches and tournaments, "Mistresses versus Pupils." Miss Duckworth was immensely popular amongst her girls.'

By this date the ideal schoolgirl had settled down into the pattern she was to maintain for the next twenty years. She was no longer ladylike, nor was she a homebody. In 1910 Angela Brazil's Patty in *The Nicest Girl in the School* was a 'cosy, thoughtful, cheery, lovable, home girl,' with a 'merry, pleasant, sunny, smiling look.' 'Merry' ten years later was still a favourite adjective, but the heroine had to be rather more dashing. 'A tall, slim girl of fifteen, with glowing brunette skin, the merriest hazel eyes, and bobbed hair,' is the heroine of May Wynne's *Peter the New Girl* (1936). 'In her long brown coat and round hat she had rather a boyish appearance, her whole person brimming with vitality . . . enthusiasm . . . the joy of life.' These girls wore their hair short; they might well insist on being called by a boy's name – Bobby, Tom, Johnnie. 'These splendid, jolly, healthy-minded, keen lassies' – as the *British Girl's Annual* called the type in 1930. Nor were they just the darling of the women writers; we meet them, 'clean-limbed', striding over the Scottish grousemoors with John Buchan.

The wild Irish girl who had to be broken in to sedate English boarding school ways was a favourite. So was the spoilt only child from a luxurious home, or the wilful and wayward one, accustomed to having her own way. She might have initial faults which would make her unpopular at first, but she was fearless and utterly straight, of course. '"She may bring a few spiders and beetles – or strew your floor with leaves and Mother Earth, but she'll never sneak or squeak."' Fun was what she was after; without it there was not much point in school – '"I fear me ye summer term at Hilford House is going to be a wash-out"' – and her teachers are tolerant on the whole. 'Mademoiselle and Miss Dale, being young themselves, had a tender spot for lassies whose sport was clean, even if at times audacious.' Though practical jokes can go too far, such as the time when Maisie puts an inflatable rubber ball under Mademoiselle's salt beef and dumplings, and persuades that poor lady, who has a horror of mice, that it is a mouse under the tablecloth making her plate rise and fall in that alarming way.

The real crimes of mean-spirited girls are cheating and sneaking and cigarettes and 'stupid, idiotic books' smuggled in from the local library. The author of *Girls and their Ways* knew all about them in real life; the sneak who not only bore tales, but tipped ink over copybooks, unpicked needlework, spilt water over drawings and spread malicious gossip. Also the toady and the backbiter. Without them, he thought, 'school becomes a kind of Eden in this workaday world.'

No. 1 OF A NEW PAPER! GRAND PLATE GIVEN FREE! OVER £100 IN PRIZES!

The Schoolgirls' Own

NOT WANTED! "You can clear out, Betty Barton!" exclaimed the snobbish girl. "We've no use for Council School kids here!" (See "Scorned by the School!" in this issue.)

2ᴰ

No. 1. Vol. 1.] PUBLISHED EVERY TUESDAY. [Week Ending February 5th, 1921.

The snobbish girl was often made a villainess. (No. 1, vol. 1, Feb. 5, 1921)

Some girls stopped at trying to influence the course of school elections with bribes of mint humbugs; others, like Angela Brazil's Netta ('rather deficient in moral fibre') were prepared to forge votes for the ballot on the Fifth Form tennis champion, to crib and to blackmail another into writing a prize essay on Carlyle for her. The reader can usually recognise the villainess because of her heavy features and the fact that she does not 'grin' or 'beam' or 'purr', but 'drawls' instead. And of course she did not have the honest, fearless eyes of the heroine. '"Don't you tell me there's any nasty, secrety ways in her, for I won't believe it. You've only to look in the child's eyes[1] to see she's honest and sweet as a May-Day."'

The favourite schoolgirl was gregarious. To come to boarding school was regarded as a privilege, for which she had often to struggle. She was sometimes even known to dress up in the uniform of the school she watched enviously (her parents, perhaps, wished to keep her at home with governesses) and act out a fantasy existence as a schoolgirl.

For school uniform was no badge of servitude; it had become the symbol of privilege. Nobody sat viciously on their Panamas or kicked the regulation felt cloche round the cloakroom. They did not wrench off striped ties and stuff them into their pockets when they were out of sight of prefects. They were proud to show that they belonged – whether it was to the Guide movement or to their school.

'This plate of Princess Mary in her Guide uniform,' said the first issue of the *Schoolgirls' Own* in 1921, 'is one you can frame and hang in your den, so that you can turn to it each day, resolving to become as fine a girl as she, and to make yourself as splendid a Guide as you know how.'

Towards their schools they feel deep devotion. These were only small establishments of between twenty and forty girls, but they commanded the same feeling as the famous boys' foundations with five hundred years of history behind them. '"Every girl when on parade

---

[1] To assess a character by looking its owner in the eye has always been a favoured English technique, particularly among the public school educated classes. Elizabeth Bowen, in *The Heat of the Day*, makes one of her characters remember ruefully his father's insistence that he and his son should look each other in the eye. 'There used to be convulsions of awkwardness when we literally couldn't unlock our looks. I suppose I could draw you a map today of every vein in his iris. The jelly of an eye . . . has been unseemly to me ever since.'

has the reputation of Brackenfield in her keeping,''' the headmistress in *A Patriotic Schoolgirl* tells a hushed assembly, '"So strong has been the spirit not only of loyalty to the school, but of innate good breeding, that up to this day our traditions have never yet been broken . . ."' (Alas, on this occasion sixteen girls have 'trailed the Brackenfield standard in the dust' by breaking out of line to cheer a French airman). The head girl feels the same and gives news of the war efforts of Old Girls.

'"Mary Walker has been nursing for fifteen months at a hospital in Cairo. She found many opportunities for interesting expeditions in her off-duty. She went for camel rides to visit the tombs in the desert, had moonlight journeys to the Pyramids, and sailed up the Nile."

"Lilian Roy has finished her motoring course at a training school. She had her van in the City during the last raid, and took refuge in a cellar . . . You see what splendid work our old Brackenfielders are doing in the world."'

Esprit de corps and zeal for games dominate the girls' stories between the wars as they had dominated the boys' stories rather earlier. The *British Girl's Annual* urged its readers to tell the editor what they wanted both for that annual and for *Little Folks*, its companion. The stories that they were subsequently given by such writers as Angela Brazil, Dorothea Moore, Ethel Talbot and Christine Chaundler presumably satisfied them. The 1930 volume brings hockey matches into nearly every story. Girls half-concussed, blinded with blood, stagger on to the pitch to score the winning goal – 'Stressa's unconquerable spirit must conquer half-stunned brain.' There are cries of '"To win matches for St Gabriel's we need grit, grip and *grind*"' and the threat of cancelling a hockey match as a punishment sends a whole form into convulsions of horror. Rules are a delight, not a burden, and everybody is thrown into a turmoil at the thought of a minor infringement – was Katie three feet out of bounds when she picked the flower?; 4a have let down the whole school by going out carol-singing, but luckily it was on a side of the town where they would not be recognised. Forms hang poised on a knife edge to know the result of the 'prees' ' [prefects'] meeting, the ballot for form captain. Hours are spent happily arranging duty rosters, finding officers for the school societies; the attention to every detail of school uniform borders on fanaticism.

The adolescent emotions that we have seen spilt out over evangelical experience, charitable works, filial pieties, sentimental friendship, have now been directed towards school.

'"I seem to have been panting for years for a game – to laugh, and shout, and sing . . . to have adventures, to be alive. You see, I've had to dream – always dream – and, though dreams are lovely, and though I've read all the books I could find about knights and heroes and splendid adventures . . . I've never been able to join in anything of the kind."'

But now she is an *alumnus* of Hilford House – all is well.

[10]

The child's heroes

I
A girl's choice

'I SUPPOSE I enjoyed them,' wrote Patricia Beer in 1968 of the books that adult taste had prescribed as 'good' in her childhood forty years before. 'I certainly did not resent or avoid them.' She was writing of *Robinson Crusoe*, *Alice*, *Little Women* and the rest, which had washed over her and left her unmoved compared to the lesser literature which she had read and re-read obsessively. None of the children's classics contained the objects of identification that she needed and found elsewhere.

This, sadly, is what is apt to happen to the book that adults thrust into children's hands. However well-written, however much previous generations have enjoyed it, when it reaches the status of prescribed reading a book's interest wanes. A child wants to find his hero for himself. He may choose it from literature that his elders consider subversive, or from that mass of material that they accept without enthusiasm, but it is not likely to be one that they would actively recommend. And though it is usually taken from a book of the moment, the qualities that children require of their heroes and heroines vary from generation to generation far less than the adult ideals. Naturally the needs of the sexes differ, as do the different age-groups, but we can trace a universal heroine such as Cinderella in say, Fatherless Fanny and Sara Crewe, and detect Jack the Giant Killer in Tarzan far more easily than we can reconcile Harry Sandford with Tom Brown.

The chapter that Patricia Beer devotes to her childhood reading in the 1920s and 30s in *Mrs Beer's House* is particularly interesting on two counts. It is engagingly frank, and it has the common touch. Too many of those who have given an account of their childhood reading have had precociously literary or intellectual tastes; others have not

The Giant endeavouring to do the trick which Jack did kills himself.

At breakfast, much the Giant stares,
For leathern bag Jack slily wears;
In which he cunningly convey'd,
The hasty pudding which was made;
Jack rip'd it open to surprize,
The Giant does the same and dies.

Jack the Giant Killer, a favourite hero of the young Georgian, was abhorred by all educational authorities.

been content to be so honest. A survey conducted among girls of eleven to nineteen in 1886, for instance, put favourite authors in this order: Dickens, Scott, Kingsley, C. M. Yonge, Shakespeare, Elizabeth Wetherell, Mrs Henry Wood, George Eliot, Lord Lytton, Longfellow, A.L.O.E. — only three writers for the young among them and those irreproachably improving. Edward Salmon, commenting on the selection, was sceptical.

There is another interesting point about her reading. She grew up at a time when there was perhaps less officious guidance over what was good and what was 'trash' in children's reading since the pre-Trimmer days. My experience in the 1930s was the same. It was possible then for the bookish child to be far less self-conscious in his choice of reading than he is in the 1970s. We knew of course that it was good to read Dickens and Scott, that a child who wanted to do well in general knowledge tests and the more tiresome sort of party games had better get through *Treasure Island* and *Kidnapped* and *The Water Babies*, and those things that the elders lumped together as 'classics', but the books that were being written for us during that period were in general an uncharted sea, and we were considered as capable of making our way through it ·as anybody else. School libraries like Patricia Beer's undoubtedly did then hold a lot that present-day teachers, steeped in the reviews of the educational journals, primed by conferences, would reject and replace by recommended authors. Girls are usually very suggestible, more anxious to please than boys when young, and so an opportunity to see what one would choose when left without direction is valuable.

The Beer family had no great literary pretensions; the mother was a primary school teacher, the father a railway clerk. They were Plymouth Brethren, members of an extreme evangelical sect, who carried into the twentieth century the distrust for the works of the imagination that we associate with the evangelical movement of the early nineteenth century. This explains why Patricia at an early age was given the street arab stories of writers of fifty or sixty years before, stories like *Little Meg's Children* and *Jessica's First Prayer* and *Christie's Old Organ* by Hesba Stretton and Mrs O. F. Walton. Published by the Religious Tract Society, they were certainly as much concerned with salvation as the Plymouth Brethren could have desired, but this was not why Patricia loved them. They fascinated her by their melodrama, for the delicious feeling of danger that could be safely enjoyed from a state of security. When the family came up from Devon on one of their day expeditions to London she could peer into an alleyway with horrified excitement, certain that down there, only a stone's throw from the broad well-lit thoroughfare in Westminster where she was walking so safely with her mother and sister, lurked danger, vice, disease; buildings that reeked with fumes of gin and tobacco and rang with the sound of groans, curses, and sobs. She liked the stories too because the children in the end won through, because comfort followed the suffering.

Vicarious suffering, when it is remote from your own doorstep and when it has a happy ending with the good and virtuous rewarded, has a great appeal. For girls it is linked with the wish to comfort and mother. Gwen Raverat in her account of her childhood in *Period Piece* described her bedtime fantasy of 'being kind to Pamela,' whom she nightly rescued from the cold and the wolves. 'And you put her into your own bed, and warmed her, and fed her, and comforted her most tenderly. This made you feel frightfully good and kind.'

It is a fantasy that countless other girls have shared, it is linked with the Cinderella story, and it is perhaps best realised in fiction by Frances Hodgson Burnett, a writer who in many ways never left her childish dreams behind but lived them out and wrote about them with unselfconscious abandon. In *A Little Princess* she describes how Sara Crewe, once rich, now poor, the drudge of cruel Miss Minchin's school, cold, hungry, forlorn – though still able to quell her persecutors by her dignity and courage – awakes in her cheerless garret to find it transformed into a place of warmth and light, full of colour and comfort. It is a moment that few girls can resist, and that many return to obsessionally, as they do to the scenes in the same book when the contemptible Miss Minchin is morally vanquished by her small pupil's superior knowledge and good breeding.

An earlier version of Sara Crewe was *Fatherless Fanny, or The Little Mendicant* (1811). Fanny, a girl of immaculate virtue, staggering beauty, compelling personality and unknown parentage, is left in Sara Crewe style in a young ladies' seminary, and is treated with either crawling deference or cruel contempt (according to whether the fees have been paid or not). She is adopted by a dashing young peer who is hoaxed by his friends into thinking that he is going to claim a lost dog, and passes through many a vicissitude before she discovers her parents and marries a duke. It was a great favourite with girls of two generations until it became recommended reading and so lost all its flavour.

Sara Crewe, poor and friendless, quelling her tyrannical teacher. Illustration
by Reginald Birch to *Sara Crewe*, 1888, the original version of *A Little
Princess* (1905).

Fanny and Sara are not only orphans who are translated from rags to riches, they have the additional attraction of being morally superior to the adults around them. This last quality was, as we have seen, a feature of many evangelical books. We find it in the compilations of pious deathbeds where the admiring adults cluster round to hear the last eloquent words of the departing child. When these were outmoded they were succeeded by the still morally superior child rebuking his elders and persuading them to abjure drink and swearing and open their hearts to heavenly influence. They might be matchgirls or boot-blacks, or rich curly-headed orphans plunged into households where the heart, not the hearth, had grown cold. But they were the ones to whom grace had been given to lead others heavenwards, and it was a type dearly loved by girls.

Few of these waifs had parents, and if they had they were poor broken reeds who had to be propped by their offspring. Patricia Beer had found the absence of parents one of the great attractions of Christie and Meg and Jessica. It is also one of the charms of Fatherless Fanny and Sara Crewe. The mother-child relationship has always presented difficulties for the author, and even Charlotte Yonge, who strove in all her domestic novels to show girls their duties in the home, was happiest when, as in *The Daisy Chain* and *The Pillars of the House*, she had sent the mother off in a decline in the first chapters or had otherwise disposed of her. Mothers have a constricting effect on the plot and on the children's activities; their love is so embarrassingly obvious that it can't be overlooked, it stands in the way of that independence that children like to imagine. This is perhaps one of the reasons why the excellent mid-Victorian family stories did not achieve great popularity. Their authors were at pains to show a happy, normal domesticity with a proper complement of parents, but it would, alas, have been so much more exciting to read about orphans fighting their lone battles, or a father comforted by an understanding little daughter, or a child who was misunderstood instead of one who was understood all too well. The writers of the holiday adventure stories which made such a showing on the juvenile book lists from the 1930s to the 1950s recognised the impossibility of fitting mothers into their scheme and they were removed from the scene of action within a paragraph or so; a decline or death in childbirth no longer being so conveniently likely, they could always be sent for to attend somebody else's sickbed.

When Patricia Beer had grown out of her orphans she turned to school stories. To a large extent these have now been ousted by the pony story, but they both satisfy the same pre-adolescent craving to belong to an elite, a clique, a gang, with its particular mystique and clothes and allusions, where outsiders are spurned, and only the initiated can understand the jokes and slang. Angela Brazil, who carried into old age her hankering for the prefects and the uniforms, the organised games and the unorganised larks that had been lacking in her own cultured and beautifully civilised establishment, supplied these needs, together with a host of other writers in the 1920s and 30s. They did not find it possible to involve themselves so closely with the characters in their fictitious schools that they could do without melodramatic elements – the girl who cheats, sabotage in the school play, spies, secret panels, buried treasure. The reader might enjoy the story in this type of book but did not identify herself with the school in it.

Elinor Brent-Dyer was one of a handful of writers who succeeded in inventing a school whose domestic doings alone could grip the reader. Her Chalet School series began in 1925 and ran for thirty years, and provided day by day – sometimes hour by hour – details of the lives of the inmates which only created among her fans a raging thirst for more. The author's own pleasure in the smallest detail of who acted what in the school theatricals, the games they play at the Christmas party, what clothes they change into and at what time, who is going to do Break Duty or take charge of Junior Library, is infectious. There is an atmosphere of calm security in this world where nobody wants to grow up, and examinations and careers are barely mentioned. The setting in the Austrian Tyrol at once removes the school from reality and saves it from being humdrum. School tea becomes delightful when it is transformed into *Kaffee und Kuchen*, and school walks glamorous when taken by the side of glaciers. And there is always Matron standing by ready to bundle anybody with wet feet straight into bed with hot milk and a bottle, and Dr Jem to minister to the more serious cases.

Enid Blyton also ministered to the girl's taste for comfort and security. Her Famous Five and Secret Seven might have encountered every desperado on the Interpol calendar, but they know and we know that they are always perfectly safe. They can roam Dartmoor and tramp the fells in the calm certainty that when they are hungry and tired there will be a rosy-cheeked farmer's wife standing on her doorstep, waiting to welcome them with cream teas and put them to bed between lavender-scented sheets. Everybody is their friend, except the criminals whom of course they will outwit.

In the easy uncritical days of the 30s and 40s Enid Blyton attracted very little attention. It was only in the 1950s when she was increasing her output (in 1950, for instance, which was a peak year, she published some thirty-two titles) that a storm of indignation broke out. Educationists thundered, librarians vetoed, the fastidious mother drew back her skirt. She was held to be intellectually and morally corrupting, and there was no end to the dangers that lurked in her flat, innocent sentences. If the critics had remembered the

Noddy, loved by the small child and execrated by his teachers.

parallel of Mrs Trimmer who made herself look so foolish to future generations when she denounced the fairy tale, they might have paused.

They reserved their special shafts for the little toy elf, Noddy. Noddy was a great figure in the lives of small children. He was somebody they could pity for being weaker and more helpless than themselves, but also love because of his willing kindness, and envy because he had a little car. When in trouble Noddy turns to Mr Big Ears, and he sets matters right – as Enid Blyton assumed all parents would. *Be Brave, Little Noddy* exhorted one of the titles, when Noddy's car had broken and he had gone tearfully to Mr Big Ears. '"You're going to show everyone how plucky you are, and how you can laugh when things go wrong,"' Mr Big Ears tells him.

'"Am I?" said Noddy.

"Of course you are," said Mr Big Ears. "Now let's make up a Brave Song . . . Think of a really nice Brave Song."'

And after a struggle to swallow down the tears, Noddy manages to quaver out his little rhyme.

> *Oh what does it matter*
> *If things go wrong.*
> *I'll sing and I'll whistle*
> *The whole day long.*
> *I'll go on smiling,*
> *I'll laugh, ho, ho!*
> *And brave as a soldier*
> *You'll see me go.*

This would have escaped without comment in the pre-war decades, but was anathema in the 1950–70 period when it seemed vitally important to all responsible adults that the child should be reared from the start on a robust literary style, and encouraged to come out from his cosy, thumb-sucking corner and look the world square in the face.

The last phase of Patricia Beer's pre-adult reading was the most deeply felt of all. She fell in love with a man and an ideal, with Ewen Cameron and the Jacobite cause in D. K. Broster's *The Flight of the Heron*. 'Looking back I feel sad,' she said. 'The feelings it roused in me were not about anything real, yet I have experienced nothing stronger since. Loch na h'Iolaire and the house of Ardroy, Ewen

Cameron and Keith Windham never existed, yet they brought me a unique joy. I have never known a greater love for any person or any land, nor half such an ardent loyalty to any cause.' Ewen Cameron was to her what the current pop star is to the younger teen-ager of the 1970s, an outlet for all the pent-up emotion that the evangelicals tried to canalise into religious experience. It was also a way of life. Charlotte Yonge's heroines had felt the same about the Cid and the Black Prince. They too dreamed lofty dreams, about chivalry and romance and the mission field and the noble savage bowing his knee to Christ. Charlotte Yonge's particular hero was Charles I, her cause the Royalist one. Many of Patricia Beer's contemporaries and their mothers before them would have waded through blood to follow the Scarlet Pimpernel, persuading themselves that it was for love of the *ancien régime*.

They were all at an age that wanted to idealise, who needed a hero who seemed to soar above sex. Patricia adored Ewen confident that he did not concern himself with women. True he has a wife, but it is clear that she makes no demands upon him, and that she accepts without repining the fact that his loyalties to his clan come above all else. There are four men in his life: Prince Charles Edward – but he is a symbol rather than a personality – Lochiel, the clan's chief; his brother Archie, and Keith Windham, the English officer whom young Cameron takes prisoner. With the last three of these he is involved in what the cynical adult eye of today would recognise as definitely erotic situations, but to the rapturous adolescent (I was one myself) of thirty years ago seemed a pure and selfless love. The chaste sexuality of these was intensely satisfying, though most readers would not have been consciously aware there was any sexual element about them.

There is a stage in the reading of most girls where romance is needed without sex. There are hosts of writers ready to provide this, and in the earlier decades of the twentieth century some who found it possible to do so with an all-female cast and still satisfy the young person. Patricia Beer was addicted to the L. M. Montgomery chronicles of life on Prince Edward Island, Canada – the stories of Anne of Green Gables and her girl friends, where there is childbirth certainly but nothing to indicate how this has come about. In England in the 1920s and 30s Elsie J. Oxenham carried this world of intense female relationships even further with her novels of the Abbey Girls. The husbands, if there are any, count for little beside the

The Scarlet Pimpernel

BARONESS ORCZY

The girl's hero – Sir Percy Blakeney, the languid aristocrat, a man of steel and decision for all his elegance.

support that the closely-knit circle of girls give to each other. They suffer each other's griefs acutely and rejoice in their triumphs, and much emotion is expended on the suffering that characters endure when female friends are torn from them by marriage. Their pleasures are simple; the thought of a week's course of folk-dancing at Chelsea Polytechnic sends girls nearly demented with excitement, and to spend the night on the floor of a friend's room in a hostel (with full permission from authority) the height of daring. The great popularity of these romances without any masculine element shows that there was a large public who wanted just that.

Children's reading seems to fall into three categories: the books adults promote; those that they merely tolerate, and 'trash' which they would like to withhold altogether. Adult opinion, as we have seen, has wavered from generation to generation. Imagination, considered so dangerous by the pre-Victorians, is now prized above all other qualities – 'stretch the child's imagination' is a catch phrase of the 1970s. We are in a phase when literary style is felt to be far more important than moral conduct; a child needs to be stimulated; to be 'improved' not by elevating his ideals, but intellectually by contact with well-written, testing material; to be encouraged to face the darker aspects of life both within and without himself. Enid Blyton would have been considered wholesome enough by the late Victorians and Edwardians; within a framework of unlikely adventure she showed happy homes where kindness and affection and trust were the qualities that mattered. But her style was undistinguished, her vocabulary limited; worse still, her readers became Blyton-addicted, therefore the 1950s and 60s classed her as 'trash'.

'Trash' is difficult to define, especially where the girl's story is concerned. To most elders it would seem to mean that sort of book that makes for compulsive, easy reading to the exclusion of anything better. Girls have not, on the whole, the boys' taste for violence and crime which present more obvious perils; adults fear more from the effects of prolonged exposure to 'light' literature. We have seen what novels did to Miss Woodland's Agatha in 1810 (see p. 35). They became such a drug that she was a prisoner of her own dreamworld, and she grew incapable of dealing with real life. Edward Salmon in 1886 deplored the penny novelettes that working class girls read; he suspected that 'the high-flown conceits and pretensions of the poorer girls of the period, their dislike of manual work and love of freedom spring largely from these. It would be a moral benefit to sweep all

girls' papers but the *Girl's Own Paper* and *Every Girl's Paper* from
the face of the earth.'

Vapid romance rather than outright immorality would have been
the main ingredient of these. For younger girls the equivalent would
have been, in the between-the-wars period before the pop-culture
developed, the highly coloured adventure, reduced perhaps to strip
cartoons. Obviously, the greater the literacy of the home the higher
the adult's expectations of his young. *Peter Pan*, desired reading for
many, was banned by at least one intellectual family. Mrs Beer
called Patricia's schoolgirl stories 'trash.' They were all borrowed
from the school library, and were no doubt harmless enough, but
Mrs Beer probably felt that her child's addiction to them was insidious. But her idea of what a 'good' book was was vague. She read
Gene Stratton Porter's *Freckles* and Helen Mather's *Comin' Thro' the
Rye* to her daughters. Both abound in sticky sentimentality, and
Comin' Thro' the Rye, where fathers are represented as tyrannical,
clergy as smugly hypocritical, and religious observance as tedious
and meaningless, could be thought decidedly subversive by people
far less strict than Plymouth Brethren.

Adults have always been distrustful of children's escape reading.
They accept the need for escape, but they like to dictate the form
that it should take. Thus a child is encouraged to escape to Narnia
and the Tolkein territories but discouraged from using the cloud
cuckoo lands of holiday adventure for the same purpose. Marghanita
Laski in her introduction to *The Patchwork Book* (1948) – an anthology
of snippets from medieval romance, travellers' stories, translations
from the classical authors – wrote disparagingly of children who
collected train numbers and played at hospitals, and whose imaginary train journeys only took them to Watford Junction – Samark-
hand or Constantinople would have been all right. Perhaps what
adult critics of children forget is this: an adventure that is prescribed
and closely watched by one's elders cannot be very exciting.

II

The boy's demands

'I think it is really easier for a boys' writer to earn a living than it is
for any other writer of juvenile matter,' said Christine Chaundler
ruefully in 1934. She was discussing what sorts of books sold so far as

boys went, and came to the conclusion that it must be one with an exciting plot, a hero of heroic dimensions, a villain of great villainy, and comedy of a primitive sort. She had found, as we have seen (see page 166) that adventure stories were the most popular and that school stories came a poor second. Even writers who commanded a huge and undisputed loyalty, like Bracebridge Hemyng and Frank Richards, had found this, and Jack Harkaway was rapidly taken from school and dispatched to foreign climes, while Billy Bunter, the Owl of the Remove, was sent puffing down the Nile in quest of missing scarabs, or bumbled round Brazil. When the readers of *The Union Jack* were asked to name their favourite stories in that paper in 1894 *The Silver Arrow. A Tale of Adventure with the Indians* was put at the top, followed by *'Neath England's Flag* and *Sexton Blake*.

Boys' reading in fact varied remarkably little over 150 years or so. In the very early years they had the travellers' tales and records of explorers in the *Evangelical Magazine* or *Sandford and Merton* or *Evenings at Home*. Mayne Reid and his contemporaries put fictitious characters in this sort of chronicle and gave them the ghost of a plot; Ballantyne, followed by Henty, Manville Fenn, Percy Westerman and their kind, took on the tradition and sent boys scurrying over pampas and veldt, surging over the seas, cutting their way through forest and jungle, and, as the century advanced and the mood of the country became more warlike, smiting the foe on the various battle-fields of the centuries. Personality mattered little, the adventures were the thing.

One might reduce the personalities to two or three stock types. Victor Neuburg, writing about chapbooks, had brought it down to two: the 'serious hero' like Robin Hood, Jack the Giant-Killer, Guy of Warwick, Tom Thumb or Fortunatus, and the comic hero such as Simple Simon. The boy wanted a killer or a buffoon, and if a little of the latter could creep into the former, so that there was a cunning rogue of the Jack Sheppard sort, so much the better. Robin Hood to Tarzan and Sherlock Holmes and Sexton Blake; Simple Simon to Ally Sloper, Billy Bunter and Just William – there are hundreds of them in popular literature. Sometimes the buffoon could apply himself to the task of defeating villainy. Billy Bunter was known to trip up rascally Greeks while pursuing cream buns, and the *Library Assistant* felt called upon in 1941 to admonish one of the D. C. Thomson publications which was persistently misleading children; one youth aided by a comic Indian could not, they said reprovingly,

rout an Axis division in Libya week after week by the simple
expedient of laying ice-cream in front of tanks.

We might add a third type, The Man of Mystery. He was noted
in an article in a privately printed journal of the 1920s devoted to late

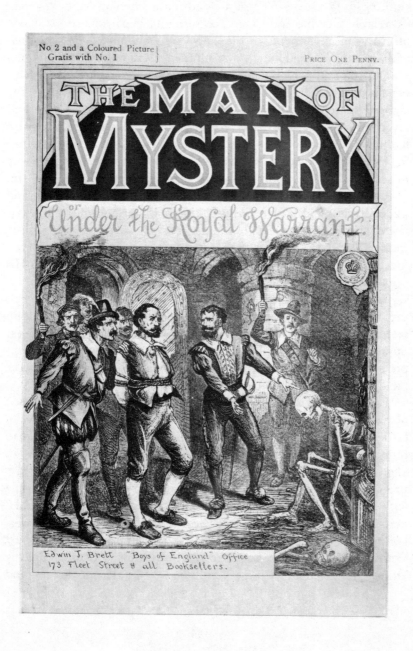

Victorian Penny Dreadfuls[1]. He appeared in many guises, sometimes as a foe, but generally as a friend of the hero, and more often than not in historical fiction. Sometimes he might be a mysterious knight, or a monk, or a dwarf or a Herne the Hunter figure. In the sixteenth century his favourite rôle was a Headsman, when his dark eyes were invariably piercing and his glance keen and sharp, and he sat, when off duty, in apartments in the Tower of London chiefly furnished with grindstones and axes, now and then rising to his feet to touch a blank stone wall which would thereupon swing open quietly revealing an aperture through which he would glide noiselessly. By the eighteenth century the massive muscularity of the Headsman had given way to a tall lithe figure with erect carriage: the deep bass voice had modulated into one pleasant and cultivated but at times assuming an icy, even, emotionless tone; the awesome anger had given way to an incisive biting politeness. But the eyes were as keen; the aim (now with a pistol) as sure, and the stroke (with a rapier) as swift and as deadly as of old. You could find him in Victorian times as Spring-heeled Jack the Terror of London, with his goat's horns sprouting from his forehead and his black bat-like wings, leaping lightly to a first floor window to snatch a swooning damsel from her bed. His appearances, often made in the midst of a spectacular thunderstorm, were usually for the purpose of confounding evil-doers, preferably titled ones. In the twentieth century he changed again into the super hero; there was Tarzan swinging through the trees; Superman (born June, 1938) jumping skyscrapers and racing express trains, and Batman (born 1939) whose feats, though spectacular, had less of the supernatural about them.

'Is it democratic sympathy, or is it that only a terribly thin crust of respectability and of self-restraint covers the old molten fires of lawlessness that lie quiescent beneath the surface of the great mass of humanity?' Howard Pyle asked, discussing the chapbook heroes in 1890. This craving for violence and roguery has always presented a problem for the elders, and many have been the attempts to grapple with it and to provide a safe literature that boys would accept, and a hero on whom they could decently model themselves. There was, however, one that was welcomed by child and adult alike (apart from a few fanatics like Mrs Trimmer) – Robinson Crusoe. Harvey Darton has given an account of his hold over readers of all ages, and

[1] *We Two*. Edited from Inveresk, Midlothian, by Matthew Hunter, 1928–9.

his influence upon writers. The imitations of him were legion, the catalogue of their names fills 'a large painstaking German volume;' the French even gave a name to the genre – *Robinsonnades*. Elders saw all manner of significant lessons to be drawn from his solitary existence; children loved him first because of the fascination of the

Possibly the most popular of all heroes – Robinson Crusoe, shipwrecked and self-sufficient. Illustration by Zwecker for Blackwood's Universal Library of Standard Authors, late nineteenth century.

island and his independence of all authority, and then because of the delicious details of how he contrived to create comfort and order out of savage nature. Hosts of storybook children set out to try to recreate a Crusoe life for themselves (in the older type of story they failed and a moral was thereby drawn). It was the island setting that made *Leila*, Ann Fraser Tytler's early Victorian idyll, so popular that Charlotte Yonge could still, in spite of its romantic, rather high-flown prose, read it aloud to absorbed parish school classes in the 1880s. In-numerable real children recalled their love for Crusoe and his island. It reached across all classes; it was an ever-popular chapbook title, and the more privileged child pored over it in his father's library. Only the twentieth century petrified it, by treating it as a children's classic, and by suggesting that it was a 'good' book that one ought to read, creating an instinctive reaction against it.

Crusoe apart, the folk heroes of the chapbooks were regarded with suspicion as soon as children's reading began to be taken seriously. The tales of the giants and their killers were abhorrent to many, so were the merry pranks of characters like Jack in *The Friar and Boy*. Jack, like some uncouth Orpheus, can play anything on his pipe. He makes horns sprout on the heads of the males, and fixes bells on the noses of the old women; he interrupts the sports of lovers and breaks into a nunnery where the nuns are all lying with friars. Everybody has to caper to his tune until he deigns to stop. As for his stepmother

> *When'er she looks upon me so*
> *Thinking to keep me under,*
> *I with her bum may then let go*
> *And crack like roaring thunder.*

James Catnach of Seven Dials in the pre-Victorian decades aimed some of his immense output of ballads and broadsides and cheap literature at the child consumer. His was the same cheerful irre-sponsibility as Newbery – only he aimed at rather lower incomes. He gave the children what they wanted, and cared nothing for what their elders might say. Among the titles we find 'the adventurous exploits of Robinson Crusoe', 'the treacherous and inveterate hatred that lingered in the bosom of Blue-Beard', 'the amusing story and career of Tom Hickathrift', 'the touching and heart-rending account as portrayed in the story of the Babes in the Wood', 'the adventures of Ali Baba', and 'the ever popular Old Mother Hubbard and her

Wonderful Dog' – tales of villainy and buffoonery all of them, with the exception of Crusoe.

In addition to this subversive literature for the children of the poor there was, after 1773, the Newgate Calendar. This biographical record of the more notorious inmates of the gaol had tremendous fascination, and there were, of course, fuller biographies of prominent individuals like Jonathan Wild the thief taker, Claud Duval, Jack Sheppard, and Dick Turpin, as well as broadsheets detailing the horrid deeds of every criminal who was executed. The Report of the Children's Employment Commission in the 1840s noted with regret that several of the children had never heard the name of the Queen, nor other names such as Nelson, Wellington, Bonaparte; but that those who had never heard even of St Paul, Moses or Solomon were very well-instructed as to the life, deeds and character of Dick Turpin, and especially Jack Sheppard. Like Robin Hood, Turpin and Sheppard achieved folk hero status. They were transformed from common criminals who pursued their own greedy ends into figures of dashing romance who defied oppression and those who sought to grind the poor. Harrison Ainsworth in his novel *Jack Sheppard* (1839) invented aristocratic parentage for his hero, and his journey to the scaffold, after his dauntless efforts to escape from Newgate have been foiled at last, takes on the nature of a triumphal procession. Good wishes pour in from all the mighty of the land, Mr Hogarth, Mr Gay and Sir James Thornhill among them, and the body is snatched from the gallows by his cousin and driven away for sumptuous burial by a carriage and liveried servants. It was Dick Turpin who survived the longest – the object of almost religious veneration. Maurice Willson-Disher commented: 'Children in the 1890s still worshipped him. Whether he robbed the rich to feed the poor mattered less than the plain fact that he successfully kicked over the traces.'

The cunning young criminal was fully aware of the abhorrence that his betters felt for these fascinating stories, and many of them tried their hand at wheedling a lighter punishment by maudlin confession of the bad influence that they had. James Greenwood, a mid-Victorian journalist who denounced the 'gallows literature' which could be bought in 'poison pen'orths' at any low newsvendor, admitted to being sceptical when he saw a small criminal trying this on with a prison governor, and wishing that he had never learnt to read 'cos then I shouldn't have read none of them highwaymen's books, sir; it was them as was the beginning of it'.

32 Pages of Romance of the Highway & a Splendid COLOURED PLATE GRATIS.

PRICE ONE PENNY.

TURNPIKE DICK

The True History of all the Celebrated Highwaymen is given in this Entrancing Story of Olden Times.

Published at 4, Shoe Lane, Fleet Street, London, E.C.; and Sold by all Newsagents.

Nos. 1 & 2.

The poison pen'orths of the 1870s that Greenwood had in mind bore titles like *The Skeleton Band, Tyburn Dick, The Black Knight of the Road, The Boy Burglar* and *Starlight Sal.* And East End audiences could to their great satisfaction see highway robberies with real horses and pistol shots performed at a 'penny gaff' – another of the curses of London to which Greenwood drew attention. The title *The Boy Burglar* and the fact that, according to Greenwood, daggers were being given away with some issues, suggests that these are boys' bloods or penny dreadfuls, published specifically for juveniles. The authorities liked them no better than the Newgate Calendar or Gothic horror type of story aimed at the mass low-minded: the *Quarterly Review*, supporting all Greenwood's sentiments, referred to them as that 'literature which has done much to people our prisons, our reformatories, and our colonies with scapegraces and ne'er-do-wells'. In this century television and horror comics have been similarly denounced. Frederic Wertham's *Seduction of the Innocents* (1954) contended that the increase of juvenile deliquency could be blamed on to the content of some of the more violent comics. He showed illustrations of eyes being gouged out, faces stamped upon, women beaten up, and a macabre baseball game where the base lines were marked out with human intestines, played with a human leg as a bat and a head as a ball.

We have seen in chapter eight some of the valiant efforts of the responsible to provide attractive alternative reading to the literature of violence. 'A pretty book, with plenty of killing,' was what boys wanted, so they were given sanctified violence in the shape of encounters with Indians, school boxing matches, the bloody defeat of pirates, the smiting of England's enemies. With many of these themes now unacceptable to the purest taste, the present decade, to the warm applause of the pundits, has evolved a new one. Here the child, in the jargon of the times, 'comes to terms with himself,' and achieves catharsis through violence. Ivan Southall's *Josh*, for instance, in 1971, is not a whole person until he has been lynched and nearly drowned by the juveniles at Ryan Creek. And in the same writer's *Finn's Folly* (1969) the two adolescent central characters realise themselves in a swirling fog in which three parents have been killed (the corpses lying beside them as they talk things out), a mentally retarded brother lost, and enough cyanide unleashed to poison the whole of Australia.

Few of these attempts really satisfied the craving of the young male.

They were either too tame and girlish, or too literary, and in any case their excitement was killed by the knowledge that adults approved of them. Jack Harkaway was perhaps a compromise. This creation of Bracebridge Hemyng who first appeared in *Boys of England* in 1871 could at a pinch be stomached by the less fastidious parent, while unquestioningly alluring his sons. There was a gentlemanly aura about Jack; his career starts in a public school, followed by Oxford, but as most of his time is spent ragging the authorities – he uses, for instance, his skill as a ventriloquist to make one of his masters say 'frogs' and 'Waterloo' to M Bolivant the French master, thereby fermenting such heat between the two gentlemen that they fight in front of their delighted class – there is nothing in the least improving about it. School however is too small a world to contain Jack, and his

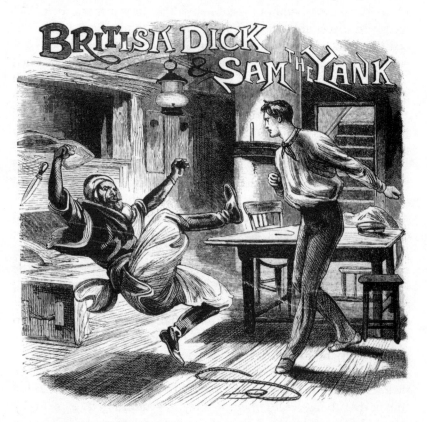

'Dick saw by the light of the lamp that his assailant was Mahmool the Arab.'
Boys like men of deeds and not of words, who can knock the stuffing out of
foreigners. Illustration from *Boys of England*, 1899.

subsequent adventures take him to most trouble spots in the world where he presides over orgies of torturing and butchering calculated to satisfy the most bloodthirsty, and calmly watches his schoolfellows and masters succumbing to the most appalling and painful disasters. But all in all he could be considered a version, at its most extreme remove from the Arnoldian concept, of the manly English boy, a robust and fearless boy with a ready fist for the foreigner and a secret tenderness for female kind.

This brief sketch of earlier reading habits will show how little fundamental change occurred. Biggles, the English boy's hero of the 1930s, only transposes into the age of aeroplanes the dreams of his readers' ancestors. True, he is law-abiding, but like Jack Harkaway he was tolerated rather than recommended by the adult. His creator, Captain W. E. Johns, who produced his first adventures in 1926, took him seriously. He told Geoffrey Trease in 1948:

'I give boys what they want, not what their elders and betters think they ought to read. I teach at the same time under a camouflage . . . I teach a boy to be a man, for without that essential qualification he will never be anything. I teach sportsmanship according to the British idea. One doesn't need blood and thunder to do that. In more than forty novels [Biggles] has only once struck a man, and that was a matter of life and death. I teach that decent behaviour wins in the end as a natural order of things. I teach the spirit of team-work, loyalty to the Crown, the Empire and lawful authority.'

It is of course difficult to deduce from this whether Captain Johns reckoned he was writing improving books or entertaining. But paradoxically it was the improving not the entertaining elements that incurred adult disapproval. Biggles began his career in 1926 when British chauvinism was acceptable, but by 1948 it was considered in very poor taste to say of a man that 'he did not look truly Western European' and to follow it up by announcing that he was everything that was crooked; while twenty-five years later such prejudices could hardly be voiced. They were, however, the negative aspect of something positive; the cult of manliness.

Biggles is the personification of Victor Neuburg's 'serious' hero. He is square-chinned, grey-eyed; he speaks laconically, nods curtly, his face is usually expressionaless. Here is the boy's ideal, a man of deeds, not words, and no silly nonsense about him thinking. On him can be pinned endless adventures (his career begins, in fact, in the Royal Flying Corps in 1916 where we watch him knocking the Hun for six, and goes on to the late 1960s where we see him, now an Air Detective, doing the same to international criminals. With Biggles the boy could escape into the dream-world that a sixteen year old remembered.[1]

> *He clambers up the stairs*
> *like it was a mountain*
> *He'd look down at the bottom*
> *and see crowds of people begging him to come down.*
> *He sprints into the bedroom*
> *dodging the cross-fire from the toilet and the workshop.*
> *Grabbing his Winchester rifle he hurriedly throws a grenade*
> *at the oncoming Germans as they start across the lawn.*
> *Suddenly from behind the gardening hut flash the Seventh Samurai*
> *From the greenhouse smash the Japanese aircraft*
> *blasting at his windowsill*
> *All is lost*
> *But suddenly the Rebs and Feds gallop down the hill*
> *and tear the enemy to shreds.*
> *He is awarded the VC at dinnertime.*
> *Then he goes to acknowledge the crowd in the park arena.*
> *Tomorrow school*
> *and that's a prison camp*
> *But he escapes for tea time*
> *He never dies.*

How much is the child influenced by his chosen heroes or by the patterns that his elders choose to put before him? Did Dick Turpin have the fearful effect that Victorian moralists feared, or Robinson Crusoe send many boys wandering? Did the industry and expansion of Victorian England owe anything to the little manuals that counselled diligence and application in the early 1800s, or the patriotism of the generation whose names are recorded on the memorials of the 1914–18 war derive much from the stories of Henty

[1] By Robert Jones; winner of a poetry competition organised by *The Observer*, 1973.

and his kind? Before we attribute too much to what the young imbibe from their books, perhaps it is salutary to remember the story that Angela Brazil told of her own childhood. She had been given Ballantyne's book *The Robber Kitten*, about a kitten who ran away, proclaiming 'I'll never more be good,' and went to live a bandit's life. Of course he came to grief and limped home to repent, but this point passed over Miss Brazil's head. She was infected by his magnificent and fascinating independence, and she too resisted all authority and stamped round chanting 'I'll never more be good.' She omitted the repentance, naturally.

It should come as an Awful Warning to all of us who write books for children; if we are remembered at all, it may well be for some point we never intended to make.

Book sources

In addition to the books specifically named in the text, the following have been used.

[1] The parting of the ways

Darton, F. J. Harvey: *Children's Books in England*, Cambridge, 1932
Hindley, Charles: *The History of the Catnach Press*, London, 1886
Hindley, Charles: *The Life and Times of James Catnach*, London, 1878
Lamb, Charles: *Letters*, edited by E. V. Lucas, London, 1945
Neuburg, Victor E. R. P.: *The Penny Histories: a Study of Chapbooks
  for Young Readers over Two Centuries*, London, 1968
Osborne Collection of Early Children's Book, The, A Catalogue,
  Toronto, 1958
Tuer, A. W.: *Stories from Old-fashioned Children's Books*, London, 1900
Vries, Leonard de: *Flowers of Delight*, Toronto, 1965

[2] The rational child

Altick, Richard D.: *The English Common Reader*, Chicago, 1957
Coleridge, Christabel: *Charlotte Mary Yonge, her Life and Letters*,
  London, 1903
[née Grant of Rothiemurchus, Elizabeth, afterwards Mrs Smith of
  Baltiboys]: *Memoirs of a Highland Lady*, edited by J. M. Strachey,
  London, 1898
Jones, M. G.: *Hannah More*, Cambridge, 1952
More, Hannah: *Strictures on the Modern System of Female Education*,
  London, 1799
Quinlan, Maurice J.: *Victorian Prelude*, New York, 1951

[3] The Sunday scholar

Altick. See chapter 2

[Burney, Fanny]: *Diary and Letters of Madame D'Arblay*, London, 1904
Coleridge. See chapter 2
Harris, J. Henry: *Robert Raikes, the Man and his Work*, Bristol, 1899
Hewitt, Gordon: *Let the People Read*, London, 1949
Jones, William: *The Jubilee Memorial of the Religious Tract Society*, London, 1850
Kendall, Guy: *Robert Raikes*, London, 1939
Mathews, H. F.: *Methodism and the Education of the People*, London, 1949
Roberts, William: *Memoirs of the Life and Correspondence of Hannah More*, London, 1834
[Shaw, Charles] 'An Old Potter': *When I was a Child*, London, 1903
Yonge, Charlotte: *Hannah More*, London, 1888

[4] The cottage child and his Sunday School prize

Arch, Joseph: *The story of his Life, Told by Himself*, London, 1898
Morgan, P. E.: 'Reward Books' (*Notes and Queries*, 31 July 1943), London

[5] The evangelical child

Altick. See chapter 2
Coleridge. See chapter 2
Cutt, M. Nancy: *Mrs Sherwood and her Books for Children*, London, 1974
Hamilton, Lord Frederic: *The Days Before Yesterday*, London, 1922
Hare, Augustus: *The Story of my Life*, vol. V, London, 1900
Hill, Rowland: *Sermons Delivered to Children at Surrey Chapel, 1823–26*, London, 1833
Jones. See chapter 2
[Keary, Eliza]: *Memoir of Annie Keary by her Sister*, London, 1882
Kelly, Sophia (ed.): *The Life of Mrs Sherwood*, London, 1857
Laski, Marghanita: *Mrs Ewing, Mrs Molesworth and Mrs Hodgson Burnett*, London, 1950
Sangster, Paul: *Pity my Simplicity. The Evangelical Revival and the Religious Education of Children 1738–1800*, London, 1963
Southey, Robert: *Life of John Wesley*, London, 1820

[6] The happy family

Grant. See chapter 2

Moberly, C. A. E.: *Dulce Domum*, London, 1911

Newsome, David: *Godliness and Good Learning*, London, 1961

Sewell, Eleanor (ed.): *The Autobiography of Elizabeth Sewell*, London, 1907

Tait, A. C.: *Catharine and Craufurd Tait, a Memoir*, edited by W. Benham, London, 1879

[7] The innocents

Acland, Eleanor: *Goodbye for the Present. The Story of Two Childhoods. Milly, 1878–88, and Ellen, 1913–24*, London, 1935

Stevenson, Lilian: *A Child's Bookshelf*, London, 1917

[8] The manly boy

Bradley, A. G., and others: *A History of Marlborough College*, London, 1893

Farrar, Reginald: *The Life of Frederic William Farrar, sometime Dean of Canterbury*, London, 1904

Firth, J. d'E.: *Winchester College*, London, 1949

Grosskurth, P. M.: *John Addington Symonds*, London, 1964

Hare, Augustus: *The Story of my Life*, vol. I, London, 1896

How, F. D.: *Six Great Headmasters*, London, 1904

Mack, Edward C.: *Public Schools and British Opinion, 1780–1860*, London, 1938

Marder, Arthur J.: *From the Dreadnought to Scapa Flow*, vol. I, Oxford, 1961

Melly, George: *School Experiences of a Fag at a Private and a Public School*, London, 1864

Minchin, J. G. Cotton: *Old Harrow Days*, London, 1898

Mulhauser, F. L. (ed.): *The Correspondence of Arthur Hugh Clough*, Oxford, 1957

O'Connor, Frank: *An Only Child*, London, 1961

Raymond, Ernest: *The Story of my Days*, London, 1968

Stanley, A. P.: *The Life and Correspondence of Thomas Arnold*, London, 1844

[9] 'Modern girls' and schoolgirls

Cruse, Amy: *The Victorians and their Books*, London, 1935

[10] The child's heroes

Darton. See chapter 1

Disher, M. Willson: 'Penny Dreadfuls' (*Pilot Papers*, March 1947), London

Greenwood, James: *The Seven Curses of London*, London, 1869.

Hindley. See chapter 1

Neuburg. See chapter 1

Pyle, Howard: 'Chapbook Heroes' (*Harper's New Monthly Magazine*, 1890), New York

Salmon, Edward G.: 'What Girls Read' (*Nineteenth Century*, October 1886), London

Trease, Geoffrey: *Tales out of School*, London, 1948

Turner, E. S.: *Boys will be Boys*, London, 1948

Acknowledgements

The author and the publishers wish to thank the following for permission to reproduce copyright material.

The Cambridge University Press for an illustration by Marjorie Whittington to the Children's Bible, 1928.

Messrs James Nisbet & Co. for the jacket front of May Wynne's *The Honour of the School*.

I.P.C. Services Ltd for a page from the *British Girls' Annual*.

The illustrations on pages 13, 17, 20, 22, 24, 26, 27, 30, 38, 39, 42, 44, 47, 49, 53, 57, 60, 64, 67, 73, 75, 78, 80, 81, 83, 85, 87, 89, 94, 95, 98, 105, 106, 113, 114, 116, 119, 122, 128, 134, 137, 139, 144, 147, 151, 154, 158, 160, 165, 168, 171, 181, 187, 191, 196, 201, 205, 210, 211, 215, 220, 233, 238, 240 were all photographed from books and periodicals in the Bodleian Library. The *British Girls' Annual* (page 208) is in the possession of Deborah Ganz, and the remaining books are my own.

Index